ReViewing
Asian
America

D1264268

Association for Asian American Studies Series

Reflections on Shattered Windows
(1987 AAAS conference, San Francisco, CA)

Frontiers of Asian American Studies
(1988 AAAS conference, Pullman, WA)

Asian Americans: Comparative and Global Perspectives
(1989 AAAS conference, New York, NY)

Bearing Dreams, Shaping Visions
(1990 AAAS conference, Santa Barbara, CA)

New Visions in Asian American Studies
(1991 AAAS conference, Honolulu, HI)

ReViewing Asian America
(1992 AAAS conference, San Jose, CA)

ReViewing
ASIAN
AMERICA
LOCATING DIVERSITY

EDITORS
Wendy L. Ng • Soo-Young Chin
James S. Moy • Gary Y. Okihiro

WSU
PRESS

Washington State University Press
Pullman, Washington 99164-5910
800-354-7360
FAX 509-335-8568

Washington State University Press, Pullman, Washington 99164-5910

Library of Congress Cataloging-in-Publication Data

ReViewing Asian America : locating diversity / editors, Wendy L. Ng
. . . [et al.].
  p. cm. — (Association for Asian American Studies series)
  Includes bibliographical references.
  ISBN 0-87422-118-8
  1. Asian Americans. 2. Asian Americans—Study and teaching—
United States. 3. Pluralism (Social sciences)—United States.
I. Ng, Wendy L. II. Series: Association of Asian American Studies
series.
E184.06R48 1995
305.895'073—dc20   95-15751
                                                       CIP

Contents

Preface

From Generation to Generation

In the fourth volume of the Association for Asian American Studies Anthology Series, *Bearing Dreams, Shaping Visions*, Linda Revilla (1993) writes about how she feels as a part of the so-called "lost generation" (Mar 1988) of Asian Pacific American scholars. While it is not my intention to duplicate Linda's introduction, she and I often discuss how we feel as part of the "other-younger" generation. And it is worth mentioning again, that the journey to Asian American Studies is as important as the movement which created the discipline. I, like Linda, have felt in some way that the "Asian American Movement" came and passed me by during my undergraduate college years in the 1970s and graduate school days when I left California for the wilderness of Oregon. Oregon was a wilderness in many more ways than I could imagine. Yet, Asian American Studies has extended its influence to many more places than one can imagine, and certainly beyond the scope of activist time periods of the late sixties and early seventies. In the 1980s, at the University of Oregon, Eugene, I was able to find copies of *Roots, Counterpoint*, and *Aiiieeeee!*. It was also there that I was exposed to John Okada's *No-No Boy*, Louis Chu's *Eat A Bowl of Tea*, Joy Kogawa's *Obasan*, and Carlos Bulosan's *America is in the Heart*. The Asian/Pacific American Student Union (APSU) was alive and expanding; one year Frank Chin's play *Chickencoop Chinaman* was performed by members of the student union. In a course entitled "Ethnic Theater," Asian/Pacific American students, all of whom grew up in the Northwest (with the exception of myself), produced a dramatic reading and performance based upon the works of Velina Hasu Houston, Lawson Inada, Robert Kikuchi-Yngojo, Chol Soo Lee, Janice Mirikitani, Nobuko Miyamoto, Shawn Wong, Nellie Wong, and J.K. Yamamoto, to name a few. We had no Asian American Studies Program, but we did have Ethnic Studies, albeit a watered-down version housed within the Folklore program at the university. Many times I felt I was in a barren wasteland where race and ethnicity were social categories which were either ignored or over-emphasized.

Despite the settlement of Chinese in Oregon in the late 19th century, the Japanese at the turn of the century, and Filipino migrant workers during the Depression, Asian faces still appeared foreign to many Oregonians. It was a place where many people, including some of my professors, thought I was an Asian foreign student or immigrant who happened to speak English fluently. In this "ethnic isolation" racial minorities stood out, and people of color within the community were forced to build multi-ethnic coalitions. The Ethnic Women's Alliance, the Black Student Union, MEChA, and the Native American Student Union worked closely together, socially, and educationally, in the spirit of multi-culturalism and unity. Being both numerical and sociological minorities amid a white majority, the building of coalitions and activism with other people of color was necessary to survive the institutional racism. Finally, ethnic and racial isolation, while forcing students to build within their organizations, also forges linkages with members of the community. Thus, Asian American Studies and Ethnic Studies are not merely academic in nature, but also draw upon the experiences and wisdom of communities of color in the area.

Yet, in spite of what I perceived as the lack of diversity, I had the opportunity to teach both Ethnic Studies and Asian American Studies as a graduate student. However, most of my Asian American and Ethnic Studies education was developed largely as a result of my fellow students, graduate and undergraduate. Imagine my amazement when I found there were actually professors who devoted their research and teaching to Asian Americans. Could I envision researching within the Asian American community and teaching about Asian Americans from a perspective which spoke truthfully to mine and other Asian American's experiences, not others' interpretation of my experiences? I have had opportunities to do this at Oregon, the University of California at Santa Cruz and San Diego, Carleton College, Minnesota, and San Jose State University. For this, I am indebted to the students in my classes who actively participated in the dialogue about what it means to be an Asian American; who honestly shared their stories with me about their experiences, cried, laughed, got angry, argued, and debated with me. They are the ones who will be our next generation. I often think that being self-taught makes one question where one's work fits in the academy. This is something academics are unaccustomed to express publicly, but may feel privately. It is not just a question of adequacy, but pioneering in a field such as Asian American Studies, our work is challenged and criticized by the traditional academy. When I left the University of Oregon and went to other places of "Asian America," I was inspired and mentored by many people. I owe much appreciation to colleagues Sucheng Chan, Gary Y. Okihiro, Ray Lou, and many more of the "other generation" of Asian American Studies who have supported and nurtured my growth in the field and who have contributed much to its scholarly development. In addition, my colleagues in the Asian American Studies Program at San Jose State University have provided a unique environment supporting the growth of Asian American Studies at our campus. Much appreciation for their hard work, humor, and esprit de corps go to Alexander Yamato, Soo-Young Chin, Hien Duc Do, Peter Bacho, and Joel Franks.

My undergraduate alma mater, Mills College, has a motto: *Una Destinatio, Viae Diversae,* One Destination, Many Ways. I think about this motto in two ways. First, I think of it as a path I and many others have traveled in Asian American Studies. There are many ways one can come to the discipline, but we all share the goals of uncovering and exploring, recording and interpreting, and most important of all validating the experiences of all Asian Americans. Questions about our identities, our relationship to our parents' generations, racism, and social change are universally held issues across generation and ethnicity. Secondly, I see the motto as a way to think about diversity in society. Asian American Studies shares with other disciplines a view of understanding, race, gender, and class relations, and cultural constructions of our identities and communities. While we do not necessarily end up in the same place, or travel along the same pathway, or even agree with one another all the time (indeed, as we shall see we frequently travel along many different shores), as Asian Americanists, we share many of the same ideals with others in the understanding of a just society.

This volume is the sixth in the series of anthologies produced by the Association for Asian American Studies with Washington State University Press. It is based on papers selected from the Association's Ninth National Meeting, held at San Jose, California, in 1992. Editors for this volume include Soo-Young Chin, James S. Moy, Gary Y. Okihiro, and myself. Soo-Young Chin and I edited the Social Science essays, Jim Moy edited the essays in the Literature section, and Gary Okihiro is responsible for the essays about East of California. In departing from previous volumes of this series, the articles in this book are arranged consecutively, with no section headings. We did this to break down the traditional distinctions of social science-history-literature-commentary. Indeed, an arrangement which crosses disciplines is supported by the interdisciplinary nature of Asian American Studies. When I think of where we have been in Asian American Studies and where we are going, I think about how it takes incremental steps, but surely, we will move forward.

WENDY L. NG
Asian American Studies Program and Sociology Department
San Jose State University
San Jose, California

References

Revilla, Linda A. (1993). *Bearing Dreams, Shaping Visions*. Pullman, Washington: Washington State University Press, xiii-xv.

Mar, Don (1988). "The Lost Second Generation of Asian American Scholars," in G. Okihiro, S. Hune, A. Hansen, and J. Liu, eds. *Reflections on Shattered Windows: Promises and Prospects for Asian American Studies*. Pullman, Washington: Washington State University Press, 37-42.

Acknowledgements

The ninth national conference of the Association for Asian American Studies was held in San Jose, California, May 27-31, 1992. The conference was organized and hosted through the efforts of a consortium of colleges and universities: San Jose State University, Santa Clara University, Stanford University, University of California-Santa Cruz, and DeAnza College. We would like to thank conference coordinators Wendy L. Ng and Stephen Fugita, and members of the 1992 conference planning committee: Marilyn Alquizola, Soo-Young Chin, Jane Singh, Alexander Yamato, Alice Yang Murray, and Judy Yung; the local arrangements committee: Joel Franks, Serena Lau, Mary Leong, Mark Pasion, Gary Quezon, Darlene Rodriguez, Patrick Lee, Richard Yuen, Maile Ho, Judy Wu, and Michael Chang, APISA and CAPE of the University of California, Santa Cruz; and the executive council of the Association for Asian American Studies: Elaine H. Kim, Franklin Odo, Judith Liu, Shawn Wong, Kenyon Chan, Margaret M. Chin, Sucheta Mazumdar, Linda Revilla, J. Kou Vang, Gregory Yee Mark, and Michael Thornton. The conference was supported by the Asian American Activities Center and Stanford Bookstore, Stanford University; Ethnic Studies Program, Santa Clara University; Anheuser-Busch Companies, Smithsonian Institution, and Takara Sake, Inc., U.S.A. The following offices at San Jose State University also provided support: Asian American Studies Program, College of Applied Sciences and Arts, College of Social Sciences, Department of Social Sciences, Office of the Academic Vice President for Undergraduate Affairs, Student Development Services, and Educational Opportunity Program. Thanks also go to Brooks and Sumi Iwakiri and George Ow, Jr. for their generous support of the Association's conference.

Betty Nobue Kano designed the cover art for this volume. At Washington State University Press, Doug Garcia designed the graphics for the cover, Jean Taylor did the copyediting, and Keith Petersen, editor, and Mary Read, assistant director, gave generously of their time and advice. The San Jose State University Faculty Development Program also provided support for this volume.

As always, the Association for Asian American Studies would like to express a special thanks to Washington State University Press for its continued support and commitment to this series.

Chapter One

Introduction
ReViewing Asian America:
Locating Diversity

Wendy L. Ng, Soo-Young Chin,
James S. Moy, and Gary Y. Okihiro

Reviewing

Reviewing: To look back on; to give a critical evaluation of; a reexamination; to study again. In April 1992, the acquittal of police officers in the beating of Rodney King sparked the largest civil uprising[1] and unrest since the 1965 Watts riots and drew national attention to the volatile, unstable nature of race relations in the United States. While much of the media focused on the violence being perpetrated by African Americans and Latinos towards European American/Anglos, the racial picture was indeed more complicated. The presence of Asian Americans, mainly Korean American immigrants in South Central Los Angeles living in communities adjacent to the areas of unrest, brought Asian Americans into the already complex racial discourse. While Asian Americans have lived in North America for over a century and a half, they are often ignored or absent from the picture. In this case, however, the presence of Korean American shopkeepers and businessmen and women was unfortunate. Many of them lost their livelihood, and some—including a number of first-generation immigrants—lost their lives.

This is not the first incident in this century or in Asian American history which resulted in loss, tragedy, and sadness. The violence experienced by Korean American merchants cannot be ignored, nor can it be treated as a mere isolated event. Asian Americans have encountered much violence throughout history, from the 1885 murders of Chinese miners at the Rock Springs Massacre in Wyoming, to the violence directed against Filipinos during the 1930 Watsonville Riots, the relocation and internment of Japanese Americans during World War II, and the killing of Vincent Chin in Detroit in 1982. Events such as these call for a closer look at inter- and intra-racial relations, and an examination of Asian America in the 1990s.

This volume is comprised of papers selected from the 1992 Meeting of the Association for Asian American Studies. The essays resound with the themes of representation, diversity, and empowerment. They address many of the questions raised by the complex nature of U.S. race relations and the relationship of Asian Americans within U.S. society. Indeed, the 1992 meeting provided a critical venue, an exploration and dialogue about the role and direction of Asian American Studies. The authors of the following essays suggest many avenues for exploring these issues, locating Asian America in its diversity, exploring the collective issues of Asian America, challenging dominant institutions, and expanding the view of Asian American Studies, the hopes and aspirations for the future of the discipline.

The changing racial demographics of this nation brought about by the sweeping revisions in immigration laws during the past 25 years have dramatically impacted the contemporary Asian American population. Older Asian American communities have expanded, new communities have emerged, and Asian Americans are no longer the quiet or invisible minority. Asian American Studies emerged from the grassroots efforts of students on college and university campuses, and today's Asian American student population continues to represent a critical point of Asian American consciousness and activism. Yet, Asian American students represent a group substantially different from previous generations, and the college classroom today has different racial and ethnic dynamics. In the first article of this volume, Lane R. Hirabayashi and Malcolm Collier address the challenges of teaching Asian American Studies to an ethnically and culturally diverse student body. Drawing upon the works of Giroux (1994) that place students as "cultural workers," they present a plan for student participation in Asian American Studies classes which places personal and individual experience at the center of learning. Using the personal experiences of Asian American students and employing collective learning strategies, diversity is validated. In addition, these differences in experience strengthen our knowledge of Asian American Studies as a discipline.

Relocating

Sociologist Robert Blauner's (1972) internal colonial model of race relations has been a leading sociological perspective for understanding race relations in the United States. An important aspect of the model emphasizes the involuntary migration of people of color to this country. Because of forced or involuntary migration, Asian Americans, along with other racial minority groups, comprise internal colonies in the United States— that is, groups that are subjected to oppressive conditions and subordination due to conditions of migration, economic exploitation, and continued cultural racism. Although Blauner describes Asian migration as "semicolonial" followed by voluntary migration during this century, he states that, "...the exclusion of Asian immigrants and the restriction acts that followed were unique blows, which marked off the status of Chinese and Japanese in America, limiting their numbers and potential power" (Blauner 1972, 54-55). Indeed, immigration restrictions, citizenship laws, and alien land laws certainly prohibited many Asian Americans from gaining a substantial foot into the major arenas of power in American society. While Blauner's theory has been dissected by many of his contemporaries (Omi and Winant 1986) it is still useful in considering the causes and consequences shaping the pattern of migration of Asians to the United States. It is not coincidental then, to look at the ways in which the migration patterns of Asian immigrants have resulted from the colonial relationship between the U.S. and Asia, and to extend the idea of forced migration to that of the most recent Asian immigrants. Particularly within the context of migration from Vietnam, Cambodia, Laos, and the Philippines, one cannot ignore the effects of external political arrangements influencing migration patterns. The first four articles in this volume reflect the interest and work in diverse, and often overlooked communities within Asian America. The authors explore the meaning of relocating for the newest Asian immigrants to America. Even with greater numbers in the total Asian American population and less restrictive immigration laws, it is significant to look at the process, conditions, and adjustments within Asian American communities to the conditions of migration.

Ellen Somekawa examines Southeast Asian refugees who have been resettled into urban, racially mixed neighborhoods in Philadelphia. In her study, she finds that refugees manage to create a sense of community. This is accomplished despite the difficulties associated with refugee status and the hardships encountered upon entering a culture and society vastly different from the one they left. In urban American contexts, refugees are surrounded by other racial and ethnic minority groups and their place and presence in the neighborhood is contested. As groups vie for space and established boundaries become realigned, dislocation becomes a multidimensional problem which manifests itself in identity, social relations, and physical actualities. New Asian refugees face challenges in establishing community; they struggle to sustain a sense of self and culture as they deal with the tensions brought by their perceived outsider status.

James A. Tyner looks at migration from the Philippines from a decision-making model moderated by changing opportunities. Because of the Philippines' long history of occupation by the United States military, there has been a constant migration between the islands and the U.S. In this article, Tyner illustrates clearly how the opportunity structure for America-bound Filipinos is regulated by policies between the Philippines and the United States. His analysis of Filipino migration links micro-level individual choices for immigration with macro-level structural opportunities and changes. In his interviews with Filipino migrants he found that family considerations were foremost in people's decisions to migrate. These individual micro-level reasons are frequently mediated by structural opportunities to migrate—such as migration policy and employment opportunities. Thus the U.S. migration policy, which gives preference towards family reunification, intersects both micro- and macro-level decision making in immigration. On the other hand, migration policy also hinders Filipino migration by forcing families to separate as one family member establishes permanent residency or U.S. citizenship before petitioning for other family members to come over.

The United States' involvement in the Korean War of the 1950s precipitated the journey of young, orphaned, Korean children to North America, a group whose relocation was not by choice. Mike Mullen's exploratory research grapples with yet another under-researched area in Asian American Studies: transracial adoption. He focuses on the identity development among Korean adoptees who were raised by non-Korean, white families. In his research, he examines the dynamics that create identification or lack of identification of adoptees as Korean Americans, and discusses the tensions that arise from the dissonance between internal and external perceptions of identity. In short, he finds that adoptees are less likely to identify as Asian Americans, and more strongly identify with mainstream European Americans in part because of their adoptive families' and society's influences.

Amarpal Dhaliwal's article raises the issue of negotiated gender roles and identity transformation of one South Asian immigrant woman. Immigration laws have dramatically affected the migration from India and the growth of the South Asian population in the United States. Many of these immigrants are educated professionals from upper- and middle-class backgrounds who have migrated with their families. Dhaliwal examines South

Asian ideas of middle-class womanhood and delineates the renegotiation and transformation of these notions to fit the American Asian context. She argues for a "gendered ideology" within particular social classes, and that the conditions of migration do not necessarily change these ideas. Traditional patriarchal structures and gender roles for South Asian women are reinforced and reproduced by the conditions of migration and resettlement in a new country. In a traditional model of assimilation, over time immigrants adopt the cultural values of the host society. A woman who immigrated to the U.S. might have greater autonomy and freedom than in patriarchal South Asian Indian society. Dhaliwal found, however, that this was not the case with the South Asian woman she studied. Although structural changes allowed her informant to engage in a petit bourgeois enterprise, something which would not occur in India, traditional gender role expectations persisted, even after immigration, and were reproduced in the new setting. In operating a small business, the woman's role was reproduced in a way acceptable to the traditional patriarchal gender structure and class structure of India. The business enterprise enabled Dhaliwal's informant to assist in maintaining her family's class status, and thus, storekeeping became an extension of her roles as wife, mother, and family caretaker.

Taken together, these pieces represent significant methodological and theoretical departures from previous work about Asian Americans. Unlike previous social science research about Asian Americans, which was conducted by outsiders, these authors are often either members or insiders to the communities they are studying. Not only must they deal with theoretical inadequacies in the literature about Asian Americans, they must develop both a methodology and analysis appropriate for understanding their subjects. The authors neither assume an assimilationist bias, nor do they assume that Asian immigrants are mere victims of subordinate conditions in the process of migration. They portray Asian American subjects as active participants in the creation of their lives, and as can be seen, diversity engenders not only conflict in roles and status, but negotiation and cooperation at many other levels.

Reaction

The events in April 1992 in Los Angeles were foremost on our mind as the Association for Asian American Studies met in San Jose. While we watched the media report about the violence, we also thought about our families and communities in the "city of angels." How did Asian Americans experience this urban uprising and what are the ways we can analyze and understand what happened? Elaine Kim, president of the

Association for Asian American Studies commented on the events in her presidential address:

> As practitioners of Asian American Studies, we are facing an enormous challenge at this particular moment. The recent events in Los Angeles have demonstrated vividly how desperately we need new visions and new tools for understanding race and Asian American identities in the 1990s. As we watched in absolute horror the destruction of Koreatown after the Rodney King verdict, many of us felt that we were watching our own dreams for a just society, which had been inspired by the African American-led Civil Rights Movement of the 1960s, being destroyed, cast aside as naive and irrelevant in the bitter and embattled 1990s. I could hardly believe my ears when I heard African American community leaders accuse Korean merchants of deliberately trying to stifle African American economic development. At the same time, I was receiving hate letters from angry white men who didn't like a subdued and intensely personal piece *Newsweek* solicited from me two weeks ago. "Go back to Korea," they wrote. " No one promised anything to you or your parents." "If you're disenchanted, go back home where you belong. Sayonara." I felt that these people could tolerate Korean Americans only as voiceless political pawns; otherwise, we would have to be deported or killed. (Kim, 1992:1)

Kim's reaction along with that of other Asian Americans has sparked an opening for a dialogue and an analysis of the events of 1992. The study of race and ethnic relations has been woefully inadequate in understanding multiracial phenomena. Social sciences have not yielded to the two-dimensional black-white dichotomy in race relations; Ethnic Studies and Asian American Studies attempt to bridge this theoretical gap. Although Korean American scholars have opened the dialogue to understanding Black-Korean conflict, there is still much work that needs to be done (Chang, 1993). Beyond analyzing the theoretical bases of race and ethnic relations, it is critical to understand how social institutions perpetuate images and ultimately, relationships between groups. Neil T. Gotanda offers an incisive analysis of how the judicial system reproduces racial and gender stereotyping in the case of *People v. Soon Ja Du.*

In 1991, Soon Ja Du, a Korean American immigrant grocery store owner, was found guilty in the shooting death of Latasha Harlins, an African American teenager. Du was tried and convicted of second-degree murder. Judge Joyce Karlin, the presiding judge in the case, sentenced Du to probation and community service. In dissecting the stereotype and gendered themes in the judge's sentencing colloquy, Gotanda suggests that the judge used the model minority stereotype to influence her sentencing of Du. Even the judicial system, in its efforts at fairness and impartiality, is still informed by damaging racial stereotypes which place one group against another. In this case, the behavior of Du is considered "reasonable" given her experiences as a storekeeper in a predominantly

African American neighborhood. She is considered to be a "law-abiding" member of a group (Asian) in which she is assumed to be a "model minority." Harlins, on the other hand, is a young, African American teenager who is "up to no good"; therefore, her being shot is seemingly considered a justifiable defense for Du. By pinpointing racism within the social structure, i.e., the judicial system, Gotanda identifies how language reinforces the climate of racism and becomes the ideological instrument of racism. Most analyses of racism merely critique institutional structures of discrimination, rarely pinpointing the ideological bases for these actions. That the Judge made inferences to a model minority and alleged "gang" members makes clear racial distinctions between Du and Harlins. Despite efforts at reducing this type of stereotyping, images and characteristics of racial minorities become imbedded within institutional structures through such racial categorization.

According to Gotanda, because this case was so highly publicized in the media, it inscribed a "gun toting grocer" stereotype to Koreans. The news media reinforced this image during the April 1992 L.A. uprising by showing numerous shots of Korean store owners brandishing guns, shooting at unseen targets (presumably African Americans). Images such as this become integrated into a range of stereotypes about Asian Americans, and one wonders whether this only supports more interracial violence in the United States.

Yet, in moving forward from April 1992, many efforts have been made to heal the wounds, mend the souls, and forge a relationship between African American and Korean American communities. Kim (1993: 215) has suggested that han: "a Korean word that means, loosely translated, the sorrow and anger that grow from the accumulated experiences of oppression," might be used to explain the complexity of the physical and psychological emotions Korean Americans faced after April 1992. By understanding han, one can understand the pain of both Korean Americans and African Americans in their quests for empowerment and justice.

In searching for essays which represent the viewpoints and reactions of Asian Americans to the 1992 events, the piece following Gotanda's was contributed by Kichung Kim. Originally, it was not presented at the 1992 Association conference, but as a speech a year later during a forum for African American and Korean American clergy in Oakland, California. His words remind us of the importance of building networks and alliances to understand the roots of oppression and commonalties in Korean and African American communities. The discussion about interracial relations must be open to public dialogue. In this essay, he draws upon the works of African American writers Richard Wright, W.E.B. Du Bois, and Langston Hughes in calling upon Korean and African Americans to look at the source of racism and oppression and to see the commonalties in their experiences.

Remembering

The next two essays describe race and ethnic relations between African Americans and Asians influenced and shaped by different time periods and historical, sociopolitical settings. As should be clear from Gotanda's reading of the Soon Ja Du case, and from Elaine Kim and Kichung Kim's response to the L.A. civil disturbance, Peter Bacho's short story reminds us that the causes and consequences of racial and ethnic tension range back to 1968: an era of civil rights, black power, and activism. Bacho's short story August 1968 begins its journey during the 1950s in a neighborhood of Seattle, Washington. Two boys, one African American, one Filipino, oblivious of their racial differences, enjoy friendship and camaraderie. Only the turbulence of the racial movements of the 1960s shatters their boyhood innocence and their reality, raising questions, tensions, and loyalty between the two young men. "Asian American writers are too nice," tells Bacho. "They don't write about conflict; we avoid controversy and confrontation. My story is different, there is no happy ending here." In all, the ending is disquieting, and leaves questions about where to make the next moves as we attempt to dismantle years of racial and ethnic conflict.

In Harmony, R.A. Sasaki explores the relationship between a young Japanese girl and her African American piano teacher. Set in pre-World War II San Francisco, Keiko Moriwaki lives in Japantown, surrounded by a multiethnic community of whites, Blacks, Chinese, and Jews. When Mr. Obediah Johnson becomes her piano teacher, her perspective about herself, her piano, and her community is transformed. Music is likened to multiculturalism, where the unique, individual sounds of instruments are brought together to create a composition, a harmony of voices; parallel to this, the beauty of our society as a whole emerges from the diversity of individual voices.

Re-Reading

Accordingly, the next three pieces by Traise Yamamoto, Rachel Lee, and Sharon Suzuki-Martinez examine some of the strategies deployed to achieve voice. Once broken, this former site of silence provides the platform for new readings of Asian America. These readings, which can provide a welcome sense of location, at once both geographic and ideological, create new difficulties. Themes of gender, power and silences, community, and institutionalization reread themselves in the literary canon of Asian America.

Traise Yamamoto eloquently brings the writing of Asian American women to a powerful position. Her moving personal account provides a sensitive individual location of personal identity as a counter to ethnic confusion. One is reminded that the silence of aporia allows dominant culture America to construct Asian America to suit its agenda. In articulating silences, Asian American women writers and poets challenge dominant institutions through their writings. "For them, silence is something to be broken, shattered, shredded; it is something solid through which one must pass in order to join one's voice to the voices on the other side." Her essay contests stereotypical images of Asian women as submissive, docile, or silent, and suggests a powerful literary movement is alive in Asian American women's writings.

Rachel Lee's article, *Claiming Land, Claiming Voice, Claiming Canon,* won the first-place award in the Association for Asian American Studies student paper competition. Lee, a graduate student in English at the University of California, Los Angeles, offers insights into how institutions legitimate and create literary canon. In her essay comparing Maxine Hong Kingston's *The Woman Warrior* and *China Men*, she notes the popular acceptance of the former novel over the latter. Despite critics' challenge that Kingston's stories are not authentic (Chin, 1991), *The Woman Warrior* has received greater literary and institutional recognition because of its gendered themes and individually centered protagonist. Lee argues, however, that *China Men* may be the more radical and significant of the two texts. *China Men*'s stories challenge power and authority in America, and give Chinese American men and women claim to America. Representation, authenticity, and voice thus become critical questions in literature as Asian American writers' works become accessible and accepted by the mainstream white audience and intellectual institutions. For it is here that Asian America can encounter problems even more daunting than the simple matter of breaking the grip of silence, as demonstrated by Yamamoto, or in challenging the institutional hegemony of one writer's work, as in Lee's essay.

Undeniably, Maxine Hong Kingston's works have made a noticeable impression among literary critics. Although these works have been criticized by writer Frank Chin in *Aiiieeeee!* and *The Big Aiiieeeee!* (Chan, Chin, Inada, and Wong, 1991), Sharon Suzuki-Martinez's postmodernist essay challenges the critics and expands the discussions of Kingston's work. By exploring the "anomalous," themes of community, and construction of identity, Suzuki-Martinez shows Kingston's use of marginalized characters and of subversive "trickster strategies" to deconstruct hegemonic institutions and her critics. The debate over Kingston's works will surely continue; diversity of opinion, as unlikely as it may seem, may be the key to forging unity within the Asian American community.

The question of how new voices will be heard and how they will be validated are the central concerns of the articles by David Mura and

George Uba. Both of these authors grapple with the dominant culture ghost of canon making, fully aware that the process of bestowing institutionalized voice upon one group at once also imposes relative silence on those excluded. Mura raises the question of authenticity and voice in the reading and interpretation of Asian American poetry and suggests that multiple challenges face the Asian American poet: correct and incorrect, authentic and fake, Asian American poets and their work are not immune from the discourse of political correctness. Asian American Studies, whether it intends to or not, defines standards in the literary canon. Mura feels that the work of Asian American poets is too often cast into discrete literary compartments by those in power, and defined only by the "Asianness," the "Asian American-ness" or the "American-ness" of the work. Such compartmentalizing is limiting. The boundaries of Asian American poets and their poetry must be decontextualized, allowing for movement from the center to the margin and from the margin back to the center again. Asian American poets must be placed within the works of other Third World writers such as Achebe, Garcia Marquez, Aimee Cesaire, and Pablo Neruda. Broadening the context of the Asian American poet's work will serve well to narrow the margins, bringing the center to a deeper understanding of multiculturalism and our very own cultural perspectives.

George Uba's essay reflects the theme of the 1992 meeting: representation, diversity, and empowerment. In his examination of Asian American poetry in the Heath Anthology of American Literature, Uba raises the question of the representatives of Asian Americans in literary anthologies. Within this literary genre, the *Heath* includes more Asian American literature than others of its kind, yet battles with the limitations in the selection of Asian American poets as particular "representatives" of Asian America in literary anthologies. In the quest for inclusiveness and representativeness, literary anthologies must often make choices at the expense of excluding others. Uba argues for reconstructing literary anthologies around a model of literature that accommodates diversity and multiple representations of Asian America. Asian American poets represent a frontier for establishing representativeness and diversity. In particular, this should also include diversity along gender, ethnicity, class, and generation lines.

Re-Visioning Asian American Studies: East

"East of California: New Perspectives in Asian American Studies" was the title of the symposium held by Cornell's Asian American Studies Program in September 1991. The meeting's purpose was to provide a forum for representatives from 23 colleges and universities from Colorado eastward to discuss their particular campuses and regions—their complexions, needs, and prospects for Asian American Studies. Their reports described the demography of their campuses, extant resources in Asian American Studies, the likely future of Asian American Studies on their campuses, and how their situations might resemble or differ from Asian American Studies in California.

Several differences emerged from the discussion. The demographics of many campuses and their surrounding communities were more dramatically homogeneous than California as a whole, both in terms of the relative absences of Asians and other minorities and the generation ages of the Asian American population. There are more "new" Asian Americans east of California, pointing to the need for courses and readings that address their interests and needs, and many of those Asian immigrants and refugees come from different parts of the world. Asian Indians east of California, for instance, could as likely have immigrated from Africa and the Caribbean as from India, and Chinese Latinos appear in Asian American Studies courses along with Chinese from Hong Kong. It is not fortuitous, thus, that the Queens College Asian/American Center in New York is broadly transnational in its approach to Asian American Studies.

Beyond the demographic impact upon the curriculum, symposium participants noted that California's programs commonly used the growing numbers of Asian Americans in the state as a justification for the existence and expansion of Asian American Studies programs. Despite the significant numbers of Asian American students on many campuses, members contend that Asian Americanists east of California do not have this luxury; instead, they must summon intellectual and pedagogical justifications other than the demographic reasons cited so prominently in California. That reality has compelled a reexamination of the bases for Asian American Studies and the tactics employed for establishing and building courses and programs.

Also and importantly, coming as it has during times of tight fiscal constraint, unlike the first programs in California that were formed during the educational expansion phase of the 1960s and 70s, Asian American Studies east of California has had to make ingenious use of scarce resources. Accordingly, there are no free-standing Asian American Studies programs east of California that offer courses and tenure their own faculties. They are all housed within units such as Ethnic and American Studies programs, or constitute multidisciplinary programs that instigate and coordinate appointments and courses in traditional departments.

Undergraduate and graduate students east of California have been as instrumental as their California counterparts in demanding Asian

American Studies courses and programs, but they have had to confront the additional challenge of virtually no staff or faculty members on their campuses with an interest in or knowledge of the field of study. Many of these students know they want Asian American Studies, but do not know precisely what Asian American Studies is or how it might be established. The campus representatives at the Cornell symposium, accordingly, resolved to form a network of schools east of California that could support one another and share resources within the region.

A final outcome of the symposium was the recognition of California-centrism within Asian American Studies curricula and scholarship. Participants argued for readings that more closely addressed the histories and concerns of Asian Americans in the Midwest, South, and Northeast. The field, for example, sees Asian America as having begun in California with the Chinese search for Gold Mountain (a few might view Hawai'i as a precursor), followed by the movement of Asians from California eastward across the continent. In addition to that migration model that reverses the Eurocentric archetype's flow from east to west, California's (and the West Coast's) communities are widely recognized as universal and paradigmatic in the field. But Asian Americanists east of California point to the Filipino communities in Louisiana of the 1760s, and Asian Indians in Philadelphia, Boston, and New York City during the 1780s as the beginnings of Asian America and as more complicated and diverse communities than the Chinatowns of California. The symposium's members thus established a committee charged with looking into the possibility of creating readings that reflected more closely the view from these "other" shores.

The next two articles by Amy Ling and Peter Kiang were commissioned by the Cornell symposium's participants to inform the field broadly of the concerns, challenges, and opportunities for Asian American Studies east of California. Ling addresses the challenges of Asian American Studies at the University of Wisconsin, Madison. As pointed out earlier, historically and demographically, the Asian American population in the Midwest is different from both the West and East coasts. Despite a critical mass of Asian American students at the University, Ling faced tremendous challenges in establishing and legitimizing a department of Asian American Studies. Her article raises the necessity of comparative Ethnic Studies, in which our understanding of Asian America is strengthened by our understanding of Native, African, and Latino Americans. As we learn from one another, we learn about ourselves.

Peter Kiang's essay brings a long-awaited recognition of Asian American Studies on the "other shore." As demonstrated by the participation of East Coast colleges and universities in the "East of California" consortium, the tide of Asian American Studies has swelled. Recognizing that there are different generations of Asian Americans and different issues today, Kiang calls for continued community and academic collaborations, reaffirming the historic link between Asian American communities and Asian American Studies. Developing Asian American Studies both in the East and the Midwest will help to bring about a broader national identity, strength, and, recognition to the discipline.

* * *

As is clear from the articles in this volume, Asian America has contributed a powerful voice in the arena of multiculturalism. Even still, the influx of diverse Asian groups to America often creates cleavages and tensions within Asian American communities and between Asian Americans and other racial-ethnic communities. As President Elaine Kim acknowledged in her 1992 presidential address, "How is the Association for Asian American Studies going to meet the challenges of our current interstitial position in the American discourse of race?…Asian American Studies is a site for what Raymond Williams has called the convergence of dominant, residual, and emergent practices…We still need to be grounded in our changing social realities, nourished by our communities of criticism, so that we can continue the work of restoring ourselves as subjects of history as we decipher what David Lloyd has called "the history of the possible."

By recognizing that anything is possible, Asian America can thrive. As we "locate" and accept the challenge of diversity throughout Asian America, we can rely on our similarities as our strength. And by facing conflict in the complex American racial arena, Asian Americans can be in the forefront of activism, learning, and leadership, forging new models of ethnic communities which recognize the interrelationships within our national and global community. Asian American Studies has much work ahead. As playwright David Henry Hwang (1993:xi) writes, "… multiculturalism must evolve into a sort of interculturalism which attempts to outline commonalities as well as differences." If we use Asian American diversity as a locus of power and knowledge, our communities along with others will be engaged in an exciting and rare dialogue, one that is empowered by the past and envisions the future.

Endnotes

The editors of this volume jointly contributed to the Introduction.

1. Several different words have been used to describe the events in Los Angeles in April 1992: uprising, civil disturbance, upheaval, rebellion, revolution, and riot. The choice of what words is used seems to relate to a matter of perspective. The

term "uprising" is used here to emphasize the reactions of powerless people responding to their perceptions of unfairness and inequality. As Cornell West writes, "What happened in Los Angeles in April of 1992 was neither a race riot nor a class rebellion. Rather, this monumental upheaval was a multiracial, trans-class, and largely male display of justified social rage....it signified the sense of powerlessness in American society," (West, 1993:3-4).

2. Interview with Peter Bacho, San Jose, California, August 1994.
3. See Yamamoto's essay in this volume.

References

Aguilar-San Juan, Karen, ed. 1994. *The State of Asian America Activism and Resistance in the 1990s.* Boston: South End Press.

Blauner, Robert. 1972. *Racial Oppression in America.* New York: Harper Row.

Chan, Jeffery Paul, Frank Chin, Lawson Fusao Inada, and Shawn Hsu Wong, eds. 1991. *Aiiieeeee! An Anthology of Asian American Writers.* New York: Penguin Mentor.

Chan, Jeffery Paul, Frank Chin, Lawson Fusao Inada, and Shawn Hsu Wong, eds. 1991. *The Big Aiiieeeee!* An Anthology of Chinese American and Japanese American Literature. New York: Penguin Meridian.

Chang, Edward T. 1993. "From Chicago to Los Angeles: Changing the Site of Race Relations." *Amerasia Journal* 19(2):1-21.

Chin, Frank. 1991. "Come All Ye Asian American Writers of the Real and the Fake," in *The Big Aiiieeeee! An Anthology of Chinese American and Japanese American Literature,* Jeffery Paul Chan, Frank Chin, Lawson Fusao Inada, and Shawn Hsu Wong, eds. New York: Penguin Meridian, 1-92.

Giroux, Henry A. and Peter McLaren, eds. 1994. *Between Borders: Pedagogy and the Politics of Cultural Studies.* New York: Routledge.

Hwang, David Henry. 1993. "Facing the Mirror," in *The State of Asian America Activism and Resistance in the 1990s,* Karen Aguilar-San Juan, ed. Boston: South End Press.

Kim, Elaine H. 1992. "Presidential Address: 1992 AAAS Conference," *Association for Asian American Studies Newsletter* (9)2:1.

Kim, Elaine H. 1992. "They Armed in Self-Defense," *Newsweek,* 18 May.

Kim, Elaine H. 1993. "Home is Where the Han Is: A Korean American Perspective on the Los Angeles Upheavals" in *Reading Rodney King, Reading Urban Uprising,* Robert Gooding-Williams (ed.), New York: Routledge, 215-235.

Omi, Michael and Howard Winant. 1986. *Racial Formation in the United States From the 1960s to the 1980s.* New York: Routledge.

West, Cornell. 1993. *Race Matters.* New York: Random House Vintage Books.

Chapter Two

Embracing Diversity: A Pedagogy for Introductory Asian American Studies Courses

Lane Ryo Hirabayashi and Malcolm Collier

The Challenges of Diversity

Addressing the contemporary diversity of Asian/Pacific Americans in an introductory class in Asian American Studies can present major difficulties.[1] In a given regional setting, students enrolled in such courses may represent a plethora of ethnic backgrounds and generational experiences, including a heady mix of "1.5," second, third, and fourth generation Asian Americans. In addition, there may be new Asian immigrants, as well as refugees from Vietnam, Laos, and Cambodia. The educational background of these students is likely to be diverse as well. One is often faced with a contingent of Asian American students whose English-language skills, either in terms of verbal or written expression, are weak and thus require sustained attention. In sum, the diverse backgrounds of students who enroll for an Asian American Studies course can present formidable challenges to the instructor, not the least of which revolves around issues of inclusion and of representation.

Specifically, while a given Asian American Studies class typically includes students from a broad range of ethnic backgrounds, credible literature on each group—let alone accurate and informative audiovisual material—is often not available. An instructor who is strong, for example, on the Chinese, Japanese, and Filipino American experiences because there are, after all, many books and videos on these groups, may shy away from similarly extended treatments of South Asian, Laotian, or Gua-manian Americans. Similarly, regionally specific studies in the field are characteristically uneven; Hmong American communities, for instance, have been studied in detail in their major areas of settlement, and yet virtually no literature is available about them in other settings.

The unevenness of scholarly resources clearly and directly impacts the decision to exclude certain Asian/Pacific American groups or com-munities from the Asian American Studies curriculum. The problem is compounded by the philosophical issue of representation in Asian Ameri-can and Ethnic Studies alike. One of the central complaints of the Asian American students who advocated for autonomy and self-determination for Asian American programs was that—insofar as the topic was even raised—professors in traditional academic disciplines expounded on Asian/Pacific American communities and experiences from detached analytic perspectives, and often in terms of frameworks undergirded by assimilatory and/or dominant society value orientations. The resulting analyses repeatedly held the Asian American communities and experi-ences up to a set of foreign standards. These theoretical misapplications often resulted in inherently substandard, if not pathological portraits of Asian/Pacific Americans. For related reasons, Asian American Studies instructors often feel an understandable reluctance to teach about Asian/Pacific American communities with which they have neither direct expe-rience nor an ongoing relationship, especially when students from such communities are in the class.

In either case, whether due to a lack of reputable materials or con-cerns over the ethics and politics of cultural representation on the part of instructors who don't belong to or work with the population in question, Asian American students may feel unintentionally left out of the focus or substance of Asian American Studies courses. Such students may be left wondering how they fit into the larger Asian American and American picture.

A Working Solution

Given our sense that the creation of Asian American Studies programs with diverse faculty and staff will be a long-term process,[2] what steps can be taken to address the issues raised above at this point in time? One solution involves introductory Asian American Studies courses that di-rectly engage the students by making their own experiences part-and-parcel of the curriculum. This can be carried out via the integra-tion of autobiographical and other paper assignments, along with associ-ated panel activities for each student, directly into course content. Our essay describes such a pedagogy and raises a series of issues and questions that have faced us over the years as we have applied this approach in different academic settings. We also share the solutions we have developed, although we acknowledge from the beginning that the overall pedagogy must be used critically and adjusted to suit the circumstances of a given situation.

The Basic Method

The prototype of the paper/panel assignment we describe here was proposed and initially developed by Malcolm Collier of the Asian American Studies Department at San Francisco State University. It was then implemented and refined by a collective of instructors who taught sections of the Ethnic Studies 220 course "Asians in America" at San Francisco State University from 1983 to the present date. Ethnic Studies 220 is an introductory exploration of contemporary Asian American life, community, and experience within the larger context of the American ethnic experience in the U.S.

The assignments require students to prepare papers in response to a fairly structured set of questions reflecting key curriculum themes. These papers are designed to draw on autobiographical and other personal knowledge.[3] On the basis of their papers, students are asked to prepare a five- to ten-minute oral presentation to share either within small groups or with the entire class.

Sample Assignment: Immigration to the U.S.

We have worked up and utilized short paper/panel presentations in our introductory course to address themes such as immigration, family values and relationships, community, and education. For the purposes of this essay, we will focus on our first such assignment, which is completed within a context of lectures and readings which provide basic information on both historical and contemporary aspects of Asian American immigration.

Background materials for lectures on immigration can be conveniently broken down into three broad sections: pre-1943, 1943-1965, and post-1965. For the period prior to 1943, key information revolves around a very basic review of relevant Asian and U.S. history, including the evolution of discriminatory immigration laws in the U.S., as well as the impact of those laws on Asian American families and communities, both past and present. The post-World War II years can be presented as a transition period, with a brief discussion of the repeal of the various exclusion acts as well as discussion of the War Brides Act and the McCarran-Walter Act.

The contemporary period is framed in terms of the 1965 Immigration Act, which is discussed in some detail. It is important to delineate the revolutionary nature of the Act as it relates to Asian/Pacific Americans, emphasizing that this was the first time that they had equal access to immigration and subsequent naturalization.[4] Equally important is an emphasis on both the growth and increasing heterogeneity of Asian American populations and communities, given that the 1965 Immigration Act profoundly shaped the configuration of socioeconomic classes, ethnic backgrounds, educational backgrounds, gender ratios, family composition, the mix of rural and urban, cosmopolitan backgrounds, and so forth, within most of the Asian American communities.

Discussion of immigration laws needs to include examination of the Immigration Act of 1990, paying particular attention to the political dimensions of its content. The points should be made that immigration regulations are always subject to change, and that anti-immigrant sentiment and agitation can develop in our society at any time for reasons similar to those that can be identified historically.

Lectures can be supplemented with videos: *Wataridori* on the pre-World War II Issei; *Carved in Silence* for Chinese who faced the Angel Island experience; *Lest We Forget* on Koreans; *Pinoy* for Filipinos; *The New Puritans: the Sikhs of Yuba City* regarding South Asians; *Saigon, U.S.A.* on Vietnamese; *Moving Mountains* on Lao; *Omai Fa'atasi*, on Samoans, are some of the readily available programs we have used in this unit.[5]

In sum, this assignment is presented in the context of basic historical and structural information on immigration so that students can begin to think about and position their own family's experiences within this larger framework. We go over the assignment carefully in class, talking about the process of oral history and identifying potential difficulties and solutions.[6] (See Appendix A for a version of the assignment.) We carefully and repeatedly advise students to take special note of anomalous findings (e.g., Japanese laborers coming in after 1908; Filipinos after 1934, etc.), as they begin to gather and analyze their family's story. They are also advised, from the beginning, to see us immediately if there are any problems. In order to reinforce this, we ask toward the end of each subsequent class if any problems or issues are coming up. Often students have similar kinds of questions, so dealing with these in class saves both them and the instructor time.[7] We give students several weeks to gather the information and write the papers.

Logistics of the Panel Assignment

With a small class (25 students or less) it may be possible to have each student speak to the entire class, but in larger classes it is usually necessary to divide the students into smaller groups for panel presentations. In the latter situation, after each student speaks to the members of the smaller group, the group is then asked to identify one or two accounts that they feel the entire class would benefit from hearing.[8] Alternatively, in place of the small groups, the instructor may select a few students to speak to the entire class, and have the remaining students make similar oral presentations on other assignments later in the term. In either case, whether breaking the class into smaller groups or in selecting people for a panel, it is important that the class hear a range of immigration experiences that reflect diversity in terms of variables such as gender, generation, ethnicity, and immigrant versus refugee experiences.[9]

As a prerequisite for the panels, it is vital that instructors articulate, explicitly, the ground rule of respect: strict attention should be given while each panel member is speaking. Because panelists basically share their lives and their families' stories for the benefit and enlightenment of class participants, instructors might also like to insist on confidentiality.[10] Information shared during the presentations is clearly not for the disrespectful or arbitrary use of other students, and definitely not fodder for gossip or criticism outside of the classroom! In short, the instructor needs to impress upon students that civility and ethics are fundamental bases of the in-class panel presentations.

To prepare for the panel, we usually suggest that students rehearse their oral presentations. Trying them out on family members or roommates, who will also time the talk, is a very valuable exercise since students, like their professors, can easily lose track of time. The class should be warned that it is undesirable (not to mention inconsiderate) for individuals to go on and on without focus or design. The instructor may also tell students, however, as the authors often have, that oral presentations will be graded on a "pass/no credit" basis to alleviate some of the pressure. They must, however, come prepared in order to receive full credit.[11]

Physically speaking, there are a variety of ways in which panels can be set up.[12] The panelists can sit in a semicircle of chairs at the head of the room, with the panel members facing the class. Alternatively, if students present their papers in smaller groups first, the individual presentations to the class as a whole can be made from wherever the smaller group is located in the room. While less formal, this can be helpful at times because the students may feel more secure with a backup of people who have already heard and indicated their interest in the account.

When the date of the panel finally arrives, the instructor should ask for a volunteer to start the session. Once people see how interesting these presentations can be, we have found they can loosen up and actually enjoy themselves and each other while they are learning. It is important in this regard to encourage subsequent questions about presentations from the rest of the class while also assuring the presenters that they may "pass" on a given question if it touches on something they would prefer not to discuss.

The instructor needs to take careful notes on each presentation and on its completion follow up with comments that bring out certain points that may have been overlooked; this, of course, should be done in a supportive manner. Even more essential is a discussion by the instructor of how particular accounts fit into larger patterns of immigration experience, history, acculturation, and adjustments, making these come alive for the class by drawing from students' own experiences.[13] It is desirable to demonstrate to the class how data and perspectives drawn from their own lives are a basis for creating knowledge and critical perspectives in Asian American Studies.[14]

Finally, it is not at all uncommon to have accounts of immigration and associated family or personal experiences that are quite extraordinary. The instructor can use these to point out that Asian Americans do not have to look toward distant celebrities as their heroes or role models. Everyday people are worthy of respect, and we have found that our assignments help students to look at themselves, their peers, and their families, anew. Students may then find that the inspiration to face and overcome the challenges that life proffers may lie closer to home than they originally thought.

Potential Problems with Papers and Panels

Over the years, a range of issues have come up in regard to the panel and the paper assignments. We have handled most of these well enough, but to be honest, problems sometimes arise that have no ready resolution. In any case, we firmly believe that identification and discussion of such problems from the beginning helps to prepare instructors to handle them more effectively. On this basis, we will indicate what problems have arisen and suggest how these might be ameliorated (without, however, intending to imply that "our" solutions are definitive).

Although it might not be thought of as a problem, what might be called the "size/time factor" is a real consideration in organizing and implementing the paper/panel approach. We have found that a class size of 25 students is ideal for a number of different reasons. Logistically speaking, if one comments extensively on the papers—especially in providing the extensive grammatical feedback some Asian American students desperately need—one can expect that grading time will take two to three times as long as it might ordinarily take. It might also be noted that papers for the immigration assignment can be lengthy, as students become personally involved in the topic. Similarly, if one has all the students in the course do all of the papers, grading three or four sets of assignments over the course of the semester involves a large commitment of time and effort. In any case, it is important to give this pedagogy a try, the first time around anyway, with a smaller class. Once you become familiar with the overall process, it is then possible to work with larger numbers. Both authors have used this pedagogy with classes of over forty.

More substantial problems have arisen when parents or other relatives claim they cannot remember or do not know the information that students need to complete assignments such as the immigration paper. In some cases this may be literally true, even when dealing with first generation parents, but this is a more common problem with families in which immigration occurred three or more generations in the past. (Interestingly enough, this also seems to be more of a problem with Euro-American families than Asian American ones of the same generational distance from the original immigrants.) In other cases, family members may not wish to discuss certain topics with their children, at least not in the context of providing information for a "research paper."

Related to this, a very complex set of problems may arise over access to and the presentation of family history or information about which parents or other relatives feel ambiguous. Issues of "face" are definitely a consideration here, if family stories reveal that seemingly "exotic" (from a Western, Christian, point of view, anyway) practices like polygamy are present, or if cultural values that differentiate family members from others in terms of a dichotomy between "insiders" as versus "outsiders" are in effect.

Almost every semester, we have had many Chinese American students whose antecedents were "paper sons" or "daughters." Sometimes family members simply don't want to talk about such matters; in other cases, students are warned by family elders not to speak of such matters publicly. The best tack, we have come to believe, is to be sympathetic and not force the issue, especially if a family's concerns are being placed on a student's shoulders. Many times the issue can be partially resolved either by having students change the way they ask questions, or talk about what the instructor has told them about illegal immigration so that family members realize that both the student and instructor have an understanding of the issue. We often encourage these students to pursue the matter on their own, and for their own information, but not to feel pressured to put this into the paper or their panel presentation. Suggesting additional reading is also a useful step, so that students can see more clearly that their family's immigration history is an integral part of the larger Chinese American/Asian American experience.

Deeper family secrets are an even more delicate issue.[15] Clearly, secrets play a dual role in ethnic communities; sometimes they are an invaluable "cloak" that hides and thus protects community members from unfair judgement and censure on the part of members of the dominant society. In other cases, including domestic situations involving conflict, violence, and abuse, the secret can become a "shroud" when and if members of the community are victimized by "their own." If so, then rules about keeping family secrets make victims unable to speak about them and thus unable to reach out to others. In the latter case, an important contribution of Asian American Studies is to bring critical attention to bear on the matter. For the health of all, that is, the nature of particular family secrets must be questioned. Who is being protected? Who is being silenced and/or ignored? Who is isolated from the support of others? To whose ultimate advantage is the secret? These questions are not easy to raise, and are often just as difficult to answer. In some cases, and for a variety of reasons, students are clearly not ready for revelation and catharsis, and we, their professors, must be sensitive to this and let the matter drop.

Similarly, papers on topics such as family relationships, roles, and values can elicit emotionally charged responses. From time to time, we have both worried about the emotional stress and distress sometimes experienced by individual students. We try to "manage" such crises by advising people not to feel compelled to present sensitive or delicate problems that clearly upset them in the oral (or even the written) portion of their assignments. We also have consciously established ongoing ties to the counseling staff at our campuses so that if crises arise, or we get over our heads, our professional colleagues are there to help us out.

Another problematic aspect of the papers involves evaluation. We try to make it clear from the start that we will be grading the papers on how well the student addresses the questions posed in the assignment, rather than on whether or not they have an exciting, funny, or unusual story. On a practical level, one can then evaluate papers based on whether the student has covered each major area as well as in terms of analytic content. This is important in explaining to students how their grades were determined. Sometimes students' feelings may be hurt if and when they feel that anything less than an "A" demeans their family story, per se. Lane Hirabayashi has had students with tears in their eyes ask why their family's story, which is clearly personally very valuable to them, only received a "B" or a "C" grade. From this experience, we sense that spending time explaining evaluation criteria ahead of time is well worth it later on. If we do this, then later we can say, "Look, it's nothing personal—you just have not gone far enough in terms of the analytic depth needed for an 'A' in executing the assignment" or "It's a very good account of what happened before arrival in the United States but you just skimmed over what happened after arrival."

At the same time, the instructor should also be aware that each paper will have to be evaluated in terms of what the student has accessible to them; a student cannot, for example, be graded "down" for having written no passages about "feelings and experiences immediately after arrival" if no one who might recall is still alive. In some cases, this can be a real problem, and one may need to generate alternative questions, or maybe even have the student do a formal interview with a non-family member.[16]

A potential problem in students' panel presentations has to do with a repetition of content. This is somewhat related to both numbers as well as to the internal diversity or lack of diversity within the class. Note, in this regard, that the more similar the students are to each other in terms of their background, and the more students one tries to process, the more likely the presentations will become repetitive. What is more, this can greatly reduce the time spent on other key curriculum topics. Making sure, in selecting students for a given panel, that a range of different ethnicities, generations, genders, forms of household composition (especially nuclear versus extended families), and so forth, are represented, goes a long way toward ameliorating this problem.

In addition, even though we see our classes as a place in which people can explore important topics and issues without feeling that they will be censured or judged, on occasion, and despite our admonitions, questions of respect and/or confidentiality can become an issue. We have no ready-made guidelines in regard to this problem, since it often revolves around particular individuals or configurations of individuals. From classroom experience, Lane Hirabayashi has observed that this seems to be more of an issue when the "mix" of Asian American students is at fifty percent or less of the total class size. Problems with respect/confidentiality have arisen explicitly in Hirabayashi's classes only in the latter situation. Malcolm Collier notes that respect and confidentiality are more of an issue when there are relatively fewer Asian American students since there may be less in the way of shared understanding and experience, and more of a sense that information is being given to "outsiders."

In sum, the ethnic mix of the class (that is, Asian versus non-Asian) necessarily affects the pedagogies one can pursue, as well as overall class dynamics. This is particularly true with regard to the approaches we are describing here. Regarding the first assignment on immigration, for example, it is not of much use to have the whole class give oral presentations if only 10 percent of these have to do with the Asian American experience. On the other hand, in a class with a primarily Asian American enrollment, accounts of immigration and other topics by non-Asian American students can often be very useful comparative statements that provide for a better understanding of the particular characteristics of Asian American experiences as part of the larger American scene.

Additional Benefits

In this essay we have emphasized that our students' diversity is a critical resource in its own right that we shouldn't resist or ignore but, rather, learn to draw from. The pedagogy we have outlined provides one approach that has enabled us to understand and represent the richness of our students' personal, family, and community backgrounds and resources. At the same time it also empowers students by allowing them to discover their own "voices," in that assignments require them to gather data, to formulate and analyze their own experiences, and to present findings to their peers. The fact that this pedagogical approach addresses issues of diversity, inclusion, and representation, is of special interest. The variability of contemporary Asian American life and history is so great that few professors (including those of Asian American descent) can be fully confident about their command of empirical, let alone the more qualitative, dimensions of such a range of groups and experiences.

There are other benefits in using the pedagogy described above. Some points are practical in nature; others have to do with philosophical questions that will be familiar to many. Beginning with the latter, Asian American Studies faculty typically have strong concerns with the kind of hierarchical, authoritarian, modes of education that Third World people are routinely subject to in Western-style institutions of higher learning.[17] "Foundational" approaches to instruction, for example, tend to reproduce authoritarian, hierarchical, relationships that revolve around vertical teacher-to-student—and at the University level, white to non-white, and male to female—patterns of transmitting "knowledge."[18] On this basis, we assert that a key objective of Asian American Studies pedagogies is to identify instructional methods that will lead to critical thinking for self-determination, and that this must be, *a priori*, a matter of both content *and* process. We want to convey to students that, to a significant degree, our courses are *their own*, and that Asian American Studies is not an abstract academic subject, but about them and for them.[19]

In sum, the pedagogical approach we have outlined above has enabled us to move somewhat away from involvement in the reproduction of authoritarian pedagogical styles.[20] Specifically, it has enabled us to pursue a process whereby students themselves are encouraged to feel more comfortable with and confident about the idea and methods of describing, situating, analyzing, and assessing their own life experiences. We and they have learned that this is a valid approach to developing new information about and insights into the Asian American experience.

The paper/panel approach also allows students with weak writing and verbal skills to develop both of these areas. The assignments require them to both write and speak, but about themselves (which may make it easier), and to their peers. Given the proper working context, peers can provide mutual support for the sharpening of anxiety-generating skills such as oral communication. At the same time, we have observed that student discussion of history and experience receives important confirmation from peers who can offer sympathetic support. Such processes are crucial because students at most of our campuses will have to take and complete writing and oral communication proficiency tests, and they need all the experience and help they can get.

Of equal importance are those magical moments of discovery and enlightenment when a student's confusion and unhappiness over biographical aspects of his/her background and life, often subtly predicated on Anglo-oriented assumptions or perspectives, become suddenly intelligible because of their overall contextualization within the larger framework of the Asian American experience.

In the context of our introductory course, then, students learn that their problems are not unique but often shared with their classmates. Problems, that is, are patterned, in the sense that they "fit" into the historical, cultural, political, and economic constraints that frame the experiences of Asian Americans and other racial/ethnic minorities in America. Once students perceive this, it can create an *esprit de corps* that often spills over into their organizations, and even their interpersonal interactions and personal lives.

The pedagogy we have described above has additional benefits. If carried out correctly, it provides a means to keep in close contact with student and community issues and needs.[19] Course papers and panel presentations can also provide a kind of ongoing "reality check" vis-a-vis available social science research publications. Though cast in the universalistic terms of social science research, the latter can be flawed by sample limitations if not outright biases of one kind or another, or by regionally specific contexts and constraints that are not necessarily valid in other settings.

In conclusion, once this pedagogy was in place in our introductory course, and once the word spread around campus about what we were doing, we ended up having to turn away hundreds of students each semester simply because there was not room to accommodate them all.

Appendix

First Paper/Panel Assignment

Your first paper is an account of your family's experiences with immigration. You must interview at least one person in your family and preferably more. In the paper you should indicate who provided what information—that is, who and what are your sources? The paper should be at least five pages in length and should include information on the following points:

1. How did immigration come to take place? Where did people come from, what were their circumstances (work, status, environment, social setting, family), there? When did they leave and why did they decide to leave?

2. The process of emigration and immigration. What did they have to do to leave and how did they get here? Try to find out the basis of which entry to the United States was gained; (n.b.: for those Asian Americans whose families came before World War Two, it is important that you set your story into the framework of prewar immigration law. For those whose families came after 1965, please specify what preference you and/or your family applied under, and what documents and procedures were necessary in order to process the application and obtain a visa.) What official steps had to be taken to leave where they were and to enter the U.S. Try also to find out what informal activities may have occurred: preparations, farewells, locating friends/relatives in the U.S., obtaining a boat, or whatever else might have been necessary to leave.

3. What happened on and after arrival in the U.S.? What were FIRST impressions, memories, feelings, surprises, difficulties, or high points? Be sure to include information about EMPLOYMENT, HOUSING, and SCHOOLS during the first few years after arrival. WHERE did people live? Who helped them obtain access to housing, jobs, and education? Who did/do they socialize with?

4. What has stayed the same, and what has changed for the family and its members after arrival in the U.S.? Include both material and non-material continuity or change. Material might include artifacts, technology, belongings, clothing, and food. Non-material culture might include roles and responsibilities, tastes in entertainment, types of employment, structure of family, attitudes and beliefs, values and desires.

5. Anything else you or your family consider significant.

IF YOU ANTICIPATE ANY DIFFICULTIES IN CARRYING OUT THIS ASSIGNMENT FOR WHATEVER REASON, including passage of time and generations, lack of people to interview, being a foreign student, or communications difficulties with family, please contact me for advice. Please note that, if your family's story is complicated, you can elect to write about only one "side" of your family. Please write your essay carefully and clearly.

Finally, you will need to prepare a five to ten minute statement, based on your paper, for presentation in class; (this will be evaluated on a "credit/ no-credit" basis). Because we are on a fairly tight schedule, you need to come prepared to talk on the day you are assigned for the presentation.

Endnotes

We would like to thank Professors Marilyn Alquizola and Wendy Ng for their thoughtful comments and editorial suggestions on an earlier draft of this paper, and to acknowledge our colleagues at San Francisco State University, as well as Professors Evelyn Hu-DeHart, Kenyon S. Chan, and Jere Takahashi, for valuable discussions related to the issues addressed here.

1. For the purposes of this paper we adapt the definition of "Asian/Pacific Americans" utilized by the U.S. Census, although we acknowledge that the resultant figures are not unproblematic (Tamayo Lott 1993). According to the 1990 Census, people of Chinese, Filipino, Japanese, Asian Indian, Korean, and Vietnamese descent made up 84 percent of the 7.3 million Asian/Pacific Americans counted (O'Hare 1992:12). According to this same source, Pacific Islanders, including Hawaiians, Samoans, and Guamanians, made up 5 percent of the 7.3 million total. For convenience, and without intending to conflate important differences between the two broad populations, we use the term "Asian American" as a synonym for the longer phrase "Asian/Pacific American."
2. Over the long-term, that is, we assume that advocates of Asian American Studies will pursue both the production of accurate studies of contemporary Asian American populations, and will fight for hiring policies that will generate a diverse faculty and staff better able to represent a range of experiences within our programs. These commitments are central to embracing diversity within Asian American Studies.
3. We note, here, that it is possible to design a sequence of assignments that provide students with a taste of a variety of methods for exploring and obtaining knowledge about their own worlds. The immigration assignment described below can be used to introduce students to the processes of oral history. Subsequent assignments, such as on family values and interaction, can provide experience with observation-based methods. Papers on community can be set up to utilize all of these methods as well as a variety of survey techniques. In each case, if the instructor chooses, it is also possible to integrate firsthand interviews or oral history research with the examination of archival and secondary sources.
4. Immigrants of Asian descent suffered differential treatment in this regard, of course. For example, Chinese immigration was cut off in 1882 and partially

restored in 1943. Korean immigration was cut off largely due to Japanese colonial policy in 1910. Japanese immigration was restricted in 1908 and cut off in 1924. The latter two groups were given small quotas again only in 1952. Chan (1990, 1991) provides accessible overviews that we have assigned in our courses concerning the history of Asian immigration to the U.S.; more detailed legal histories are also available (e.g, Hing 1993).

5. The National Asian American Telecommunications Association (346 Ninth Street, San Francisco, CA 94103) has made many of these titles available for purchase or for rental.

6. Dunway and Baum (1984) is a useful resource, especially in terms of Okihiro's reprinted selection in which he highlights the enfranchising and empowering aspects of oral history methodology for research in Asian American and Ethnic Studies (Okihiro 1981).

7. Both authors have also handled students in groups during office hours if they come with general questions about the assignment. Another point in this regard is that we have sometimes found that we can best get the assignment "across" to students who are unclear about our expectations by making exemplary papers available as models. See Collier (1993) for examples of student papers produced in response to this assignment as well as others.

8. There are both advantages and disadvantages to the small group, selected panel sequence. On the negative side, the class as a whole hears only some of the range of experiences reflected in the class. On the positive side, presentations in smaller groups can be more extensive and less formal, allowing more questioning and interaction among students, and the individual panel presentations can go on longer. Generally speaking, the instructor's own personal contact with students, and the benefit of other pedagogical dimensions of the method (such as the generation of intragroup solidarity among the students), will probably go "up" in direct proportion to everyone's participation in all aspects of the assignment.

9. It is therefore useful if the instructor has basic biographical information about each student at hand. We usually obtain these data on the first day of class by asking each student to fill out an "information" sheet, including points such as ethnicity and generation, as well as a short autobiography. We then use this information to ensure as much diversity as possible in small groups and panels.

10. Both authors also reinforce this by emphasizing that panel presentations are an integral part of course materials, and advise students before the panel presentations to be sure to take notes—i.e., that the information presented by their peers is as important as information from the course texts, lectures, and videos. It might also be specified that panel information will be central to success on exams. If an exam question asks about the "fifth preference," for example, students will get full credit for the answer when they can not only define this item but also illustrate it with case study information garnered from their fellow students' panel presentations.

11. If students still complain about the panel assignment (and some have indeed expressed deep terror, stating that they have never had to speak in front of such a large group before), making the following points can help. The first is that the instructor and their fellow students will assist them and that it is not graded, per se. Second, students can bring maps, photos, artifacts, etc., as "aids" (but the main focus should still be on their verbal presentation). Third, it is important for them, scholastically and in terms of their future careers, to become practiced in making oral presentations to an audience. Fourth, it is a required course assignment and

everyone who signs up has to fulfill it—no exceptions allowed! Beyond this, we advise instructors to take the time to think through the entire process carefully, describe the process to students well in advance, and then set forth the context and rules for each panel.

12. Parenthetically, it should be noted here that there is very little discussion in the Ethnic Studies literature in regard to the proxemic dimensions of pedagogy— that is, concerning how classroom "set ups" impact patterns of communication among racial minority students (see Collier 1983).

13. For example, the impact of U.S. immigration laws on Asian Americans can be made immediately relevant to new Asian immigrants' lives by asking that such students list and discuss the specific preference category that allowed their family members to come to the U.S., or by inviting students whose parents came as "refugees" to find out what specific legislation the latter came under (typically not the seventh preference of the 1965 Immigration Act). In both cases, we have found that parents will often give extended accounts of these processes that students have not necessarily heard about before. In the same light, this is also an excellent point at which to stress the "family reunification" issue—both practically, since so many new Asian immigrants arrived via nuclear and extended family ties, and as a reflection of Asian and Asian American values and commitments.

14. In creating this larger context, we have often been able to delineate the "international underpinnings" of Asian American history vis-a-vis explications of our students' families' immigration histories (Mazumdar 1991:41).

15. This section draws from an article by Chabrán and Hirabayashi (1986).

16. Similarly, there may be some students for whom the information requested in the assignment is simply not available or not applicable. This includes students whose ancestors arrived many generations ago and others who are not immigrants, as well as foreign students who do not plan on staying in the United States after the completion of their education. In such cases we recommend flexibility. On occasion, we have provided alternative assignments such as interviewing an Asian American friend, a classmate from another class, or a neighbor. With foreign students we sometimes suggest a presentation of their own stories about coming to America as compared to the account of an immigrant. For students with longtime roots in the United States, it is possible to rework the assignment into a family history that traces internal migrations, economic shifts, and other changes over generations here in the United States. This has been productive with many non-Asian American students, as well as for fourth and fifth generation Asian American students who may have little access to information about their family's immigrant story. Our colleague, Professor Ben Kobashigawa, has devised yet another variation on the immigration assignment that is suitable for such situations. In one of his introductory courses on Asian American history, when he saw that there were too few Asian Americans in the course to set up panels, Kobashigawa created study groups that included at least one Asian American. Each study group was then issued the assignment (such as the immigration assignment we have described above) and the group as a whole selected an Asian American individual and collectively conducted the interview. Then each student in the group was required to write up the assignment.

17. See, for example, Hirabayashi (1973), Nash (1988) and Chan (1989).

18. Kenneth A. Bruffee, 1993, *Collaborative Learning: Higher Education, Interdependence, and the Authority of Knowledge*, Baltimore, Maryland: The Johns Hopkins University Press, 126-141.

19. This pedagogical orientation is not distinctive to Asian American Studies or Ethnic Studies, of course. Giroux (1992) provides an excellent series of essays introducing a pedagogy that highlights his vision of educators as "cultural workers" whose efforts demand an ongoing engagement with related critical and political perspectives. Professor Jere Takahashi also suggests that Asian American Studies faculty can look into the growing literature on "cooperative/ collaborative learning" at the university level (e.g., Cooper and Mueck 1989, Bruffee 1993), for insights on how to develop alternative educational contexts and processes (personal communication, 1991).

20. A related but somewhat unexpected by-product of the assignments occurred when students began to approach the instructors with personal problems and asked either for advice or referrals. In other cases, Collier, in particular, was able to spot individual educational and personal difficulties and counseled students in nonthreatening terms to seek additional advising.

References

Bruffee, Kenneth A. 1993. *Collaborative Learning: Higher Education, Interdependence, and the Authority of Knowledge*. Baltimore, Maryland: The Johns Hopkins University Press.

Chabrán, Mrytha, and Lane R. Hirabayashi. 1986. "The Cloak and the Shroud: On the Dual Nature of Ethnic and Family Secrets among Third World People in the United States." *Images: Ethnic Studies Occasional Papers Series*. School of Ethnic Studies, San Francisco State University, 44-62.

Chan, Sucheng. 1989. "On the Ethnic Studies Requirement. Part I: Pedagogical Implications." *Amerasia Journal* 15:267-280.

———. 1990. "European and Asian Immigration into the United States in Comparative Perspective, 1820s to 1920s." In Virginia Yans-McLaughlin, ed., *Immigration Reconsidered: History, Sociology, and Politics*. New York: Oxford University Press, 37-75.

———. 1991. *Asian Americans: An Interpretive History*. Boston: Twayne.

Collier, Malcolm. 1983. *Nonverbal Factors in the Education of Chinese American Children: A Film Study*. (A report on research conducted with the assistance of National Institute of Education grant NIE-81-0115.) Available from ERIC.

———. 1993. *Asians in America: A Reader*. Dubuque, Iowa: Kendall/Hunt Publishing Co.

Cooper, James L., and Randall Mueck. 1989. "Cooperative/ Collaborative Learning: Research and Practice (Primarily) at the Collegiate Level." *Journal of Staff, Program, and Organizational Development* 7:143-148.

Dunaway, David K., and Willa K. Baum, eds. 1984. *Oral History: An Interdisciplinary Anthology*. American Association for State and Local History in cooperation with the Oral History Association.

Giroux, Henry. 1992. *Border Crossings: Cultural Workers and the Politics of Education*. New York: Routledge.

Giroux, Henry A., and Peter McLaren, eds. 1994. *Between Borders: Pedagogy and the Politics of Cultural Studies*. New York: Routledge.

Hing, Bill Ong. 1993. *Making and Remaking Asian America Through Immigration Policy*. Stanford: Stanford University Press.

Hirabayashi, James A. 1973. "Research and Studies." In George Kagiwada, et al., eds., *Proceedings of National Asian American Studies Conference II: Tool of Control?*

Tool of Change? Davis, California: Asian American Studies, Department of Applied Behavioral Sciences, 25-28.

Mazumdar, Sucheta. 1991. "Asian American Studies and Asian Studies: Rethinking Roots." In Shirley Hune, Hyung-chan Kim, Stephen S. Fugita, and Amy Ling, eds., *Asian Americans: Comparative and Global Perspectives.* Pullman, Washington: Washington State University Press, 29-44.

Nash, Phil. 1988. "Creating Critical Consciousness: Paulo Freire and the Mechanics of Teaching Asian American Studies." In Gary Y. Okihiro, Shirley Hune, Arthur A. Hansen, John M. Liu, eds., *Reflections on Shattered Windows: Promises and Prospects for Asian American Studies.* Pullman, Washington: Washington State University Press, 101-116.

O'Hare, William. P. 1992. "America's Minorities—The Demographics of Diversity." *Population Bulletin,* Vol. 27, No. 4.

Okihiro, Gary Y. 1981. "Oral History and the Writing of Ethnic History." *Oral History Review* 9:27-46. [Reprinted in Dunaway and Baum 1984.]

Tamayo Lott, Juanita. 1993. "Do United States Racial/Ethnic Categories Still Fit?" *Population Today,* January 1993, 6-9.

Chapter Three

On the Edge:
Southeast Asians in Philadelphia
and the Struggle for Space

Ellen Somekawa

As Asian Americans, many of us experience the sense of being out of place, of being told to go back where we belong, of belonging neither completely to the communities where we live nor to Asian ancestral homes. This felt lack of place reflects an immediate material reality, especially for Asians living in eastern U.S. cities. Our small numbers and the ideological construction of Asians as perpetual outsiders are legacies of our history of exclusion and set the conditions for the struggle of Asian Americans to open up space for ourselves. A historical and cultural geography of Asian American communities must examine not only community formation where it occurs, but also the denial of community and our struggle as Asian Americans to create a place for ourselves.

Struggling for space is part of the lived experience of getting up and going through each day, especially for recent immigrants. To wear what one wants and to speak the language of one's choosing, to sit on the front steps, to hold a public celebration, to observe one's religion, and to use a library or walk on a sidewalk are forms of struggling for space. For Asian American communities past and present, struggling for space has meant reconstructing communities dislodged by the forced removal of Japanese Americans during the Internment; resisting developers' encroachment on Chinatown; and overcoming neighborhood opposition to a Cambodian Buddhist temple. Fighting for "turf" is often represented by the media and the police as the petty and juvenile concerns of young gang members, but in actuality it can mean contending for the right to participate in basic human activities.

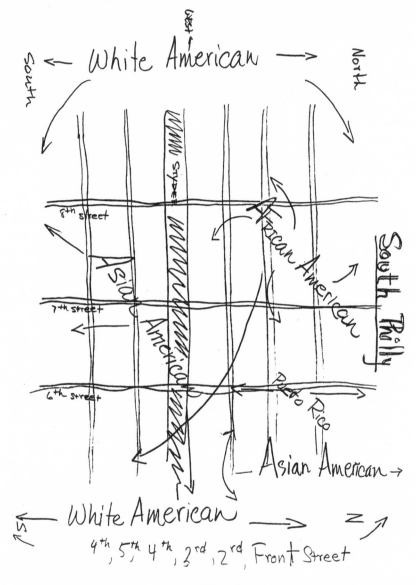

Figure 1

Accordingly, this map of his South Philadelphia neighborhood, drawn by Phin Phoeung, a seventeen year old Cambodian youth, portrays the swirling and complex racial patterns that he lives in and negotiates every day. [Figure 1] [1]

In Phoeung's depiction, African Americans, Asian Americans, and Puerto Ricans relate to each other in a cramped and dynamic frenzy. The adamantly drawn border running east-west and labeled "Snyder" signifies a distinct racial divide between the African American and the Asian American sections of the neighborhood. "White American" territory surrounds and encloses it all. The absence of detail about the White American zone reflects its unexplored and unknown quality, being an area off-limits to a Cambodian American youth. When Philadelphia Mayor Ed Rendell singled out the public library at Seventh and Snyder Streets for closure, the African American and Asian American children whom it served lost a vital resource. Many openly expressed their fear of crossing the borderline into the white area to go to another library, and recounted stories of being beaten and harassed by white youth there. Some Asian residents mistakenly and earnestly believed that this library—Whitman Library—was called "Whiteman Library." By contrast, Seventh Street south of Snyder has developed into a hub of Asian activity featuring Southeast Asian restaurants, groceries, beauty shops, video stores, saté stands, kids playing, youth hanging out, and older people strolling, shopping and playing chess on the sidewalk.

Over the last two decades, new Asian communities have come into being in Philadelphia. From an almost nonexistent population to a population of over 20,000, Southeast Asian refugees have entered Philadelphia at a time when the processes of abandonment and gentrification are reshaping many of the nation's inner cities.[2] The deindustrialization of cities and the transformation to a service economy have had dramatic repercussions on the development of urban residential areas. Caroline Adams, David Bartelt, et al. have described the process by which those areas of Philadelphia that house the prosperous segment of the service-sector work force or that bolster powerful service sector institutions are being revitalized, while the neighborhoods that relied on the manufacturing base for their prosperity are tending to fall into decline.[3] Neighborhoods affected by both ends of this process of urban restructuring—gentrification and decline—are vulnerable to high levels of displacement and abandonment. Housing in and on the edges of gentrifying neighborhoods can become vacant when rising rents force lower income people out or when real estate speculators "warehouse" properties for future development. Housing in many working class neighborhoods is abandoned as manufacturing jobs leave the city, and as their populations age. Some neighborhoods are rising while others are having the floor fall out from under them, but in both cases the lives of poor and working class people are disrupted.[4]

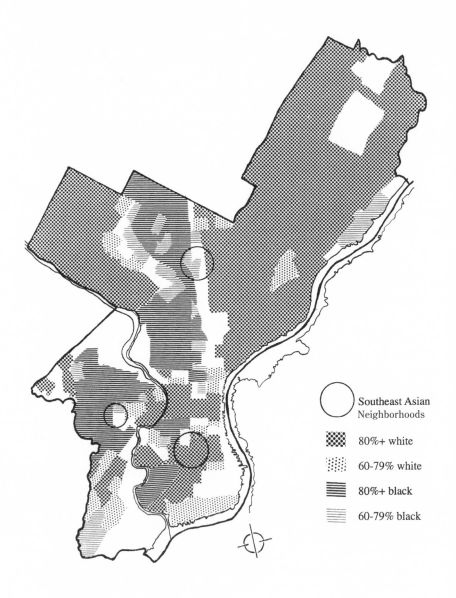

Figure 2

City of Philadelphia. Pattern of segregation based on 1980 Census.

The vacant and deteriorating housing created by these stressful and conflict-ridden processes became home to many Southeast Asian refugees. Dislodged from Southeast Asia in large numbers and with few resources, refugees learned that few housing opportunities were open to them in this country. Resettlement agencies received government contracts and funding to place and provide services to refugees. Faced with the need to find large numbers of vacant low-rent housing units on short notice, the agencies ended up creating concentrations of Southeast Asians in neighborhoods that were undergoing decline or racial and economic transition.

These new communities have also developed in the context of sharp residential segregation. According to Adams, Bartelt et al., in 1980, the average black Philadelphian lived in a census tract that was 82 percent black, and the average white Philadelphian lived in an area that was over 90 percent white.[5] This map (Fig. 2), based on the 1980 census, is a rough visual description of residential segregation in the city at a time when the largest waves of Southeast Asian refugees were settling in Philadelphia. In a city so dramatically divided into black and white areas, where was the social space available for new Asian migrants to settle?[6]

The Setting

Concentrations of Asian residents have in many cases developed in boundary areas—that is, between demarcated African American and white communities. In Philadelphia, the several neighborhoods where Southeast Asian refugees have concentrated illustrate a pattern of being "on the edge." Three main areas of Southeast Asian refugee resettlement became clearly defined in the period from 1979 to 1982: one in West Philadelphia, one in North Philadelphia in the Olney/Logan area, and one in South Philadelphia (Fig. 2). These are the areas of largest concentration, although some new pockets have emerged (Figs. 3-4). We can see very clearly this phenomenon of Asian communities on the margins, inserted in the spaces between other larger communities.

Casual observers might think that Asian refugees were resettled in the poorest areas, in predominantly black neighborhoods, but what we notice from looking at these maps is that the refugees tended not to be resettled in large numbers in the heart of African American, Latino, or white neighborhoods, but rather in border areas. These are charged areas. They are arenas of contention between different groups, and all are going through some sort of painful transition. The vacant housing which made these neighborhoods convenient locations for refugee resettlement is itself a mark of dislocation and change.

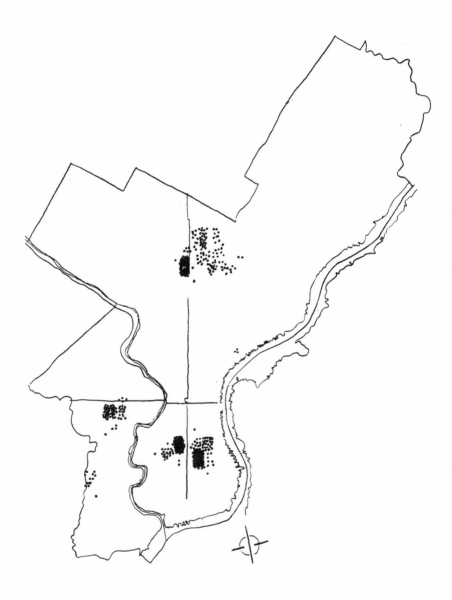

Figure 3

City of Philadelphia. One dot (•) represents 10 Cambodians or 10 Laotians.
(1990 Census Tract Data)

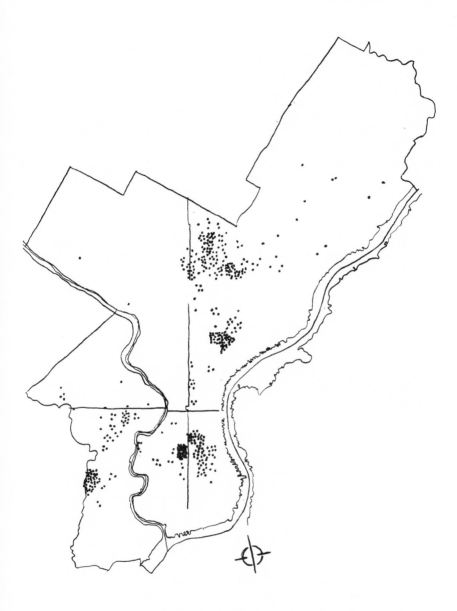

Figure 4

City of Philadelphia. One dot (•) represents 10 Vietnamese.
(1990 Census Tract Data)

One of the areas that numbers of Southeast Asian refugees moved into is West Philadelphia. In particular, Asian refugees were being moved into the area on the borders of the black community and on the border of the University of Pennsylvania community. On the one side is the University of Pennsylvania, Drexel University and other large institutions which have been expanding since the 1960s. As a consortium of universities, hospitals, and research centers, along with city planners, implemented their vision of urban renewal, they cleared the way for the massive expansion of these institutions and for housing their work forces. The University of Pennsylvania, in particular, made conscious efforts to expand student housing and to encourage its faculty and staff to live in the West Philadelphia neighborhood.[7]

To the west of the University of Pennsylvania is Walnut Hill, which had developed into a stable, predominantly black, middle-class neighborhood during the 1950s and 1960s. Walnut Hill is now the site of upscale housing and rising rents right alongside housing being allowed to go vacant and deteriorate. It is into these vacant and deteriorating housing units that numbers of Asian refugees were resettled during the late 1970s and early 1980s. The position of being on the edge describes not only a spatial reality but also an aspect of the social relations in the neighborhood. To be on the edge is to be in a precarious position, at the site of economic transition. Asian refugees were an unwelcome visual reminder and a confirmation of the changes in the neighborhoods that until that time had occurred gradually and if not imperceptibly, at least quietly. In the decade between 1970 and 1980, the neighborhood had lost one-fourth of its households and almost a third of its rental units.[8]

Neighborhood Responses

To the African American residents who had been living in the West Philadelphia neighborhood of Walnut Hill, the resettlement of Asians was sudden and unexpected. One African American resident told the story of two large apartment buildings in this way:

> It didn't just happen like one day you looked up and the neighborhood had changed, no. It was over a period of years. The Admiral Court situation, now, I'm going to truthfully say that was an overnight deal at Admiral Court. One day you walked past, the building is empty, the windows are broken; it's just empty and everybody moved out. And this big orange slip of paper from the City telling that it was unfit. You go to bed, you wake up the next morning. There's three hundred Asians all over the place. And everybody's saying, "Where did they come from? How did this happen?" And that's basically what I remember. I'll never forget because I used to walk past.

Because I remember how the building looked and then to see it just sitting there and nothing going on and then the next day to come past and to see all of these Asians all over the place. And the trucks were still coming. They came in tractor-trailers, not tractor trailers, but long trucks I guess would it be eighteen wheelers? And the people were all in the back. And they opened the back of the truck and here they come. . .

And that's basically what happened with Admiral Court. Same thing with Stoneleigh Court. One day the building is—they didn't even have time to board it up, rather they didn't even take the time to board the building up. The people who lived there left. The last people who just stayed there because they had no place else to go finally left. You go to bed, you wake up the next day; the place is filled up with Asians. And truckloads are still coming, emptying more Asians into the building. And so you have people there with no light, no electricity, no running water, and you know, like what's going on. And it just never stopped. It seemed like it went on for days and days. And then the people in the community started making phone calls, yelling and screaming, and children fighting. Black children fighting Asian children. "You don't belong here. What are you doing here?" It was just total confusion. It was just so crazy. You wouldn't have believed it. It was just like a war broke out in West Philadelphia, that's just what it was like.[9]

Was this a classic case of housing filtering? (As one group moves up and out, a new group having fewer resources comes in and the housing stock goes through a progressive decline.) There is evidence to suggest that a different process was at work here: landlords chose to milk their properties as a strategy for making profit. The economic interest of these landlords coincided with the needs of the resettlement agencies who had to place large numbers of refugees in a short period of time.

In the weeks and months after the movement of refugees into Stoneleigh Court, some Walnut Hill residents mobilized to respond to the influx of refugees into their neighborhood. In January of 1980, the Walnut Hill Community Association. an organization made up predominantly of African American home owners, put out a flyer reading:

Strangers
(Southeast Asians)
Living in UNFIT houses
apartments, etc.—in Walnut Hill . . .
Who is responsible?
We should have been consulted . . .
Public hearing very soon . . .[10]

Long-standing residents' opinions about the Asian refugees were varied, but some common themes emerged in public forums such as community meetings, negotiations with politicians and resettlement agencies, and the press. Resentment of privileges which refugees were purported to receive was a frequently articulated grievance against Southeast Asians.

A leader of an African American institution in West Philadelphia was quoted in the *Daily News* saying:

> It's really a paradox. These are some of the same people who black people were told to fight against [in Vietnam].
>
> A Cambodian refugee who comes into the U.S. gets a $250 resettlement grant when he sets foot in the country, has cheap housing set up for him before he's here, goes on welfare when the $250 runs out, and can count on nonprofit agencies to give him English lessons and help getting a job. The ancestors of black Americans, didn't have a chance when they came to America—they were 'kidnapped'—and their descendants haven't been given the leg up the refugees have gotten. [11]

Another critique of refugee resettlement went beyond general resentment and argued that the way in which refugee resettlement was being conducted was hurting the efforts of African American residents to improve their own condition. One representative of the Walnut Hill Community Association put it this way: "We have a right to know who's coming to dinner . . . There's no more food at the table. Poor is poor . . . Why when this country is so wide open do they have to put the refugees in the black community where we've been fighting for better education, housing and jobs for so long?" [12]

In a heated meeting, members of another West Philadelphia community group questioned a staff member from one of the resettlement agencies. First, why was the agency putting people in apartments owned by slumlords when residents were trying to fight the landlords and get people not to move into those apartments? Second, what was the agency doing to train the refugees to keep their properties clean? Third, would the agency commit itself to assisting its clients in filing Licenses and Inspections claims against their landlords? The staff member from the agency noted that "The major concerns were similar to those always brought up." [13] On the one hand, refugees were viewed as bringing down the neighborhood—living in unfit housing, in overcrowded conditions, and not properly disposing of garbage. On the other hand, Asian refugees were seen as instruments of white business. A struggle between black residents and white landlords was being played out with the Asian refugees constructed as passive objects in the process. [14]

These arguments implied that the refugees were taking away opportunities from black residents, and that refugees moving into these apartment buildings were setting back the struggle of the black residents against slum landlords. It was not simply that refugees took limited affordable housing away from black residents, but that the refugees were viewed as being exploitable and therefore as weakening the bargaining power of tenants struggling to hold their landlords accountable for basic services. [15]

These perceptions were not without a basis in the real interactions that occurred in the neighborhood. The owner of the Stoneleigh Court apartment complex actively approached the refugee resettlement agencies about renting out his buildings to them. The Executive Director of one of the resettlement agencies said,

> That particular landlord [of Stoneleigh Court], that's an interesting story. He was the only landlord that ever approached us and said, 'I want to do a good job for these refugees. And I have two large or three large . . .' I think he had three or four large buildings. He was also a tax delinquent, which we did not know at the time. But we were impressed that he came to us. [16]

The resettlement agencies and the landlords developed a reciprocal relationship. The necessities facing the agencies made them receptive to the idea of establishing ongoing relationships with landlords who could provide them with quantities of vacant housing on short notice. For the landlords' part, the agencies, and their refugee clients, provided a regular source of rent. Since the landlords knew that the first months of the refugees' expenses would be guaranteed by the government, they were assured that they would be regularly paid rent even for housing that was declared unfit for habitation. The Asian refugees provided a peculiar combination of attributes—they were poor enough and powerless enough that they would, at least for a time, put up with deplorable housing conditions. The large family size and low income of many refugee families meant that they had to rent from landlords who would allow severe overcrowding of their housing units. At the same time, the landlords would have a regular source of income and some oversight that would assure that they would be paid rent.

Rumors were circulated in Walnut Hill that the resettlement agencies had made agreements with the landlord and removed black residents from Stoneleigh Court. At least one agency denied the charge at the time. Reports appeared in the local African American newspaper that refugees were being placed in abandoned or condemned housing from which African Americans had been forced out. [17] In a recent interview, the Catholic Social Services employee in charge of resettling all the surviving members of one Cambodian village in Stoneleigh Court recalled that:

> I think there were one or two Vietnamese families living in the building at the time. And this landlord had sort of kept the place going and then when he found out, I think what he did was he evicted a lot of people who were marginal payees, who weren't paying their rent regularly. He knew he was going to get the regular money from Catholic Social Services for these people so he saw this as an opportunity to fill up the building with paying

customers. So when we finally moved in the place was a— the windows were all busted up, the heating system, the radiators were kind of not working or part of the building was working and the rest was not working.

. . . we eventually got to the point where once we got the people on welfare and once they were getting their checks we made sure they paid their rent on schedule every month. [18]

In this case, the competition between blacks and Asians for housing was direct. It was not that the Asians were taking housing which was unavailable for blacks. There was much vacant housing in the neighborhood. But the Asian refugees who were moving in were operating under a different set of rules—rules which particularly benefited landlords, which allowed landlords to milk their properties to collect rents without putting anything back into the maintenance and upkeep of the buildings.

Since there was almost no established Southeast Asian community in Philadelphia at the time, the resettlement agencies became the intermediaries between the African Americans, white residents, and the refugees. These agencies showed little interest in helping the efforts of tenant organizations to challenge the practices of landlords. However, as the Asian communities become more established and the role of the resettlement agencies is reduced, the systemic features that made refugees particularly exploitable will no longer be built into the situation. A successful rent strike by the Cambodian tenants of a West Philadelphia apartment building in 1985 belies the various cultural interpretations which construct Asian refugees as politically passive by nature.

Street Responses

Living on the edge describes the broad geographic pattern of Southeast Asian resettlement and a relationship to economic transition; it also describes a street level reality. The Philadelphia Commission on Human Relations puts out a report on the state of intergroup relations every year. The PCHR statistics for 1988 and 1989 showed that although Asians comprised an estimated three to five percent of the population of the city, they were victims of 25 to 30 percent of the interracial incidents reported to the PCHR. The tensions created by the placement of refugees in racial border areas and in areas undergoing economic and physical distress were played out on the street.

Anti-Asian violence represents the rawest form of coercion by which Asians are taught where the boundaries are—where they do not belong. In the early 1980s, elderly Hmong women in West Philadelphia were forced to give up the garden they shared after being attacked and stoned repeatedly. After a series of attacks and one particularly brutal assault on a

Hmong man in the Powelton section of West Philadelphia in 1984, most of the Hmong people left the city altogether.[19] From a population of over 3000, only a few hundred Hmong still remain in Philadelphia.[20]

One young Vietnamese American man said of his Southwest Philadelphia neighborhood, "You know where to walk and where not to walk." He described his friend's experience of first moving into the neighborhood and not knowing where it was safe to go. His friend went to get a movie and walked past a group of white guys. They started to harass him and then chased him all the way to his home where he escaped inside. They then stayed outside and threw rocks at the house until they broke a window; then they left. [21]

A Lao man in West Philadelphia talks about the lack of social space for older Asians in that neighborhood: "Coming home from work and staying home all the time. Go to your friend's home everyday, you would like to have some place for them to go to play cards or to talk or to do whatever. . . It's just a sad thing, like being a prisoner in your home and nothing to do." He also talks about the attempts of young Asian men to carve out a space for themselves: "So they form a group and, 'hey, this is my neighborhood.' It's like everybody, every kid, protects the turf. 'So this is my turf. You come in and look me down, you spit on me, you try to insult me, I'll beat you up.' So that's the way the kids think." [22] A Cambodian community leader explained that:

> The refugees who were there at the beginning were robbed a lot. Were beaten up a lot . . . At the beginning they think we're easy prey. And the young ones, the youngsters formed their own groups and fought back . . . and although we don't condone that thing, anything that helps is appreciated. So that's one of the things that stops some of the crimes against Asians.[23]

Individuals are cast into the role of expanding or defending existing space accessible to themselves and their families. Youth "fighting back," as a mode of negotiating the use of social space, can exact a heavy price in terms of the devastation of human lives. On a contested playground in Southwest Philadelphia, white and Asian teens clashed when the whites tried to force the Asians to leave the park. A young white man died, and six young Asian men are spending years of their lives locked in prison. White community hysteria, media hype and the racially inflammatory prosecution of the case increased the vulnerability of Asians in the city to attacks and to a justice system more interested in placating an angry community than in meting out justice. Just as the young men would not be chased from the park and accept constrictions on their lives imposed by white power graffiti and physical threats, adults organizing to defend the accused youth constituted an act of defending space for Asians.

In this city, blood on the ground and young men behind bars has sprung from urban restructuring and the dynamics of the housing market. Most Southeast Asian refugees had little initial choice about where they would live and no control over the economy and housing market of the aging industrial city they were placed in; but once placed, people became active agents in constructing their own lives. Creating a community, in both its social and physical sense, arose out of a tension between freedom and necessity, between choosing affirmatively to live among those who share one's culture and history and being forced into narrowly proscribed zones through the "unseen hand" of the housing market or the heavy hand of resettlement agencies complicit with landlords.

We struggle to create a place for ourselves—by organizing to save a library, fighting in the street, planting a garden, building our organizations, teaching our daughters to sew, or standing on the corner. While some attempts at opening up space affirm our cultures and our humanity, others pose challenges to our deepest values and risk societal censure. We may yearn to be able to use our creativity and energy in other ways, but we continue to struggle on because the alternative may well be to remain always out of place, always on the edge.

Endnotes

1. Phin Phoeung has since moved to Wisconsin to complete his education.
2. Population estimates are from Robert P. Thayer, "Who Killed Heng Lim? The Southeast Asian Experience of Racial Harassment in Philadelphia" (M.A. Thesis, School for International Training, Brattleboro, VT, 1990), p. 2.
3. Caroline Adams, David Bartelt et al., *Philadelphia: Neighborhoods, Division, and Conflict in a Postindustrial City* (Philadelphia: Temple University Press, 1991), chapter 3.
4. See Peter Marcuse, "Abandonment, Gentrification, and Displacement: The Linkages in New York City," in *Gentrification of the City*, ed. Neil Smith and Peter Williams. (Boston: Allen & Unwin, 1986), 172; also Joe R. Feagin, "Urban Real Estate Speculation in the United States: Implications for Social Science and Urban Planning," in *Critical Perspectives on Housing*, ed. Rachel G. Bratt, Chester Hartman, and Ann Meyerson (Philadelphia: Temple University Press, 1986).
5. Adams, Bartelt, et al., pp. 94-95.
6. An analogous question might be asked in relation to the Latino population of the city. A significant stretch of the long, narrow north-south blank strip on Figure 2 between the heavy concentrations of African Americans and whites has become home to a large Puerto Rican community.
7. Group Planning and Research Inc., "The Market for Housing in University City: Urban Renewal Area Unit III," Preliminary Draft, prepared for the Redevelopment Authority of the City of Philadelphia, ca 1964, Redevelopment Authority Record Group, Municipal Archives, Philadelphia; "University City: Brainsville on the March," *Philadelphia Inquirer Magazine*, 19 July 1964; *Sunday Bulletin* 15 August 1965.

8. Philadelphia City Planning Commission, "Center City and Its People: A Working Paper," September 1985, p. 76.
9. Interview with Jacqui Simmons, Philadelphia, 22 March 1990.
10. Nationalities Service Center Records, Urban Archives, Temple University, Philadelphia, PA.
11. Sister Falakah Fattah of the House of Umoja in West Philadelphia, quoted in the *Philadelphia Daily News*, 25 July 1979.
12. *University City News*, January 1980.
13. Memo dated 4/10 from W. L. to Gabe. Nationalities Service Center Records, Urban Archives, Temple University, Philadelphia, PA.
14. See various memos in the Community Relations Project files of the Nationalities Service Center Records, Urban Archives, Temple University, Philadelphia PA, *Philadelphia Tribune* 27 January 1980; *Philadelphia Daily News* 25 July 1979.
15. W.L. Memorandum to Supervisors, April 10 (no year) Nationalities Service Center Records, Urban Archives, Temple University, Philadelphia, PA.
16. Interview with Michael Blum, Executive Director of the Nationalities Service Center, Philadelphia, 6 June 1990.
17. *University City News*, January 1980; *Philadelphia Tribune*, 27 January 1980; interview with Michael Blum, 6 June 1990.
18. Interview with Lloyd Romero, ex-consultant to Catholic Social Services, 1 April 1991.
19. Interview with Ruth Adams, block captain of the 4400 block of Powelton Avenue, 25 April 1990; *Philadelphia Inquirer*, 8 September 1984, B1; conversation with a Hmong community leader, 11 September 1993.
20. Population estimate from Robert P. Thayer, p. 14.
21. Anonymous interview by Neeta Patel, Philadelphia, March 1992.
22. Interview with Dan Sengsourysack, West Philadelphia resident, 5 February 1992.
23. Interview with Samien Nol, Executive Director of Southeast Asian Mutual Assistance Associations Coalition, Philadelphia, 6 February 1992.

Chapter Four

Individuals, Institutions, and Structure: The Decision-Making Process of Philippine International Migrants

James A. Tyner

Filipinos reside, either temporarily or permanently, in over 130 countries and territories. However, individual migrants do not actively choose among this wide range of alternative destinations. Indeed, it is highly unlikely that any one individual would be aware of many alternative destinations. Research on Philippine immigration (Medina and Natividad 1985; Carino et al. 1990) is consistent with other migration literature (Lansing and Mueller 1967; Goodman 1981; Roseman 1983), in that Filipino migrants have only a few alternative destinations—perhaps one or two—at the time of migration decision-making.

Often, the selection of alternative destinations is predicated on family reunification and chain migration. In the Philippines, family networks exert a major influence on migration decisions (Carino et al. 1990; Lindquist 1993). According to Timberman (1991, 46), the extended family is the most important social and economic unit in the Philippines. This alone does not explain, however, why some migrants go to the United States while others find temporary employment in Asian or Middle Eastern countries.

To begin to understand the decision-making processes involved within a global system of Philippine international migration, it is necessary to address the migration process at both a macro-structural level as well as a micro-individual level. Throughout this paper I argue that a focus on the production of opportunities—defined as alternative destinations for potential migrants—will better enable researchers to focus on the determinant variables involved in the decision-making process of international migrants. In particular, I situate the decision-making process of Philippine international migrants within a context of changing opportunities. In this way I am able to link micro-level individual decision-making with macro-level structural changes.

Data Sources

Interviews were conducted during March and April of 1992. With the help of a Filipina assistant, respondents were selected (in a nonrandom manner) in medical offices and retail stores throughout Long Beach and Carson, California. This study is neither comprehensive nor exhaustive. Rather, the intent is to provide a preliminary examination of the decision-making process of Philippine migrants within the context of changing opportunities. Interviews were completed either in person or by phone, depending on the preference of the respondent, and lasted between 30 minutes and two hours. Questions were open ended, and focused specifically on the migration histories of individuals, alternative locations that were considered, and motivations behind each movement. I focus on single moves of individuals as the unit of analysis. In this way, I am able to isolate each move, and situate the move within its own unique context. I use Roseman's (1971) distinction of partial and total displacement[1] as a surrogate for local and long-distance moves. While not initially formulated to encapsulate international migration, a modified version of the total/partial displacement classification—consisting of partial displacement moves, total displacement moves, and international moves[2]—provides a framework for discussing aspects of the migration process (Roseman 1971, 593). In total, 22 interviews (18 females and 4 males) were completed. The average age of the respondents was 32, ranging from 19 to 49, while the average age at the time of first migration to the United States was 22, ranging from 10 to 32. The sample had a total of 103 moves; the average number of moves per person was 4.7, with a range from 2 to 12 moves.

The Context of Migration

Considerable difficulty has arisen in providing a mode of discourse between competing theoretical perspectives in migration research. Macro-level theories state that migration is directly related to structural processes (Shrestha 1987) and focus on such variables as unemployment levels, wage rates, and immigration/emigration policies. A strict structural emphasis, however, often loses sight of individual migrants and thus downplays the micro-level decisions involved prior to movement

(Pedraza-Bailey 1990). Micro-level theories, conversely, view migration as a behavioral response to macro-level constraints and opportunities (Shrestha 1987, 331). Thus, while acknowledging structural variables, it is the networks developed by the movement of people back and forth that sustain migration over time (Portes 1991; Lindquist 1993). Micro-level theories are often criticized, however, for their portrayal of migrants as free-choice, rational beings (Shrestha 1990, 48).

Satisfactory explanations of migration require balance and integration between various levels (Ward 1981, 75). Throughout this paper I contend that migration results from the matching of macro-level opportunities with micro-level decision-making. A key tenet of this is that at any given time for a specified location, there are a finite number of potential destinations (opportunities) available to prospective migrants owing to such factors as immigration and emigration policies, labor recruitment policies, and citizenship rights. Opportunities to migrate are produced primarily by macro-level institutions such as local and national governments, schools, military institutions, and labor recruitment agencies. In essence, alternative destinations are bounded by certain parameters that are often beyond the control of individual potential migrants.

At the micro-level decisions are made within the confines of these parameters and hinge on two main aspects. First, potential migrants need to be exposed to various opportunities. In this sense, social networks and personal experience weigh heavily as explanatory variables. However, even though an opportunity may be known, not everyone is eligible. Opportunities often have specific requirements (e.g., age, sex, education and occupation levels) stipulating who may take advantage of the various opportunities. Thus, individuals not only need to be exposed to opportunities (a space-time match), but the potential migrants must also match the specific requirements of the opportunity presented.

Philippine International Migration

Philippine international migration may be broadly classified as occurring in two phases: pre-1970s and post-1970s.[3] Prior to the 1970s, opportunities for Philippine migrants were influenced primarily by the actions of United States institutions in a colonial, and later post-colonial, context.[4] However, the opportunities to migrate internationally were developed and maintained by U.S. institutions, and these initial patterns have been reinforced through the development of social networks and chain migration. Following the 1970s, international migration of Filipinos was more and more influenced by Philippine institutions in response to changing global political-economic relationships.

Pre-1970s

When the Philippines became a colony of the United States following the Philippine-American War, 1899-1902, the creation of certain institutions and the implementation of certain policies by the United States had a direct impact on the movement of Filipinos. Opportunities were basically a reflection of ties to the United States with migration flows directed towards the United States and her possessions—chiefly Hawaii. The development and maintenance of these opportunities can be attributed to three broad institutional processes: education, immigration policies, and the military.

Education contributed to Philippine international migration in two fundamental ways. The U.S. government, after taking possession of the Philippines, initiated that country's first public schools—albeit to effectively assimilate the Filipinos under American control. Through novels, songs, and American teachers in public schools, education provided many young Filipinos with an awareness of opportunities outside of the Philippines. Additionally, educational institutions offered the chance for Filipinos to migrate to the United States as students. In terms of numbers, the migration of Filipino students during the first decades of the twentieth century was small, yet its impact was great. On returning to the Philippines, students would share their experiences with other Filipinos, speaking of widespread opportunities in the United States (Posadas 1986-87).

United States immigration policies have both directly and indirectly influenced Philippine international migration. Indirectly, this has occurred through United States immigration policies addressed to other countries and immigrant groups. The Philippine-Hawaiian system was one such case. Beginning in 1852, the powerful elite in Hawaii had conducted labor recruitment campaigns in search of cheap labor (Teodoro 1981, 8). First, Chinese immigrants were imported, and beginning in 1869, Japanese immigrants were working on the plantations. However, the Chinese Exclusion Act of 1882 severely limited Chinese immigration, and the Gentlemen's Agreement in 1907 impeded Japanese immigration. Thus, in response to labor shortages, sugar growers in Hawaii began to search for alternative sources (Chan 1991, 18; Teodoro 1981, 10). Classified as U.S. nationals, Filipinos were excluded from most U.S. immigration policies and international agreements; thus the Philippines was a logical choice. Philippine migration to Hawaii began in earnest in 1909.

The Immigration Acts of 1921 and 1924 were also indirect influences on Philippine international migration. Initially, shifting patterns of international migration to the continental United States resulted from an oversupply of laborers in Hawaii. However, following the 1921 and 1924 Immigration

Acts, which placed quota restrictions on immigrants by country, U.S. farmers were concerned over a ready supply of labor. The Chinese Exclusion Act and Gentlemen's Agreement previously limited the supply of Chinese and Japanese farm laborers to the United States, and now farm owners feared that Mexican migrants—previously a source of cheap labor—would be limited by quota restrictions. Similar to the Philippine-Hawaiian system, Filipinos were not subject to quota limitations and were able to take advantage of employment opportunities in the United States.

Not until the migration of Filipinos was considered to have a detrimental impact on the United States were specific migration policies implemented. Ostensibly for the purpose of granting the Philippines independence, the passage of the Tydings-McDuffie Act in 1934 gave the country commonwealth status. Thereafter, Filipinos were not considered U.S. nationals, and were thus subject to quota restrictions. Philippine immigration to the United States was restricted to just 50 migrants per year.

A third institution, the military, has been highly influential as well. Carino (1987, 312) identifies two fundamental ways in which the continuing presence of the U.S. military in the Philippines has contributed to migration. First, there is the kinship-based immigration through international marriages between American military personnel and Filipino women. This was particularly relevant following World War II with the passage of the War Brides Act and the Fiancees Act. Second, the U.S. military presence in the Philippines has facilitated the recruitment of Filipinos into the U.S. military. As soon as the American military forces had pacified the Philippines, Filipinos were hired by the Navy. By 1930, there were an estimated 25,000 Filipino Navy enlistees. Many recruits eventually qualified for American citizenship, a fact that has had a significant impact on subsequent Philippine immigration (Carino 1987). Indeed, as an opportunity, getting into any of the branches of the U.S. armed forces was a major access route to the United States for many young and able-bodied Filipinos (Salazar 1987, 468). Moreover, Filipinos in the U.S. military have been stationed in various destinations throughout the world (Salazar 1987, 468). In this way the U.S. military indirectly opened up global exposure and opportunities for many Filipino servicemen.

Post-1970s

In the 1960s, Filipino migrants began to disperse geographically—in large part owing to liberalized immigration policies of certain countries (e.g., Australia, Canada, New Zealand, and the United States). However, in terms of institutional control, Philippine international migration was still regulated primarily by U.S. institutions. Even the migration into Canada was influenced strongly by U.S. institutions. Many of the first arrivals in Canada were postgraduate students from the United States who were required to leave that country following completion of their studies or technical training (Ramcharan 1982, 26). Yet following the Immigration Act of the United States—fully effective in 1968—Philippine immigration into Canada lessened. With newly opened opportunities to stay, many Filipinos elected to remain in the United States.

It was not until the 1970s—and in particular, after the declaration of Martial Law by former Philippine President Ferdinand Marcos—that patterns of institutional control changed. Under the Labor Code of 1974 the Philippine government assumed control of overseas employment.

In general, opportunities for Philippine migrants following martial law reflect the changing political and economic relations between the Philippine government and other countries. Thus, as political and economic ties developed, so too did opportunities for temporary employment abroad—primarily in Asia and the Middle East. Settlement migration, however, has continued to flow primarily to the United States, with smaller flows to Canada, Australia, and New Zealand.

The Decision to Migrate

In the Philippines, the powerful influence of the family shapes most social, political, and economic interactions (Timberman 1991, 17). Indeed, studies generally find that migration decisions of Filipinos are most often made by entire families (Arnold and Abad 1985; Medina and Natividad 1985; Lauby and Stark 1988; Root and DeJong 1991). However, Trager (1988, 186) contends that family strategies are not necessarily focused on migration per se; rather, families are concerned with ways of maintaining and/or advancing household capital by bringing in income and other resources. Thus, migrants from individual households may be viewed as those individuals that would best fulfill familial responsibilities. In the Philippines, this most often refers to women. Lauby and Stark (1988, 485), for example, found that families in the Philippines may be willing to rely on daughters to supplement their income because, traditionally, daughters maintain close ties with their families of origin even after marriage.

However, the specificities of opportunities significantly influence the development of family strategies. As such, Filipino immigrants to the United States have adjusted their lives around institutional determinants such as migration policy and employment opportunities. This, in itself, is not new. Considerable research has examined how families develop strategies to utilize U.S. immigration policy to their advantage (Medina and

Natividad 1985; Reimers 1985; DeJong et al. 1985-86; DeJong et al. 1986; Jasso and Rosenzweig 1986; Arnold et al. 1989; Carino et al. 1990). Specifically, the preference systems of immigration policies provide guidelines concerning age, marital status, occupation level, and kin relations in determining the volume and timing of entry.

Respondents in this study differ little from the preceding discussion. Immigration policy—and changes therein—significantly influence migration behavior. One Filipina nurse, for example, migrated to the United States during the mid-1960s through an exchange visitor program for a two-year term. Having no desire to return to the Philippines when her visa expired, she applied for a visa to work in Canada. However, before her original visa expired, U.S. immigration law changed and she was able to adjust her status and remain in the United States.

An overwhelming number of Filipino respondents made personal sacrifices for other family members and friends. As a result of U.S. immigration policy, many spouses were forced to separate for years. Often, the initial mover in a family would migrate to the United States while the spouse would stay in the Philippines. Only after the migrant was granted U.S. citizenship could the couple be reunited. Other respondents were forced to leave their children behind, planning to reunite after establishing themselves. In fact, it is quite common for children to be shuffled around from relative to relative, country to country. One Filipina explained that when she was two, her father (who was divorced) took her to the United States for a vacation and kept her. Another Filipina said that her children were still in the Philippines staying with relatives; she would not bring her children to the United States until she had saved enough money.

Very few respondents in this study migrated as a result of employment transfers. Exceptions were those individuals serving in the U.S. Navy. However, even in this instance, some Filipinos were able to utilize the institutional process to their advantage. One couple, for example, was initially stationed in South Carolina, a location they each disliked. Subsequently, the husband applied for a transfer to San Diego and the couple was able to reunite with relatives in southern California.

In general, respondents indicated that they, or their relatives, took the first available opportunity to migrate. Often, respondents, or relatives of the respondents, would go to labor recruitment offices and take whatever job was available. This differs from traditional interpretations that immigrants will look through various alternatives and weigh the cost/benefits. The few exceptions were those who had an opportunity to come to the United States if they were willing to wait a little longer. One Filipina, for example, had an opportunity to go to Germany as a nurse, but her sister told her that if she was willing to wait a little longer, she would petition her to the United States. This is not to imply, however, that the United States is always the primary destination. One Filipino applied for tourist visas first to Saudi Arabia, Canada, and Australia. The respondent felt that life would be easier in these locations and he could earn a tax-free salary. In each instance, however, he was denied entry. The basis of his denial was that he might potentially overstay his visa since he was still in his prime working age and did not qualify financially. Ironically, the respondent's uncle had overstayed his visa in Australia, and the respondent himself was planning to do the same.

This study likewise reveals a relationship between the spatial extent of migration and the motivation behind migrating [Table 1].

Table 1
Primary Motive for Migrating

	PD	TD	X
Family Reunification	4	10	15
To Join Spouse	1	1	7
Occupation Transfer	0	1	2
Search for New Employment	3	6	5
Schooling	0	4	1
Leave Home/New House/Apartment	35	3	6

In general, shorter distance moves are related to families separating, whereas longer distance moves are related to families coming together. Partial displacement moves (PD), for example, are motivated primarily by the search for new housing. This may result from a desire to move out on one's own, as is the case with young adults, or it may result from the birth of a child, or even a divorce. International moves (X), and total displacement moves (TD), however, are motivated predominantly by family reunification.

The Selection of Alternative Destinations

The selection of destinations is based, in part, on the motivation to move [Table 2]. Consistent with other findings (Medina and Natividad 1985; Carino et al. 1990), the majority of respondents selected the destination of international moves with respect to the location of family members. Partial displacement moves, however, while also selected in part on the location of relatives, were chosen primarily because of familiarity with the location and proximity to work.

Filipino respondents, when not capitalizing on the first opportunity, often considered only a small number of alternative destinations at the time of migration. When Filipinos migrate with the first opportunity available, such as with labor recruitment, they have no choice concerning the destination. In other instances, Filipinos may not actively construct a search space since the move they are planning is often dependent on social networks. Destinations of migrations that are motivated by family reunification are determined by the location of the relatives.

Table 2
Primary Reason Given for Destination Selection

	PD	TD	X
Relatives in Destination Area	12	17	23
Friends in Destination Area	1	2	2
Spouse in Destination Area	1	1	7
Occupation Transfer to Destination	0	1	2
Study in Destination Area	0	4	1
Lower Rent	7	0	0
Familiarity/Close to Work	22	0	1

Conclusions

Throughout this paper I have examined the decision-making process of Philippine international migrants set within a context of changing opportunities. Structural changes involving immigration policies, recruitment mechanisms, and citizenship rights have been shown to be important variables in "bounding" the decision-making of Filipino migrants.

By integrating both structural and individual perspectives, it is possible to systematically document the changing nature of opportunities and illustrate the various ways in which individuals and households are able to adjust. In short, it is imperative to understand the formation of opportunities—within the Philippines as well as overseas—and how these are utilized by individuals and households.

Endnotes

I extend thanks to Belinda Patricio for her assistance during the interview stage of this study. I also thank T.B.

1. The distinction between partial and total displacement migration is based on weekly movement cycles. Total displacement moves result in moves that displace all aspects of the weekly movement cycle. With partial displacement movements, the center of gravity—the home—changes location, but the location of other nodes, such as job site, remains unchanged (Roseman 1971, 593).

2.   Most international migrations are total displacement moves. However, total displacement and international moves differ in that the latter case represents the crossing of an international border. In certain cases, such as Mexican immigration along the U.S.-Mexico border, international moves may likewise be partial displacement moves.

3.   Philippine immigration to the United States has been described as comprising either two (Melendy 1974; Smith 1976), three (Allen 1977; Crouchett 1982; Knoll 1982), or four waves (Yu 1980). However, for all of these waves, U.S. institutions were still the dominant agents influencing the direction of flows. Thus, it is perhaps best to view these various waves as subsystems of the pre-1970 phase of Philippine international migration.

4.   This is not to say that the Philippine government had no control over migration. Indeed, there are many instances where it influenced specific aspects of emigration. See, for example, Teodoro (1981, 11).

References

Allen, James P. 1977. "Recent immigration from the Philippines and Filipino Communities in the United States." *The Geographical Review* 67(2):195-208.

Arnold, Fred and Ricardo Abad. 1985. "Linkages Between Internal and International Migration: The Ilocos Norte Experience." *Philippine Population Journal* 1(2):1-17.

Arnold, Fred, Benjamin Carino, James T. Fawcett, and Insook Han Park. 1989. "Estimating the Immigration Multiplier: An Analysis of Recent Korean and Filipino Immigration to the United States." *International Migration Review* 23(4):813-838.

Carino, Benjamin V. 1987. "The Philippines and Southeast Asia: Historical Roots and Contemporary Linkages." In J.T. Fawcett and B.V. Carino, eds., *Pacific Bridges:The New Immigration from Asia and the Pacific Islands*. Staten Island, New York: Center for Migration Studies, 305-325.

Carino, Benjamin V., James T. Fawcett, Robert W. Gardner, and Fred Arnold. 1990. "The New Filipino Immigrants to the United States: Increasing Diversity and Change." *Papers of the East-West Population Institute*. Number 115. Honolulu: East West Center.

Chan, Sucheng. 1991. *Asian Americans: An Interpretive History*. Boston: Twayne Publishers.

Crouchett, Lorrain Jacobs. 1982. *Filipinos in California*. El Cerrito, CA: Downey Place Publishing House.

DeJong, Gordon F., Brenda Davis Root, Robert W. Gardner, James T. Fawcett, and Ricardo G. Abad. 1985-86. "Migration Intentions and Behavior: Decision Making in a Rural Philippine Province." *Population and Environment* 8(1-2):41-62.

DeJong, Gordon F., Brenda Davis Root, and Ricardo Abad. 1986. "Family Reunification and Philippine Migration to the United States: The Immigrant's Perspective." *Working Paper No. 1986-10*. The Pennsylvania State University: Population Issues Research Center.

Goodman, John L. 1981. "Information, uncertainty, and the microeconomic model of migration decision making." In G.F. DeJong and R.W. Gardner, eds., *Migration Decision-making: Multidisciplinary Approaches to Microlevel Studies in Developed and Developing Countries*. New York: Pergamon Press, 130-148.

Jasso, Guillermina and Mark R. Rosenzweig. 1986. "Family Reunification and the Immigration Multiplier: U.S. Immigration Law, Origin-country Conditions, and the Reproduction of Immigrants." *Demography* 23(3):291-311.

Knoll, Tricia. 1982. *Becoming Americans: Asian Sojourners, Immigrants and Refugees in the Western United States.* Portland, Oregon: Coast to Coast Books.

Lansing, John and Eva Mueller. 1967. *The Geographic Mobility of Labor.* Ann Arbor: University of Michigan, Institute for Social Research.

Lauby, Jennifer and Oded Stark. 1988. "Individual Migration as a Family Strategy: Young Women in the Philippines." *Population Studies* 42:473-486.

Lindquist, Bruce A. 1993. "Migration Networks: A Case Study in the Philippines." *Asian and Pacific Migration Journal* 2(1):75-104.

Medina, Belen T.G. and Josefina N. Natividad. 1985. "Filipino Chain Migration to the United States." *Philippine Population Journal* 1(4):67-94.

Melendy, H. Brett. 1974. "Filipinos in the United States." *Pacific Historical Review* 43(4):520-547.

Pedraza-Bailey, Silvia. 1990. "Immigration Research: A Conceptual Map." *Social Science History* 14(1):43-67.

Portes, Alejandro. 1978. "Migration and Underdevelopment." *Politics and Society* 8(1):1-48.

Posadas, Barbara M. 1986-87. "At a Crossroad: Filipino American History and the Old-timers' Generation." *Amerasia* 13(1):85-97.

Ramcharan, Subhas. 1982. *Racism: Nonwhites in Canada.* Toronto: Butterworths.

Reimers, David M. 1985. *Still the Golden Door: The Third World Comes to America.* New York: Columbia University Press.

Root, Brenda Davis and Gordon F. DeJong. 1991. "Family Migration in a Developing Country." *Population Studies* 45:221-233.

Roseman, Curtis C. 1971. "Migration as a Spatial and Temporal Process." *Annals of the Association of American Geographers* 61:589-598.

——. 1983. "A Framework for the Study of Migration Destination Selection." *Population and Environment* 6(3):151-165.

Salazar, Zeus A. 1987. "The Outflow of Filipinos to the Bundesrepublik Deutschland Since the 1960s." *Philippine Journal of Public Administration* 31(4):463-486.

Shrestha, Nanda R. 1987. "Institutional Policies and Migration Behavior: A Selective Review." *World Development* 15(3):329-345.

——. 1990. *Landlessness and Migration in Nepal.* Boulder, Colorado: Westview Press.

Smith, Peter C. 1976. "The Social Demography of Filipino Migrations Abroad." *International Migration Review* 10(3):307-353.

Teodoro, Luis V. Jr. (Ed.). 1981. *Out of This Struggle: The Filipinos in Hawaii.* Honolulu: University Press of Hawaii.

Timberman, David G. 1991. *A Changeless Land: Continuity and Change in Philippine Politics.* Singapore: Institute of Southeast Asian Studies.

Trager, Lillian. 1988. *The City Connection: Migration and Family Interdependence in the Philippines.* Ann Arbor: The University of Michigan Press.

Ward, R. Gerard. 1981. "Decision Makers in Migration—Papua New Guinea." *Population Geography* 3(1-2):69-79.

Yu, Elena S.H. 1980. "Filipino Migration and Community Organizations in the United States." *California Sociologist* 3(2):76-102.

Chapter Five

Identity Development of Korean Adoptees

Mike Mullen

Introduction

While there may be some difficulties associated with adoption, under most circumstances it is not a highly charged political debate. However, in the United States, the practice of interracial adoption catapults it into the arena of modern-day race relations. Issues of identity, community, and culture, when used by both proponents and opponents of interracial adoption, confound more than clarify the situation. The practice of inter-country adoption adds another layer of complexity and moves the issue into the international arena. A million American families, almost exclusively white, seek to adopt healthy white children, but only about 1 in 30 are so lucky. There are long waiting lists, and the cost of adopting a healthy white baby is upwards of $40,000 to $50,000 (Gubernick, 1991). Adoption fees for children who do not fit that narrow description are a fraction of the price, and there is no wait (Rothschild, 1988). Those who do not want to wait or do not care for domestic adoption possibilities look abroad to adopt. South Korea supplies the largest number of children for overseas adoption to the United States as well as worldwide. In the United States over 60 percent of all children adopted abroad have come from South Korea (Rothschild, 1988). Nearly 70,000 Korean children have been adopted by American families since 1950. In 1985, the peak year, over 14,000 Korean children were adopted (Wang, 1989).

One of the primary issues facing the white families that adopt a non-white child from overseas is the identity development of the adopted child.

Certainly, growing up in a family with different cultural practices has some effect on the child. And at some point both the child and the family inevitably have to confront the race issue; if the issues are not raised within the family, the issues will be brought to them from outside.

The purpose of this paper is to explore the identity of Korean adopted children and to examine what factors affect their identity development. A non-white adopted by whites may never be able to come to grips with being a minority. He or she may lack a sense of belonging with other minorities and fail to possess the common feeling among minorities of not being accepted as Americans. What, if anything, can and should adoptive families do to help their children develop a healthy identity?

Most of the literature on identity development among interracially adopted children focuses on black children and white adoptive families. In the 1970s, the National Association of Black Social Workers advocated ending all placements of black children in white homes. The rationale for this was that black children, if raised by white parents, could not develop an adequate sense of values, attitudes, or self-concepts. Other research supports the idea that transracially adopted children would be robbed of their heritage and identity and exhibit a "white bias," especially as they approach adolescence (Ladner, 1977), However, some research contradicts this perspective and suggests that neither biological nor adopted children exhibit racial preferences: that black adopted children perceive themselves as accurately as white children perceive themselves (Simon and Altstein, 1977); that adoptees' environment is a more critical factor in self-perception; and that age of adoption and conditions prior to adoption are more significant for a child's development (McRoy and Zurcher 1983). Black children living with white families in white communities tend to feel an affinity and preference for whites, while black children who live in racially mixed environments acquire an affinity towards both races. Black psychiatrist James Comer urges continued placement of black children with white families, insisting that a child can develop a positive sense of self with the proper nurturing, love, and care from parents regardless of racial differences (Ladner, 1977). In all, professionals working in transracial adoptions, parents, and adoptees agree that a childhood spent in institutions is least desirable for healthy developmental outcomes, and that the transient nature of institutional life often leaves lifelong scars (Ladner, 1977).

There is a paucity of research on adopted Asian children, and very little information on the diverse cultural backgrounds that might affect the adopted children's development. The lack of sources that specifically address adopted Korean children compelled me to embark on an exploratory study to illuminate the primary factors that influence identity.

Methodology

The study I conducted employed both structured questionnaires and open-ended interviews using Atkinson, Morten, and Sue's Minority Identity Development (MID) model (1979) as a general guideline for assessing identity of Korean adoptees. The MID was used as a starting point because Korean adoptees are perceived by members of the majority culture as minorities. The questionnaires and interviews were designed as complementary parts of the inquiry. While the questionnaire is a good gauge of baseline sentiments around many issues, there are also many ambiguities since the informants are forced to choose among a set of ratings without elaborating on the reasons for the beliefs. Additionally, informants may have gone through many changes throughout their lives regarding any or all of the items, and the process of change and reassessment cannot be ascertained from the questionnaire. While the questionnaires garnered information about an adoptee's identity, the interviews provided full exploration of the issues.

Informants

Eleven Korean adoptees participated in this study. They were contacted with the help of the Korean Identity Development Society. Participants were self-selected since only adoptees with some interest in or connection to identity development agreed to participate in the study. The five males and 6 females who participated were between the ages of 17 and 35, with the average age being 26. Of the sample, 4 were of mixed race; these 4 participants were also married and all over 26 years of age. All 11 participants completed the questionnaire and 6 agreed to be interviewed. Clearly, the sample was one of convenience. It is not large enough to draw definitive or reliable generalizations, but it allows for an exploratory investigation of an area which has previously been under-researched.

Questionnaires

The questionnaire was designed such that participants read statements and rated them on a Likert scale from 4 to 0, with 4 indicating "strongly agree," 3 indicating "mildly agree," 2 indicating "no opinion," 1 indicating "mildly disagree," and 0 indicating "strongly disagree." The numbers were then applied directly or inversely to calculate averages for questions and groups of questions, depending on the nature of the question. For example, when considering a subject's awareness of racism, "Racism is not a big factor in American society today" would apply inversely, since an answer of "strongly agree" would indicate a perception that racism is not a problem and "strongly disagree" the perception that it is. Meanwhile,

"Whites have done a lot of harm to my people" would apply directly, for the opposite reasons.

All the items in the questionnaire were constructed around five components of self adapted from the MID model: self-identification, identification with same minority group as Asian; identification with same minority group as Korean; identification with other minority groups: and identification with the majority group.

While questionnaires lend themselves to statistical analysis, statistical significance was not the aim of the study. Analyzing the questionnaire data in conjunction with the interview materials gained insights for this study's primary goal: exploring features that influence identity development for Korean adoptees.

Interviews

One-hour interviews were held with six adoptees. Each informant was asked open-ended questions about three main themes: recollections of being adopted, first awareness of and reaction to differences between child and parents, and the importance of teaching Korean culture to the adoptee's children. Participants' responses guided additional probes along varying themes. Additionally, items on the questionnaire were discussed.

Findings

One of the most interesting findings of this preliminary study was the differences evident between adoptees and other minorities with regard to identity development. Using questionnaire data as a starting place for investigation, interview material offered provocative rationale for the differences. Identification with the majority group and with other minority groups were two areas that differed between participants in the study conducted by Atkinson et al. and the adoptees that participated in my study. According to Atkinson, Morten, and Sue (1979), members of minority groups first try to identify with the dominant group, often to the exclusion of the culture or group of origin. Upon finding this untenable, individuals reject the dominant group and immerse themselves in their own minority group(s) or culture(s). Finally, individuals may achieve an equilibrium between identifying totally with the dominant or the minority group. It was also noted that not all members of a minority group follow the pattern in the order delineated; some may become stuck in one stage of the model, or repeatedly bounce between the same stages (Atkinson, Morten, and Sue 1979). However, few of the informants in my study expressed rejection of the dominant group, and those who did were not immersed in minority communities or cultures.

While the aggregated ratings of the items questionnaire were in a fairly narrow range, identification with minorities was the lowest (2.01), while identification with the dominant group was 25 percent higher (2.59), and indeed the highest. The ratings indicated that, on the whole, there was no evidence of adoptee immersion in the same or other minority groups, and that adoptees did not reject the majority culture. Unlike other minority informants, adoptees were not compelled to stray from the first stage of the MID, and they felt comfortable with interactions with the dominant group. Several participants echoed the sentiment that they did not view themselves as minorities, but simply as part of the majority. According to one,

> I grew up here thinking, "I'm an American." When I applied for college, I had a couple of acceptance letters that said, "Congratulations, you're an outstanding minority student." You know, I'd laugh at that and say, "Look at this, I'm a minority student," and my parents would say, "Well, gee, sorry to inform you, but yes, you are." And, I never thought of myself that way.

Another subject expressed the ease he had while among whites.

> . . . do I feel comfortable with whites? . . . I feel incredibly comfortable with them. I grew up in a white community, and all of my friends, until recently, have been all white.

He went on to explain that standing out as a minority was not something he preferred at all.

> In fact, when I was growing up with my family, I just didn't want to see any Korean people. My parents would take me to a Korean restaurant . . .and they would take me there so I could speak my language. And, I would just hide behind them and not say anything. You know, I'd feel like "I'm in America, I don't want to be picked out as someone who is particularly special in any way" . . . I like integration. Yeah, I like integration. And, that may mean that you have to help them keep their heritage a little bit, so they can have time. But, after some time, if it's working right, why try to stand out by doing something extraordinary?

Adoptees are less prone to reject dominant culture or condemn all whites as some members of minority groups may, because their families are white. Rejection was particularly uncommon among those who had good relations with their families. Even among those who expressed some modicum of rejection, recurrent resistance to repudiation of the dominant culture was tied to their attachment to their families.

> M: You talked about the immigration of the Europeans. "They made the Native Americans 2nd class citizens in their own country": the history of racism in America. Do you ever get mad at whites about racism in America?

I: I used to, when I was a freshman in college. I'd come home for the weekend and get into a heavy discussion with my parents. I feel so sorry for them.

M: Why?

I: Because they had to listen to me talk. I felt like the white people–

M: Were you angry at white people?

I: No, I wasn't angry. I was just generalizing. Not all people are like that, but I generalized, like I did with Koreans.

M: So, what were you saying?

I: White people steal from the little people. White people did this and that.

M: But, how could you really believe that? Your parents are white, and you weren't accusing them of that.

I: No, I wasn't. I saw them as friends.

One subject was upset because of some problems she had experienced in interactions with whites, but resisted connecting the problems with people themselves.

M: Does anything come to mind about the way white people act that disturbs you?

I: I just feel like they're very—the way they relate to people, they're very on the surface. And, like, when I see a friend, they're like, "Oh, hi, how are you?" and I answer, "Good," and they don't really care about how that person is really doing . . . They don't actually try to spend time with you or go out and do stuff with you. It just bothers me. I'm not saying this about white people; I think it's white culture.

Awareness of Racism

Calculating individual scores for "awareness of racism" produced the largest gap in identities. Each respondent's value was obtained from answers to the statements that directly pointed to racism in society: "Minorities have to work twice as hard to make it in American society," "Racism is not a big factor in American society today," and "Whites have done a lot of harm to my people." Three of the participants had noticeably lower values than the others, and they were grouped separately from the other eight. The two groups' scores along the MID categories were recalculated, and those with lower awareness of racism had the lowest score (1.05) for identification with other minorities. Not surprisingly, identification with the dominant group was very high (2.78).

Those with higher awareness of racism scored more evenly in terms of identification with minorities (2.38) and with the dominant group (2.47). It is understandable that being around racist comments or actions against minorities might tend to heighten one's awareness of racial differences and weaken identification with the majority. One informant said that her family makes comments against non-whites, and that the comments inevitably force her to align herself with other minorities:

. . . a lot of my younger cousins still like to call blacks "niggers" like that, and I just want to say, "Hey, listen here. I'm not black, but I'm not white, either. You know, don't say that stuff around me." I've had some of my American friends make fun of the Asians, and I'm like, "Wait a minute here." I guess they just think of me as being white, as American.

Another participant seemed to indicate that, although she was unaware of past racist acts against minorities, she did not want to know for fear that it would disturb her association with the dominant group.

So, I guess that's where I'm coming from—that's why I strongly disagree [that "whites have done a lot of harm to my people"]—because I'm not exposed to all the things that have been done, and I don't know if I want to know because that may give me a different view that I don't really want against Americans.

Importance of Age

When the subjects were separated by age, contrast between identification with other minorities and identification with the majority was stark. Those below 26 years old (17, 21, 21, 23, 23, 23, and 25 years of age, respectively) had fairly equal ratings for both (2.35 for minorities, 2.49 for dominant group), while those older than 26 (30, 34, 34, and 35 years of age) had very low ratings for identification with minorities (1.43)—just over half their rating for the majority (2.67). This awareness of racism may be due to a cohort effect since those below 26 exhibited a stronger awareness than those above.

It is also quite possible that awareness of or concern with racism declines with age. According to MID, the stages of bonding with minorities, rejecting the dominant culture, to a more moderate stance are developmental. One adoptee who reported that she had gone through a stage of rejecting dominant culture states:

I don't care anymore, because I didn't give a shit about other people here, so why should I care about what they say? I think I grew out of that stage when I was a teenager. When you're a teenager, everything is coming apart, when you're trying to understand what's going on. And, Frank [her husband] did help me understand that I'm Korean, but that doesn't mean we have to live like Koreans. We're in America. We can do whatever we want, just like everybody else.

However, the data are confusing because the same informants who are above 26 are also those of mixed racial background, and the difference in identification may be due to the latter feature rather than age. Three of the mixed-race participants were half-white, the fourth was half-Hawaiian. One reason the MID model asserts for bonding with minority groups is a lingering sense of not fitting in with the majority group.

It is quite plausible that those of mixed race are more accepted in the U.S. because they don't stand out as much. Another reason given is the feeling that minorities have suffered the same oppression at the hands of the dominant group. Experiencing less racism from the majority group, the mixed-race adoptees would lack feelings of common oppression; this lack would lower identification with minorities and sustain identification with the dominant group. One subject explained that because his sister looked more Asian than he did, she experienced greater prejudice.

> My sister was full-blooded Korean, and she tended to run into a few more problems than I did. A lot of people would look at me and think, well, I'm probably Hawaiian or something, and being from somewhere like Hawaii is a lot more accepted than being from somewhere like Japan or China or Korea. People could understand being from Hawaii. Whereas Rebecca definitely looked Asian, and so she heard some name-calling, some feelings of bias, but I never really felt that.

Conversely, a non-mixed-race interviewee admits her Asian looks set her apart, and lended to a constant feeling that she didn't belong.

> M: Does it make you feel uncomfortable when you're with a group of whites and somebody points out to you that you aren't white?
> I: Oh, yeah, I had that happen to me just recently. Um, and that was with my brother down in Auburn, at this RV Center. I just walked in to find out where he was located in the area, in the trailer area, and they kind of looked at me and stared at me. "Like what's your problem?" That was my reaction.
> M: What do you think they were thinking?
> I: That she's different, she looks different.

In fact, despite what she perceived as many similarities between she and her classmates, her physical differences were constantly pointed out to her as undesirable, and this became an issue.

> M: When did you first start having emotions about the fact that–
> S: That I was different? In elementary school, when some people would make comments or say that I had a flat face, or I remember one time when I was just standing against the wall, and people were teasing me.
> M: But, you fit in pretty well, didn't you?
> S: Oh, yeah, I feel that I am a very outgoing person and I don't criticize or pass judgment on other people and so—and that was just like one or two incidents, and I felt like, I realized that I was different. And, so, what I would do sometimes when, like, when the person made a comment that my face was different, because we do have really flat–
> M: Relatively speaking.
> S: So, when I was in band, I would tilt my head a certain way so that it wouldn't look, it's kind of silly–
> M: So that it wouldn't be so noticeable.
> S: Yeah.

Despite ratings on items that indicate that mixed race adoptees identified more strongly with the dominant group, there is some indication that they may be more likely to feel uneasy on two fronts: there is still some difference from the dominant group as well as the same minority group.

> I can go over there and the Koreans in Korea look at me and say, "Oh, you're American. You look white, you look American, whatever." But, when I'm over here, a lot of people ask me if I'm at least some type of Asian . . . So, it just kind of made me more and more realize that there's this whole group of people that's mixed-race, and we're kind of in this situation where Korea might be our heritage, but we don't really belong to Korea because they think we belong over here; sometimes, people over here think we look Asian so we must be from somewhere else, even though we've spent our whole lives here.

However, despite the fact that they may feel added uneasiness because of their mixed race, their identification with other minorities was not supported.

Age of Placement

Age of placement also influenced identification patterns. Those who were placed younger had the highest ratings of identification with the dominant group (2.80). Children placed earlier in their lives have a higher likelihood of bonding with the adoptive family, internalizing their ways, and forgetting the culture of their biological parents. Those who came to the U.S. at an older age probably had their habits more firmly ingrained, and being in a new environment, a new family, came as more of a shock. One participant who was placed at the age of 10 describes the process as re-learning to live.

> I: I think identity is the only thing you have a problem with when living with Caucasians.
> M: Did you have a problem with that?
> I: Sort of. First of all, you were brought into a culture style, and then all of sudden you've got that cut off, and then you have to learn a new culture.

All other participants, regardless of age of placement, related strong feelings of acceptance into the mainstream. However, those who were placed younger viewed Korea as a more distant, foreign place, and their interest in Korea and Korean culture was more exploratory in nature, rather than returning to one's roots.

> I just sort of, for myself, wanted to know what Korea was. And, now that I've been over there half a dozen times or so, to me it's just a place to go visit. I don't really think of it as a homeland or anything.

Views of Adoption

The informants' view of adoption played a role in their identification with minorities. Those with very positive views of adoption had a much lower rating of identification with minorities (1.71) than those with mixed feelings (2.46); however, both had almost identical ratings toward the dominant group. Views toward adoption were figured from answers to the statements "Being adopted has serious advantages," "The exporting of babies for adoption from Korea should stop," and "Adoption has been an effective way to deal with the problem of unwanted children in Korea." One possible explanation is that dissatisfaction with the adoption process resulted in stronger identification with minority culture.

A common reason for supporting adoption was the understanding that adoptees are not treated well in Korea. The prevalent belief was that if the children are not adopted here in the U.S., they would be stuck with a miserable life in Korea. According to one informant,

> . . . the problem is that kids are not getting adopted to be family members. Older kids are being adopted to be servants, which is not good . . . These children are not going to be treated as equal family members. They would have better chances in life here, than there.

They believed that, had they not been adopted, they very well might be one of those living miserably. Another informant said:

> But, you know, I can look back at what would have happened to me if I'd have stayed in Korea, and at that time, there probably would have been a good chance I wouldn't have been even alive. The kids that are orphans in Korea, the Korean word for it literally translated means "a nonentity, a nobody person." And, you see them over there, even now, gathering bottles and washing them, doing whatever they can to scrape up a little money just to live, because they don't have the social welfare programs that we do . . . if you're not handicapped, they basically tell you, "Do it on your own." And, it doesn't matter if you're four years old or whatever.

Given adoptees' beliefs about life in Korea, it is not surprising that those with very positive feelings toward adoption felt that they had avoided a miserable life because of the compassion of strangers in a foreign country, and gave high ratings toward the culture that took them in. Many of the informants expressed discomfort, and even anger, towards Koreans because they felt rejected by Koreans. Feelings of rejection probably tempered their interest in being, and identifying, with Koreans.

> I told you when I came here, before I came to the U (University of Washington), my identity as far as I can see, was Korean. I wanted to be around Koreans; I thought I was Korean. And, then I come here and people questioned me being Korean because I was adopted and I'm living with a white

family. And that hurt me a lot. I was proud of being Korean. That was my identity. When I came here, people were saying, "Well, you're not Korean because you're living with a white family." And, what happened—I went to a KSA (Korean Student Association) dance when I was a freshman. And at the orientation, where they introduced all the freshmen, they came to me—and my last name is Sanders, right—and he said, "Why is your last name different from ours?" And, I said I was adopted, and he asked me if I was Korean, and I said yeah. And, it hurt my feelings. Korean adoption is a big thing in Korea. I think people should know more about it and accept it because it's part of them.

For one interviewee, the pain of the rejection of being put up for adoption was greater than the hardships of being of mixed race.

S: Koreans are one of the racists out there. They're racist among their own people . . . I resent the fact that Koreans do not accept me as Korean. Because I was adopted by Americans, therefore I am not Korean.

M: Do you think the lack of acceptance the Koreans have toward you was the result of 1) the fact that your parents aren't Koreans, or 2) that you had some Caucasian blood in you, or perhaps both?

S: Both.

M: Do you think one is greater, as it has affected you?

S: I think adoption, itself, is taboo in Korea. So, I think that was it more than anything. They didn't mind the part that I had Caucasian blood in me. They could accept that, but the part about being adopted, they thought my parents were, my mother was a prostitute. They didn't even ask, "What happened to your parents?" or anything. They assumed all this and they start talking about it, and I resent that. My mother was not that kind of person.

Childhood Environment

Separating the subjects by the ethnic makeup of their childhood environment suggests that the environment adoptees grow up in affects their attitudes (McRoy and Zurcher, 1983). Of the 11 participants, two did not describe the ethnic makeup of their families as "white," and one did not describe the ethnic makeup of her neighborhood as "white." Those who described their environment as "white" had a larger gap between their ratings of identification with the dominant (2.65) and with minority (1.82) groups. Those who described their environment as "mixed"—the two subjects from "mixed families" and the subject from a mixed neighborhood—actually had higher identification ratings toward minorities (2.52) than toward the dominant group (2.30): the only instance of such a pattern.

All three from the "mixed" environment group expressed discomfort when being in a group of only whites.

> . . . this past summer, I went to my cousin's wedding in Minnesota . . . and it was just strange being there. There was not one minority there. It was all white. I just felt weird because I've always been—you know how here in Seattle, my school, and just walking down the street, I'm just used to seeing so much culture.

Being in a non-white environment on a regular basis can act as a vehicle for identifying with minorities since the probability of interacting with non-whites is higher. As no one rated him/herself as "somewhat Korean" or "very Korean," participants were divided between those who rated themselves "equally Korean/equally American," "somewhat American," and "very American." Ratings of affiliation with Koreans fell in an expected fashion, with "equally Korean/equally American" having the highest rating (2.59), followed by "somewhat American" (2.21), and "very American" (1.84). The same pattern repeated itself for ratings toward minorities, but this time the gaps between the groups were even greater (2.76 to 2.21 to 1.57). Identification with the dominant group was consistent with the other findings, falling in reverse order. Those who rated themselves "very American" had the highest rating (2.70), followed by those who rated themselves "somewhat American" (2.67), and then by those who rated themselves "equally Korean/American" (2.19). One informant who felt very American definitely did not want people thinking of her as strictly a Korean or as Asian.

> I: Yeah, I do, I feel like Susan Thompson, and I don't feel like Chung Hui Sun, and that's home to me, and a lot of people say, "Well, did you have a Korean name," and I say yeah, and sometimes they say, "What is it?" and I say, "Why?" I don't want to say. I kind of feel weird saying it because then it's going to attach me to being more Asian than American.
>
> M: You don't like that?
>
> I: No, I have some feelings toward Asians that I don't like, and I don't know if it's because of the way I was brought up or if because I was surrounded by American people . . . I don't know if it has something to do with me having something against Asians or Asian countries or not, I think there has to be more, but I don't know what it is.
>
> M: How does it make you feel when you're with a bunch of other Asians and you notice, you feel that you're with other Asians, and you walk by the other white people? Do you feel like you are being categorized with the other Asians, even though you probably fit in better with them?
>
> I: Uh-huh, I want to tell them that I'm American, I'm more of an American than I am an Asian. Naturally, people are going to categorize me as Asian, as someone of a different nationality, different cultures from our own, and I want to let them know that I have an American family and I was raised the same way they were, and that I'm not purely Asian.

Discussion

Informants in this pilot study departed from the Minority Identity Development model put forth by Atkinson, Morten, and Sue (1979). The middle phase of "rejection" of the dominant group and "immersion" with other minorities was barely perceptible in the adoptees' questionnaires and interviews. While this was initially surprising, there are reasons for the differences. Atkinson et al. suggest that in the first stage, when minorities try to conform to the dominant group, the individuals "repress their awareness of their distinguishing physical and/or cultural characteristics" and "depreciate themselves at a subconscious level." This self-denial is the root from which grow subsequent feelings of dissatisfaction. Korean adoptees in white families simply do not have strong feelings of dissatisfaction because they feel indebted to their families for having taken them in. Acceptance of the dominant group comes quickly and easily, assuming no problems with the adoptive placement. Their lack of awareness of themselves as minorities is due not to repression, but to lack of exposure to and experience with situations that might bring issues of minority/majority to the fore. In short, when adoptees are young, they can feel white, act white, and feel accepted by whites; only later, when consciousness of physical differences becomes greater do adoptees begin to question issues of race. However, even the questioning does not foster a tremendous amount of dislike and distrust of the majority group nor initiate immersion into minority cultures or groups.

All the participants had thought a great deal about the issue of who they were and where they fit in since they were selected from the Korean Identity Development Society. It appears that those who explored issues of identity had liberating experiences; they were able to avoid a lot of the categoric dogma surrounding the "what it is to be American and what it is to be a minority" debate. Many of them came to the conclusion that the answer would continue to be elusive, but they would just be whoever they were, whatever that was. An attitude like this does not contradict Atkinson et al.'s final stage of awareness of oneself as an individual with autonomy beyond issues of minority or majority status.

Acceptance of one's identity is a source of pride. This sense of pride, the desire to learn more about themselves as individuals was a primary reason for adoptees' interest in minority groups and cultures. Interest and involvement came not out of anger at being outcast or not accepted, but from trying to understand what that meant. Not one of the informants expressed regret or anger about being adopted; curiosity was the more common response when the adoptees' affinity with whites was called into question. Korean children who have been adopted by white families have a fairly distinct identity development process and diverge from a more traditional minority identity development approach. More research is needed on the issues that have been raised in this paper, as well as other issues that were not brought forth in this study, to understand identity development among Korean adoptees more fully.

References

Atkinson, Donald R., George Morten, and Derald Wing Sue. 1979. *Counseling American Minorities*. Dubuque: William C. Brown.

Benet, Mary Kathleen. 1976. *The Politics of Adoption*. New York: Macmillan.

Chun, Byung-Hoon. 1989. "Adoption and Korea." *Child Welfare*, March/April: 255-260

Gubernick, Lisa. 1991. "How Much Is That Baby in the Window?" *Forbes,* October 14: 90-98.

Ladner, Joyce. 1977. *Mixed Families*. Garden City: Burrough Press.

Loeb, Vernon. 1991. "Koreans Defying Adoption Taboo." *The Honolulu Advertiser,* October 12: E12.

McRoy, Ruth C., and Louis A. Zurcher, Jr. *Transracial and Inracial Adoptees: The Adolescent Years*. Springfield: Charles C. Thomas Publishing, 1983.

Rothschild, Matthew. 1988. "Babies for Sale." *Progressive*, January: 18-23.

Simon, Rita James, and Howard Altstein. 1977. *Transracial Adoption*. New York: Wiley and Sons.

Tahk, Youn-Taek. 1986. "Intercountry Adoption Program in Korea." *Adoption in Worldwide Perspective*. Ed. R.A.C. Hoksbergen. Lisse: Swets and Zeitlinger.

van Loon, J.H.A. 1990. Report on Intercountry Adoption. Proc. of Hague Conference on private international law. April, The Hague, Netherlands.

Wang, Jung-Hwa, and Si-Nae Kang. 1989. "Taking a Closer Look at Adopted Children." *The Sungshin Mirror*, March 10: 3.

Chapter Six

Gender at Work: The Renegotiation of Middle-Class Womanhood in a South Asian-Owned Business

Amarpal K. Dhaliwal

This paper addresses the linkages between gender, class, and culture as these various factors intersect in the life of one female South Asian immigrant business owner residing in the United States. The analysis focuses on how gender ideologies[1] are created and maintained in the everyday activities and interactions of one woman working in small business; it also examines how participation in the workplace, the family, and the process of migration are contexts in which a middle-class, South Asian immigrant woman is defined and constructed.

In Asian American Studies, considerable research has focused upon business proprietorship.[2] Recent work on Asian American-owned business ventures has highlighted the theoretical legitimacy and value of contextualizing the variables examined in social scientific studies.[3] While the importance of contextually studying variables such as gender, ethnicity, and social class has been acknowledged, the understanding of the interface of multiple and shifting contexts such as gender ideologies, cultural systems, and class stratification has been more elusive. Too often one of the variables is studied to the exclusion of another; this results in the depiction of these variables as independent from one another. This is evidenced in approaches to the study of Asian-owned businesses that pay attention to issues of ethnicity or class and devote less consideration to issues of gender. Such treatment, particularly the lack of focus on women, is troubling in light of the fact that many Asian American businesses often tend to be stores that are "built on the backbreaking labor of the family, most frequently of women." As many scholars have noted, in order to keep these businesses profitable, Asian American women perform a wide range of duties, frequently seven days a week. (Mazumdar 1989, 17)

Research on business ownership has either ignored gender or employed the construct uncritically. In the latter instances, when gender has been mentioned in studies of Asian American businesses, the approach has been limited to concern with the effects of gender arrangements on business proprietorship (or vice versa). Park, one of the few researchers who does address gender, sees it as integral to changes in conjugal relationships and the household division of labor. (Park 1989, 142-143) Park recognizes that the support and work of women as wives is critical in the success of middle-class Korean businesses, but leaves the *conceptual relationship* between gender systems and business proprietorship largely unexplored. Feminist philosopher Sandra Harding has noted such conceptual limitations, and contends that research programs employing positivistic philosophies of social science have been "systematically inhospitable to gender as theoretical category . . . [and that positivistic social scientists] have been willing to add gender as a variable to be analyzed in their subject matter—as a property of individuals and their behaviors rather than also of social structures and conceptual systems." (Harding 1986, 33-34) One significant theoretical consequence of such research programs is that scholarship concerned with the roles of Asian American women in small businesses has neither examined the transition of immigrant women into positions of business ownership nor explored the impact of business operation on the crafting of gendered subjects. Toward addressing these omissions, this paper will illuminate the role work plays in creating and maintaining gender ideologies.

The Migration Experience of a Middle-Class South Asian Woman

To better comprehend how notions of middle-class immigrant womanhood are constructed and renegotiated in a small business context, a case study methodology was employed. One informant was extensively interviewed over a five-month period. Some open-ended questions were initially posed to the subject, named Kaur, and responses to these questions structured subsequent questions. Generally, however, the interaction was characterized by a narrative style in which the subject recounted her experiences as an immigrant woman specifically in relation to employment concerns. Of particular significance for analysis were areas of tension or conflict around gender expectations, class status, and the negotiation of change. The methodology was not necessarily intended to lead to representative or generalizable conclusions, but rather to help mark as gender-specific some sites of conflict and contradiction within migration processes. This marking, intended to highlight gender-related reconstitutions of culture, is evidenced in the following narration:

The subject, Kaur, is a middle-class, Sikh, South Asian immigrant woman, 48 years old at the time of the interviews. She is married and the mother of three children. She is one of 16,929 South Asians who migrated to the United States in 1972. (Xeros, Barringer, and Levin 1989, 15) She and her five-year-old daughter followed her husband Singh;[4] he had immigrated two years previously under the post-1965 immigration laws, which eased entry into the United States for those with post-secondary educations. (Mazumdar 1989, 13) Kaur's husband has a graduate degree in mechanical engineering. Like the vast majority of South Asian immigrants of the early 1970s, Kaur is also well educated. (Saran 1985, 31)[5]

Educational attainment of Indian women of Kaur's cohort reflects the gender ideology of that time period. According to Mazumdar (1976, 49-50), the notion was that, "Education would not turn the women away from their familial roles, but improve their efficiency as wives and mothers and strengthen the hold of traditional values on society . . ." For Kaur, then, growing up in Punjab and of middle- to upper-middle-class Sikh background, a college education was both acceptable and expected. According to Kaur, "Although I went to college, it was not thought that I would work at a job or have a career. College was something I did in between [high] school and getting married. College was preparation to get married." This class-based gender ideology rests on the definition of womanhood in terms of wifely and motherly duties, and education is often part of the path to proper womanhood. Hence, women like Kaur were encouraged to pursue college educations to be good wives and mothers, not to be employable. Exclusion from the paid labor force is predicated on a South Asian middle-class gender ideology which dictates that the public sphere is masculine and the domestic or private sphere feminine. For Sikh women, exclusion from the public domain in terms of employment is a cultural expectation that reflects both class and gender.

Upon immigration to the United States, Kaur had to cope with a relative drop in financial and class status as well as the lack of family networks. After arriving, she felt she had no choice but to seek employment. She states that she was "poor" in comparison to her previous status in India, and part of her perceived need for employment was to restore her previous class standing. Kaur and Singh were preoccupied with "making it," establishing the relative social standing that they had in India, a task that in the United States requires two paychecks.

Experiences in the Paid Workforce

As with many South Asian women in the 25 to 44 age group who immigrated between 1970 and 1974, when Kaur participated in the paid labor force, she accepted employment that was not commensurate with her educational level. Additionally, Kaur was only sporadically a member of the paid workforce. For several years, Kaur devoted herself primarily to maintaining the household and taking care of her three children, two of whom were born in the United States. It was Singh's job as an engineer which allowed them to steadily achieve some semblance of their previous social standing by the early 1980s. According to Kaur,

> This was when we bought a new car and our first house. We had to borrow a lot of money to do it, but we were so happy to have our first house seven years after we came to America. We also moved to a different town, one in which our younger daughters got to take things like ballet lessons. Of course, money was still tight. But things were finally getting better.

Up to this point Kaur did not work outside the home. Kaur's restriction to the private sphere simultaneously symbolized her class privilege and her subordination to patriarchal control. After all, who but the wealthiest of immigrants could afford to support a family in the style that Kaur and Singh had lived in India without the income of all the adult members of the family? Kaur's constriction to working in the home thus reveals an embeddedness in a class-specific version of femininity. Upholding a middle-class lifestyle can be difficult for immigrants, however, in the face of the racist realities of the United States. As Kaur highlights:

> [A]lmost at the same time, it became harder and harder for my husband to put up with the discrimination at work. He was always stressed out. This affected the whole family. The thing about the discrimination that always seemed weird was that he kept getting raises in terms of money but no promotions.

While Singh's job did provide financial stability, he was not advancing at the same rate as his colleagues; he and his wife attributed his difficulties to job discrimination based on national origin.

It was at this point that Kaur's husband began to pressure her to seek employment. Kaur stated:

> I had always wanted to help out with the money, but he would not let me work. He'd say that I couldn't find a job anyway. But when I did he would be irritated and he would not help watch the kids. He would let me know how inconvenienced he was. Or he would put down any job that I got because it did not pay much, or was in a factory, or something.

For many years Singh did not encourage Kaur to join the paid workforce although she sporadically did so. When he permitted her to be employed he expected her to instantaneously succeed in finding employment adequate to their social standing. Kaur's employment during these initial years in the United States consisted of a few part-time factory jobs, a barely used real estate license, and a baby-sitting career in her home. While she did hold a few jobs over the years, it was without sufficient support from her husband, who refused to help with childcare.

For Kaur and her husband, it was the perception that Singh's work status had become tenuous which permitted Kaur's shift to the workforce to go uncontested. However, Kaur's restriction from, as well as compulsion into, employment were influenced both by her husband and his patriarchal, upper-middle-class notions of conjugal roles. When it was convenient for Singh that Kaur remain at home, she did. When he demanded she join the labor force, she attempted to comply even though there was little support for working. Accordingly,

> When he said I should work, I read the paper every day. Most of the jobs were too far away and paid so little. Others required me to go back to college which I did not want to do [because it was too costly and time-consuming]. My husband would get mad at me for this.

Locating a job was difficult for Kaur not only because her Indian degree was not recognized and her job experience was insufficient, but also because she had to consider her primary role as homemaker and care provider for her children.

Business Proprietorship:
Reinterpreting Workforce Participation

After deliberating many years about moving to California from the Midwest in order to be geographically closer to relatives and to embark on some type of money-making venture, in 1985 Singh decided that Kaur would manage a small grocery story they had purchased in a small town in the central valley of California. Singh determined that Kaur would manage the store while he continued to work as an engineer. This is reported to be a common scenario for Asian-owned businesses: the wife, often with the help of her children, manages the store while the husband works for a salary. Through Kaur's experience we can explore the factors that influenced her husband's change in attitude concerning her employment.

The store catered to a wide range of customers of diverse ethnic and class backgrounds. Managing the store allowed Kaur to be in contact with many different types of people and clearly marked her entry into the public sphere in a manner previously unimaginable to Kaur. Until she began managing the store, her husband's attitude towards her employment had been ambivalent and contradictory. Working in the store marked the first time her membership within the public sphere became socially sanctioned.

It is important to examine the destabilizing factors which created the shift in this family's work arrangements. Singh's perceived lack of employment security and the concomitant threats to class status became destabilizing enough to create a significant change in gender-related work arrangements. But this change in gender arrangement also needed to be contained; to do this, Kaur's participation in the public sphere was negotiated in a manner reconcilable with previous gender arrangements. This was achieved in a number of ways. First of all, Kaur's duties in the private realm continued to be defined as primary; she was responsible for the maintenance of the household and the rearing of the children. As she puts it:

> I still do all the housework. My husband does not help at all. The most he does is sometimes heat his own dinner, and that's only because of the microwave. If I say I am tired or would like some help, he tells me to have one of the girls help me. But, they are busy with their schoolwork and their friends.

Furthermore, because Kaur does a substantial amount of paperwork for the business at home, the family is constantly reminded of the blurred boundaries between home and work, and thereby constructs her work as part of her home responsibilities.

> I have a desk at home where I do my paperwork. This way I can be home when my daughters get home from high school, and when my husband gets home from work so I can serve him dinner right away.

Additionally, Kaur outfitted the store with appliances that permit her to fulfill some of her duties as a wife and mother at the store as well as combine work and household errands. According to Kaur,

> I bought a stove for the store on which I cook meals for my husband and children during the hours when business is slow at the store. Everything I do is set around the hours the store is open, which is 7 am to 9 pm, seven days a week. The rest of my family also plans according to the needs of the store, but not nearly as much as I do. I try to combine my housework with the store work such as grocery shopping. When I go shopping I buy stuff for home and for the store.

The fluid boundaries between business and home create a flexible framework within which to manage the multiple and changing demands on Kaur's time. Bringing work home is a culturally acceptable and appropriate strategy to attain the stabilization of both her class and gender standing.

It is precisely the ability to take the office home and vice versa that makes family businesses so inviting, and makes them acceptable journeys into the public sphere for middle-class Indian women. While managing the store alters the pre-existing gender system, the new gender arrangement (Kaur working outside the home) is made consonant with previous gender expectations and ideologies by framing Kaur's work as an extension of family and household responsibilities. She herself reads the task of managing a business as an extension of household duties:

> Running the store is like running a larger household. I have to keep it clean, I have to keep it stocked, I have to be nice and pleasant to any guests or customers, I have to keep everyone happy, I have to organize many things, I have to look presentable because you never know who is going to stop by, and I always have to keep the house in order.

Indeed, there is a striking similarity between managing a household and managing a store. The two types of work share many characteristics. First, both domestic and business duties are:

> twenty-four hour jobs. I am always worrying about the store and about the house. Even at night I sometimes wake up thinking about it. It [the store] has "taken over our lives," as my youngest daughter puts it. Sometimes my family gets jealous of the time I put into the store. But I have to do it.

Clearly the repetitious, never-ending, and labor-intensive nature of both managing a store and running a house are apparent. For Kaur, as for many other similar small business owners, survival depends on the number of hours the store is kept open. (*Time,* July 8, 1985, p. 42) Hence there is a reliance on family contributions of labor, frequently across generations. While Kaur is not the sole worker, she bears the primary responsibility of managing her family's schedules so that she can keep the store open on American holidays such as Thanksgiving and Christmas.

Working at the store is not seen to compromise Kaur's domestic obligations, obligations which act as the core of her middle-class feminine identity. For many middle-class women such as Kaur, then, entry into the public sector "signals a partial emergence into a different kind of economic sphere into which they carry the constraints of conduct inculcated by the private sphere." (Sangari and Vaid 1990, 13)

Framing Kaur's entry into the public sphere in a manner highlighting the parallels between operating a store and doing housework actually serves to facilitate the shift from housewife to small business proprietorship in the Sikh South Asian context. Like housework, managing stores affords little time and opportunity for women who run them to develop other skills or to establish close friendships; more often, it fosters isolation and alienation. (Mazumdar 1989, 17)

The manner in which her work is socially constructed exploits gendered traits such as women's presumed ability to cook, clean, organize, and serve. Furthermore, it reinforces the cultural notion that because Kaur is an upper-middle-class Sikh South Asian woman, she can do little else; the idea that such work is the only solution for her, in turn reinforces the limited range of employment possibilities for upper-middle-class Sikh South Asian immigrant women. Kaur's work is thus molded into ideas of appropriate womanhood which link her to gender-bound domestic and familial obligations. Thus, the type of work women do and the conditions under which women work are sustained by historically specific and shifting cultural notions of gender and class.

Conclusion

While Kaur's work experience is not representative of all South Asian women who migrated to the United States in the early 1970s, throughout the nation many middle- and upper-middle-class women experienced similar kinds of tensions regarding participation in the workforce and the perceived need to be a wage earner. In fact, many Indian women in the United States did and do have jobs. (Helweg and Helweg 1990, 204) According to an analysis of the 1980 census data, the ratio of female to male income earners among South Asians is 45 percent. (Xenos, Barringer, and Levin 1989, 34-35) Employment for women is seen as an economic necessity for family survival. (Bhagat and Kedia 1986, 134; Ashcraft 1986, 64). The conditions and conflicts surrounding this are gender and class related.

The conditions under which Kaur works and the manner in which her work is understood are both sustained by cultural and contextual notions that are class and gender specific. These notions are fluid, simultaneously reconstructing gender ideologies by integrating new contexts into existing notions and creating an image of constancy. The family's definition of Kaur's work as an extension of her domestic obligations stabilizes patriarchal ideology in the face of migration-related change. Paradoxically, the capacity for continual revision actually permits the image of continuity of Sikh upper-middle-class patriarchy.

The constant negotiation of who is suitable for different types of work is based on the complex interface between histories of social class and gender relations. Work is perpetually re-inscribed with gender ideologies into which changes are constantly integrated. Gender hierarchies obtain their hegemony from collective understandings of behaviors that solidify and sustain existing ideologies. Collective understanding occurs in terms of how change is discussed and how individuals and communities respond to and participate in changes in gender systems. Kaur's foray into the public domain was condoned when it could be interpreted as resonant with South Asian middle-class notions of appropriate womanhood for her family and others in the Sikh South Asian American community. Such formations and reformations of cultural standards often rely on collective interpretations of what it means to be a woman in each community and context.

Migration-related changes are frequently understood in ways that actively continue to uphold certain configurations of power among men and women. This investigation explores the gendered experience of work and shows that work is not only affected by class and gender, but is active in the construction of class and gender, and the crafting of feminine identity. This simultaneous construction of multiple sets of social relations is central to the formation, recomposition, and reproduction of cultures. This paper hints at some gender related or gender inscribed ways in which social, cultural, and personal tensions are mediated by South Asian immigrants and how these mediations reconstitute cultural systems.

Endnotes

The author wishes to acknowledge the contributions of Satinder Dhaliwal, Kanwarpal Dhaliwal, and Jagbir Dhaliwal. This paper would not be possible without the incredible work they have performed and to them it is dedicated.

1. The broad operational definition of "ideology" that is used is Eagleton's: "The largely concealed structure of values which informs and underlies our factual statements" as well as "those modes of feeling, valuing, perceiving and believing which have some kind of relationship to the maintenance and reproduction of social power."

2. Specifically, in research on businesses in the field of Asian American Studies, Lou states that, "Studies of Asian American success in business have been a notable part of the literature." (Lou 1989, 98) For example, in the 1989 Association for Asian American Studies publication *Frontiers of Asian American Studies: Writing, Research, and Commentary*, two out of five social science papers directly address the topic of Asian American businesses. These papers critique extant scholarship on Asian American business ventures by highlighting its narrow focus on *either* economic factors *or* cultural ones. The authors of these papers attempt to expand our understanding of Asian American businesses by focusing on multiple aspects of business proprietorship. For instance, Park does so by investigating how involvement in small businesses affects the domestic lives of Korean Americans and Lou does so by critiquing existing research for its emphasis on "traditional culture" as an explanation of the success of Vietnamese American businesses (Lou 1989, 98; Park 1989, 140-150). Lou concludes that "Perhaps due to the focus on cultural variables as the primary explanation for

Asian American success in enterprise, studies of Asian Americans have tended to examine these groups in isolation from their *societal context* [author's emphasis]" (98). Lou's criticism of decontextualized studies of Asian American business ventures is crucial. It is not only a valid criticism, it is heuristically important as well because of its implications for future research.

3. This has been emphasized by R. Lou and K. Park in reference to the study of Asian American businesses. (Lou 1989; Park 1989) Also see Mazumdar 1989.

4. "Kaur" is a "pseudo" pseudonym. It is actually the middle name of the informant as well as the middle name of many Sikh women. Singh is the parallel name to Kaur for Sikh men and is the pseudonym for the informant's husband.

5. This is evidenced by the fact that both had master's degrees. Of those who emigrated from India to the United States between 1970 and 1974, 90.8 percent of females and 95.2 percent of males had high school diplomas; 51 percent of females and 76.5 percent of males had completed four or more years of college (Xenos, Barringer, and Levin, 26, 28). Their college educations also meant that they had moderate proficiency in the English language, or at least in formal British English. In this respect, Kaur and her husband fit the typical profile of the second wave of South Asian immigrants: they were highly educated, English-speaking, had come to the United States for economic reasons, and had immigrated together as a family. See also Takaki 1989, 420, 445.

References

Ashcraft, Norman. 1986. "The Clash of Traditions: Asian-Indian Immigrants in Crisis." In Richard Harvey Brown and George V. Coelho, (Eds), *Tradition and Transformation: Asian Indians in America*. Studies in Third World Societies, Publication number 38: 64.

Bhachu, Parminder K. 1986. "Work, Dowry, and Marriage Among East African Sikh Women in the United Kingdom." In Rita James Simon and Caroline B. Brettell (Eds), *International Migration: The Female Experience*. Totowa, New Jersey: Rowman & Allenheld: 229-240.

Bhagat, Rabi S. and Ben L. Kedia. 1986. "Coping in the Workplace: Indian Professionals in the U.S. Organization." In Richard Harvey Brown and George V. Coelho (Eds), *Tradition and Transformation: Asian Indians in America*. Studies in Third World Societies, publication number 38: 134.

Eagleton, Terry. 1983. *Literary Theory: An Introduction*. Minneapolis: Minnesota University Press.

Endo, Russell, 1989. "The Social Science Frontiers of Asian American Studies." In Gail Nomura, Russell Endo, Stephen Sumida, and Russell Leong (Eds), *Frontiers of Asian American Studies: Writing, Research, and Commentary*. Pullman, Washington: Washington State University Press: 81-84.

Fernandez, Marilyn, and William Liu. 1986. "Asian Indians in the United States: Economic, Educational and Family Profile from the 1980 Census." In Richard Harvey Brown and George V. Coelho (Eds). *Tradition and Transformation: Asian Indians in America*. Studies in Third World Societies, Publication number 38: 168.

Harding, Sandra. 1986. *The Science Question in Feminism*. Ithaca, New York: Cornell University Press.

Helweg, Arthur W., and Usha M. Helweg. 1990. *An Immigrant Success Story: East Indians in America*. Philadelphia: University of Pennsylvania Press.

Jayawardena, Kumari. 1986. *Feminism and Nationalism in the Third World*. London: Zed Press.

Kay, Diana. 1988. "The Politics of Gender in Exile." *Sociology* 22: 1-21.

Lou, Raymond. 1989. "The Vietnamese Business Community of San Jose." In Gail Nomura, Russell Endo, Stephen Sumida, and Russell Leong (Eds), *Frontiers of Asian American Studies: Writing, Research, and Commentary*. Pullman, Washington: Washington State University Press: 98-112.

Mazumdar, Sucheta. 1989. "General Introduction: A Woman-Centered Perspective on Asian American History." Asian Women United of California (Eds). *Making Waves: An Anthology of Writings by and About Asian American Women*. Boston: Beacon Press.

Mazumdar, Vina. 1976. "The Social Reform Movement in India." In B. R. Nanda (Ed), *Indian Women from Purdah to Modernity*. New Delhi: Vikas Press.

Mohanty, Chandra Talpade. 1989. "Under Western Eyes: Feminist Scholarship and Colonial Discourses." In Chandra Talpade Mohanty, Ann Russo, and Lourdes Torres (Eds), *Third World Women and the Politics of Feminism*. Bloomington: Indiana University Press: 51-80.

Park, Kyeyoung. 1989. "Impact of New Productive Activities on the Organization of Domestic Life: A Case Study of the Korean American Community." In Gail Nomura, Russell Endo, Stephen Sumida, and Russell Leong (Eds), *Frontiers of Asian American Studies: Writing, Research, and Commentary*. Pullman, Washington: Washington State University Press: 140-150.

Sangari, KumKum and Sudesh Vaid, (Eds). 1990. *Recasting Women: Essays in Indian Colonial History*. New Brunswick: Rutgers University Press.

Saran, Parmatma. 1985. *The Asian Indian Experience in the United States*. Cambridge, Massachusetts: Schenkman.

Takaki, Ronald. 1989. *Strangers from a Different Shore: A History of Asian Americans*. Boston, Massachusetts: Little, Brown.

Time, July 8, 1985, p. 42.

Xenos, Peter, Herbert Barringer, and Michael J. Levin. 1989. *Asian Indians in the United States: A 1980 Census Profile*. Paper number 111 of the East-West Population Institute.

Yu, Eui Young. 1982. "Koreans in LA: Prospects and Promises." Center for Korean American and Korean Studies, California State University, Los Angeles: 54-55.

Chapter Seven

Re-Producing the Model Minority Stereotype: Judge Joyce Karlin's Sentencing Colloquy in *People v. Soon Ja Du*

Neil Gotanda

I. Introduction

Following the Los Angeles civil disturbances of April and May, 1992, commentary on race and the judicial system have focused on the acquittal and re-trial of the police officers charged with beating Rodney King and the trial of the two African Americans charged with severely beating truck driver Reginald Denny. However, another incident has proven to be of greater significance for Asian Americans and has cast an even longer shadow over racial relationships involving Asian Americans. *People v. Soon Ja Du*[1] preceded the Rodney King case and attracted widespread local attention but little national coverage.[2] Du Soon Ja,[3] a fifty-one-year-old Korean immigrant mother and store owner, shot and killed a fifteen-year-old African American girl in a dispute over a bottle of orange juice. The incident itself generated anger and apprehension in the African American and Korean communities. But the extremely lenient sentence of the trial judge, Joyce A. Karlin, elevated the shooting, trial and sentence into a shorthand summary of resentment and outrage at the judicial system's treatment of African Americans.

Judge Karlin was well aware of the deep concerns of both the African American and Korean communities in Los Angeles over the Du trial. The barrage of local media coverage reinforced the high visibility of the trial.

In response to this visibility and the general requirements of the judiciary, Karlin took special care to present her sentence as fair and impartial. She sought to emphasize her impartiality through the use of a "color-blind" rhetorical device called "racial nonrecognition."[4] There are brief references to "Korean" and "African American" at the beginning and end of her short sentencing colloquy, but in the body Judge Karlin avoids any explicit racial references. Instead, she uses disguised racial references, including demeaning racial stereotypes of both African Americans and Asian Americans.

Judge Karlin's disguised use of race, moreover, is done in a manner which differs from the usual White/Black bi-polar racial model. Instead of staying within the traditional racial framework of White/Black or White/Non-white, Judge Karlin creates a three-tier White-Asian-Black, racially stratified hierarchy. The three-tier racial hierarchy is produced through a stereotypical demonization of the victim Latasha Harlins and the placement of the defendant Du Soon Ja into a "model minority" middle position.

During the violent May 1992 civil disturbances, and continuing to the present, Latasha Harlins' death is mentioned as contributing to deep skepticism as to whether any African American could receive justice in the legal system. Since the end of the Los Angeles civil disorders, incidents involving Asian American shopkeepers and African American patrons have continued to be flash points of controversy.[5]

Outside of the African American community, published comments about Judge Karlin herself have been sympathetic. The *Los Angeles Times*'s summary of the civil disturbances suggested that Karlin had acted to reduce tensions. Karlin is quoted as seeking "healing, not revenge. . . a catalyst to confront an intolerable situation and . . . create solutions."[6]

Karlin's sentence is characterized as being a well-meaning error of judgment, nothing more.

I believe this impression is incorrect. This article reviews closely the text of Karlin's sentencing colloquy. While much of the anti-Karlin sentiment sprang from the perceived injustice of probation without jail time, her sentencing colloquy proves to be much more revealing. The content of the colloquy shows that Judge Karlin did not make a sentencing decision based upon the individual background of the defendant Du Soon Ja, but improperly relied upon stereotypes of Koreans and African Americans. Her use of these stereotypes contributed to Du's sentence, with its subsequent impact upon Asian American/African American relations.

II. Stereotypes and Demons in Karlin's Colloquy

My examination of the text of Judge Karlin's colloquy will show how Karlin clearly sympathizes with defendant Du Soon Ja. In contrast, Karlin presents the victim Latasha Harlins in an unfavorable light. These contrasting portrayals are presented by associating Du and Harlins with various racial stereotypes. These linkages to stereotypes are hidden by the color-blind technique of racial nonrecognition. Judge Karlin is thus not making an "objective" presentation of the Korean identity of Du or the African American identity of Harlins. In the next sections, I will refer to the text of Judge Karlin's sentencing colloquy, which begins on page 84 at the end of this article.

A. Distancing and Demonizing by Judge Karlin

Judge Karlin differentiates between the defendant Du and the victim Harlins by humanizing Du but "demonizing" Harlins through harmful stereotypes.[7] There are a number of opposing stereotypes which are loosely connected to Du and to Harlins. In that process, Latasha Harlins is criminalized while Du is favorably portrayed.

Karlin describes Du as a 51-year-old woman who is a victim of circumstances (P. 29), including gang terror (P. 29, 33) and a gun altered by unknown thieves (P. 29). Further, Du was present on the day of the killing only because of her maternal loyalty to her son (P. 33-34), to shield her son from the repeated robberies (P. 33), and "to save him one day of fear" (P. 34). And Karlin is generally sympathetic to the hardships faced by innocent shopkeepers who are under frequent attack (P. 24-26).

Judge Karlin portrays defendant Du through reproduction of the Korean shopkeeper as an "innocent victim." In the colloquy, Du is a hard worker and has no criminal record (P. 19). Gangs terrorize Du's family while they operate the store (P. 29-33). The actual killing was the result of the assault by Harlins upon Du (P. 38) and the modification of the revolver by unknown thieves who had rendered the revolver "defective" (P. 29).[8]

In contrast, Karlin portrays Latasha Harlins as a criminal. Harlins is described as having likely committed a criminal assault upon Du (P. 26-29) after an act of shoplifting (P. 25). Harlins is an example of shoplifters who attack shopkeepers after being caught in the act (P. 24-26). Further, Karlin associates Harlins with gang theft and terror (P. 33-34); Harlins is the person who caused Du to commit a criminal act when Du had previously led a crime-free life (P. 38).

Judge Karlin also stereotypes Harlins through continued references to gangs and gang terror. These references to gangs are not an allegation that Harlins was herself a gang member. The use of stereotypes with Harlins is indirect and involves linking Harlins to a racial group identity.

Judge Karlin's portrayal of Harlins therefore operates within the context of an existing social consciousness of "gangness." That is, street gangs exist in society and while a serious social problem are imagined to be pervasive.[9] In line with images in popular culture, Karlin constructs and imagines members of these street gangs as violent criminals, dealing drugs and engaging in theft. She further connects "gangness" with African Americans, ignoring the widespread prevalence of gangs comprised largely of Asians. Judge Karlin emphasizes her appreciation of "gangness" by using the word "terror" three times in her colloquy: "victimized and terrorized by gang members" (P. 29); "the very real terror experienced by the Du family" (P. 33); "repeated robberies and terrorism in the same store" (P. 33).

Judge Karlin's omission of any humanizing information about Harlins also works to demonize her. Karlin might have done well to note a number of facts related by the Court of Appeals about Latasha Harlins:

> The probation report also reveals that Latasha had suffered many painful experiences during her life, including the violent death of her mother. Latasha lived with her extended family (her grandmother, younger brother and sister, aunt, uncle and niece) in what the probation officer described as "a clean, attractively furnished three-bedroom apartment" in South Central Los Angeles. Latasha had been an honor student at Bret Hart Junior High School, from which she had graduated the previous spring. Although she was making only average grades in high school, she had promised that she would bring her grades up to her former standard. Latasha was involved in activities at a youth center as an assistant cheerleader, member of the drill team and a summer junior camp counselor. She was a good athlete and an active church member.[10]

The absence of these observations from Karlin's comments, their presence in the probation report, and their inclusion by the opinion of the Court of Appeals, suggest that these facts may not have been overlooked by Karlin but actively judged by her to be unworthy of mention.

B. Avoiding the Question of Punishment

One significant consequence of Karlin's "humanizing" of Du and "demonizing" of Harlins occurs in the question of *punishment*. Karlin omits any direct consideration of punishment. Instead, Karlin *balances* Harlins against Du, African American against Asian American.

Karlin quotes the statutory requirements at the beginning of her discussion on sentencing (P. 7). After briefly noting and dismissing most of the statutory criteria, Karlin turns to the crucial question of "punishment" and rhetorically asks, but does not directly answer, "Is state prison need[ed] to punish Du? Perhaps" (P. 14). She then directs her discussion away from "punishment" to the sufficient but not necessary question of whether Du's situation is an "unusual case." If it is, she can avoid the "presumption against probation" when a firearm is used, which would usually result in a prison sentence.[11] In the discussion of probation, Karlin focuses on whether Du is likely to engage in criminal conduct in the future (P. 37). Karlin never directly returns to the question of punishment.

The District Attorney addresses the issue of punishment by characterizing the social response to Du's wrongful taking of Harlins' life in terms of "protection" of a "black child's life." Karlin characterizes the District Attorney's suggestion that probation would "send a message that a black child's life is not worthy of protection" as an effort at "revenge" (P. 4). Specifically, Karlin states, "This is not the time for revenge, and my job is not to exact revenge for those who demand it" (P. 4). Karlin thus equates a call for a prison sentence as punishment with unfair retribution ("revenge"). Karlin further particularizes this demand for a statutorily allowed judicial punishment as emanating from an amorphous "those" rather than from a community frustrated by its perception of a lack of fairness and justice.

In lieu of a direct inquiry into punishment, Karlin resorts to her preconstructed racial stratification through her analysis of the statutory criteria for probation. Karlin's use of "demonizing" stereotypes of Harlins is not a simple effort to "blame the victim." Karlin does not directly judge Harlins's social status to see if she was such a socially dangerous personality—such a menace to society—that any harm, including her being shot, was indirectly deserved. Further, Karlin's analysis is more of a balancing of Harlins and Du against each other. Karlin engages in a set of comparisons between Harlins and Du, rather than measuring Harlins against a generalized social standard to decide if her summary "punishment" was appropriate.

First, Karlin balances Du against Harlins by noting that in determining whether probation is appropriate, she must determine "the *vulnerability of the victim*" (L. 53). Although the issue of vulnerability is in theory applicable only to the *victim*, Karlin proceeds to apply it to both Harlins *and* Du. Because Harlins "used her fists as weapons," Karlin declares that she was not vulnerable. Karlin does not mention the fact that Du had shot Harlins in the *back* of the head, which logically demonstrates that Harlins was "vulnerable" to an attack by Du. Karlin follows this with a non-sequitur implying that Harlins was not vulnerable because she was an accused shoplifter and therefore had not been justified in her assault upon Du (P. 24). In contrast, Karlin describes Du's situation sympathetically: shopkeepers like Du seem unable to even accuse customers of shoplifting without fear of being assaulted.

Second, Karlin states that under the statute she is to consider "criminal sophistication" in deciding the propriety of probation. Although the consideration is meant to apply to the criminal sophistication of the *defendant*, Karlin ultimately balances Du's criminal sophistication against the victim's alleged criminality (P. 27). Karlin describes Du as lacking "any degree of criminal sophistication in her offense," a woman "who would not be here today" but for "unusual circumstances" (P. 28, 29). Judge Karlin believes that Harlins, on the other hand, would have had charges filed against her had she "not been shot" and had the "incident which preceded the shooting been reported" (P. 26).

C. Redirecting the Question of Deterrence

Similarly, Karlin fails to address explicitly the question of deterrence. The shooting incident occurred in an extremely tense context—a Korean grocery store in a poor neighborhood.[12] Karlin perceives Du's use of a gun against a suspected shoplifter to be predictable, even if extreme. Karlin finds the courts "filled with defendants who are charged with assault resulting in great bodily injury as a result of attacks on shopkeepers" (P. 25). Possession of such a firearm by a shopkeeper in this context is expected and normal. "The [presumption against probation because a firearm was used (P. 15)] is aimed at criminals who arm themselves when they go out and commit other crimes. It is not aimed at shopkeepers who lawfully possess firearms for their own protection" (P. 18).

Karlin goes far beyond discussing the "reasonableness" of Du's use of a handgun as part of the question of mitigation in determining Du's sentence. Instead, her comments go towards a revision of the issue of deterrence. Karlin's admonitions on the use of guns do not speak to deterring shooting of unarmed shoplifters, but rather to deterring shoplifters and armed robbers from attacking shopkeepers. Karlin addresses herself to the training of shopkeepers in the proper use of handguns and avoiding revolvers modified to have light trigger pulls (P. 30-31; App 827).

In her own defense, Karlin is reported to have complained that critics were not taking into account the dozens of Korean shopkeepers who have been killed in shootings. Such comments only reinforce my interpretation that any deterrent effect of the sentence was directed at future shoplifters and burglars, not at shopkeepers who improperly use guns.

Karlin's version of deterrence—use a gun to save your store—was later memorialized in the media images on television, in newspapers, and in magazines, of gun toting Korean shopkeepers defending their stores during the Los Angeles disturbances.[13] Karlin thus expects such use of firearms in self-defense to occur in the future, and her failure to discuss deterrence when granting probation strongly suggests that such conduct is condoned, especially within the context of a highly publicized trial.

D. Gendered Roles: Good Woman vs. Bad Woman

1. Good Wife vs. Criminal Daughter

Karlin reinforces her social hierarchy through the use of various gendered images of Du and Harlins. Du is portrayed as a good wife—loyally working in the family store. She is even more dramatically portrayed as a good mother—volunteering to work in the store to protect her son. Karlin also focuses attention upon Du Soon Ja's status as spouse and wife by never directly mentioning Du's husband. There are references to Du's family and her son, but her husband is omitted. The context for these images is the traditional stereotype of the family as a strength of Asian cultures.

By contrast, any of the available positive gendered images of Harlins as dutiful daughter, church member and student are ignored and she is portrayed as a criminal. This contrast between Du and Harlins reinforces the social hierarchy through the greater social distance from Judge Karlin—a female law-giver.

2. Battered Woman vs. Aggressor Criminal

An alternative interpretation of Judge Karlin's preference for defendant Du over victim Harlins is that Karlin is privileging a "feminized" defendant Du over a "masculinized" Harlins.

This genderizing can be seen in the following steps. Karlin casts the victim Harlins into the role of criminal aggressor and casts the defendant Du into the role of an innocent victim. This reversal of roles has been noted earlier. The aggressor/victim reversal can also be seen as evoking the structure of the "battered woman" criminal defense.

Du Soon Ja is presented as having the characteristics of a battered woman who strikes back against her aggressor. Harlins is described as having used her "fists as weapons." (P. 23) It is not a difficult leap to link this image of fists beating a helpless woman to the stereotypes of an abusive male battering his spouse or girlfriend. Similarly, Du's use of the gun as a response to a physical assault is a scenario which we associate with the most dramatic instances of women striking back against their abuse. Du not only draws more sympathy, but takes on the character of a feminized victim of physical abuse. Du's testimony that she did not recall the actual shooting[14] also safely distances her from the male images on television and in the newspapers of Korean men defending their stores during the Los Angeles civil disturbances. Gun-toting Korean shopkeepers shooting into the dark are an extremely provocative image and evoke far less sympathy than a physically abused woman.

Latasha Harlins is further masculinized by association with crime and gangs. The structural implication of male batterer is reinforced by the multiple associations to "gangness" and gang terror. Gangs have most often been constructed as having a strong African American male identity. Harlins as a "masculinized male batterer" is then placed in opposition to Defendant Du's "innocent battered woman victim." Karlin's favoring of Du and identification with Du thus become a choice of the battered woman over Harlins's constructed role as the abusive male.

III. Racial Stratification: The Model Minority

The myth of the "model minority" is a very recent and modern innovation, perhaps only two decades old. The "model minority" is a complex resurrection of previously existing constructed stereotypes of Asian Americans consolidated with new images, especially that of social and economic prosperity. The old images constitute the collective set of stereotypes and constructed identities of Asian Americans accumulated over a century of anti-Asian activities. The transformation of the Asian American from the "heathen chinee" and the "yellow horde" into a "model minority" has been dramatic and rapid.

A. The Ideological Content of the "Model Minority"

The sharp change began in the middle of the 1960s with the appearance of several articles in major national news media commenting favorably upon the success of the Asian Americans, at that time mostly second- and third-generation Japanese and Chinese Americans.[15] Especially noteworthy was a 1966 *New York Times Magazine* article entitled "Success Story: Japanese American Style."[16] Those early articles, however, rather than focusing upon their economic success, emphasized overcoming adversity.[17]

In the past decade the stereotype has shifted to emphasize economic success based upon an extremely aggressive work ethic and strong family cohesion. Lisa Lowe has described the model minority myth as including the image of Asians as "aggressively driven overachievers" who "assimilate well."[18] This version of the "model minority" places Asian Americans into a reasonably well-to-do class position vis-a-vis other minorities, especially African Americans. A typical response from socially concerned Asian Americans has been to argue that Asians as a "model minority is a myth."[19] Such a response, however, denies the possibility that as a group, Asian immigrants and their descendants have actually acquired certain social and economic advantages over African Americans.

"Model" includes two notions. First it includes a sense of being "exemplary," and therefore in some higher status than some non-exemplary group—African Americans. Second, "model" includes a sense that the "model" is directed at that other group for emulation.[20] "Minority"—the second half of "model minority"—has been less explored. The word suggests that Asian Americans remain in a subsidiary position to the White racial majority. One might argue that the term is simply descriptive of the numerical demographic position of Asian Americans. But "minority" here is linked to "model," hardly a neutral term. This linkage strongly suggests that in this usage, the ideological implications are paramount.

The term "model minority" thus includes references to three distinct and different levels of racial status—a three-tier racial stratification. At the top, there is the White majority. In the middle are Asian Americans, role models for another racial group in need of exemplars for their own conduct. At the bottom are African Americans, who are directed to emulate Asian Americans with the goal of someday achieving a higher racial status.

B. Karlin's Re-Production of the "Model Minority"

The individualized racial characterizations by Karlin of Du and Harlins coincide with and reproduce the image and structure of Koreans and Asian Americans as a "model minority." Karlin emphasizes Du's "model minority" status through an emphasis upon the race and class nature of the "innocent shopkeeper." Karlin understands, and expects others to understand, that Du is a *Korean* shopkeeper.

The "shopkeeper" stereotype is a complex one with a substantial history. There are the references from the beginning of the century to the hapless Chinese laundryman or the villainous Japanese merchant.[21] In the legal curriculum, the most famous case involving a person of Asian ancestry is the 1886 U.S. Supreme Court decision in *Yick Wo v. Hopkins*, involving a San Francisco ordinance discriminatorily applied to Chinese laundries.[22]

The "middleman minority" cited in the work of Edna Bonacich emphasizes groups which have successfully occupied various economic and social niches between larger social groupings.[23] Those groups have often been shopkeepers and operators of small commercial enterprises. In the modern context, the image of the Korean grocery store owner has become the dominant media image of an Asian American.[24] Sales transactions between Korean grocers and African American patrons are now exemplary of all social interaction between Asians and African Americans,[25] and the actions of Korean grocers are exemplary of all Asian American cultures.[26]

Judge Karlin characterizes Du Soon Ja as a successful shopkeeper and by implication presents the Korean community as a successful "model minority." This presentation thus provides Judge Karlin with an ideological framework to both distance herself from Latasha Harlins individually, and also more generally to absolve non-Blacks, especially those in the highest tier of the three-tiered system of the "model minority," of any social responsibility for the effects of racial subordination upon African Americans.

In contrast, Harlins was closely tied to criminal conduct and gang terror. As noted earlier, Harlins's personal background as an honor student in Junior High School and an active participant in her church and social groups is omitted by Judge Karlin. This omission invites the inference that Harlins, an African American living in a poor neighborhood, was a participant in a crime and welfare subculture who did not have any middle-class aspirations to education and economic success.

C. Asian American as a Racial Category

It has become commonplace to say that race is not biological or natural and that race is "socially constructed."[27] Even with that intellectual understanding, there is often resistance to appreciating the ways in which that "social construction" can take place.[28] In *Racial Formation in the United States* Omi and Winant emphasize the open and contested nature of race in America. They argue:

> . . . there is a continuous temptation to think of race as an essence, as something fixed, concrete and objective . . . In our view it is crucial to break with these habits of thought. The effort must be made to understand race as *an unstable and "decentered" complex of social meanings constantly being transformed by political struggle.*[29]

When Judge Karlin presents Du and Harlins in a racially stratified context, she is both creating as well as reproducing the idea of race as tiered with multiple levels rather than simply consisting of White and non-white. This use of race as changing, and subject to constant negotiation between individuals and within society, is unfamiliar to most legal scholars.

Karlin makes reference to Koreans, but she never uses the term "Asian American." That is a term I have added in my interpretation of her colloquy. I have done so with full recognition that there is no simple way to describe how persons of Asian ancestry—immigrants and subsequent generations—have been and are grouped together.

My approach in this article is based upon the idea that the Asian American category is a racial category, subject to the "constant negotiation" described by Omi and Winant. I used the concept of "racial categories" to describe a number of aspects of modern American race:

While the social content of race has varied throughout American history, the practice of using race as a commonly recognized social divider has remained almost constant. . . [T]he term "racial category" refers to this distinct, consistent practice of classifying people in a socially determined and socially determinative way.[30]

Exploration of "Asian American" as a racial category would examine whether or not social and economic privileges attach to those persons classified as Asian American. In economic relations, research could determine whether real property values declined when an Asian American integrated a formerly all-White neighborhood. Central to my suggestion that the Asian American racial category is an intermediate category between White and African American would be a comparison of whether the decline in values, and any associated racial "tipping," was more severe for African Americans than Asian Americans.[31] An analysis of social attitudes might also reveal a differential between African Americans and Asian Americans around such issues as crime and morality.[32] Similar studies could be carried out on other areas such as income, job discrimination and portrayals in popular culture.

Whatever the results of this suggested research, historical materials do not demonstrate a strong, consistent terminology. Outside of legal scholarship, writing on the subject of "Asian Americans" uses the term either without definition, or as a problematic mixture of race and ethnicity.[33] While explorations of "ethnicity" are extremely valuable, I choose not to discuss "ethnicity" here because I believe that at least for examining legal ideology, using race is more productive. It is beyond this short article to pursue a careful analysis of the social or ideological linkages from Du Soon Ja, a Korean American, to Asian Americans generally. Any stronger statement about how one can legitimately move from Korean (or any other immigrant group from Asia) to Asian American must await further academic examination and social development.[34] The social growth and acceptance of the term "Asian American" will depend in large part upon if and when the various Asian "ethnic" communities choose to feel comfortable among themselves with the label of Asian American. That day may be approaching, but it has not yet arrived.

D. The Political Significance of the "Model Minority"

The response of Asian American academics has been to deny that all Asian Americans have "made it." Most recently, Ronald Takaki noted:

[I]n their celebration of this "model minority" these media pundits have exaggerated Asian American "success." . . . Actually, in terms of personal incomes, Asian Americans have not reached equality. While many Asian Americans are doing well, others find themselves mired in poverty.[35]

Takaki suggests that Americans can find a basis for celebrating our multiculturalism in our common struggles for a better life. This effort to recognize past discrimination against Asian Americans and thus build a common bond with other oppressed groups, especially African Americans, seems to me inadequate. As a basis for bridging racial antagonisms, such historically based claims have proven of limited value.[36]

Instead of denying shifting economics and demographics, we should recognize the half-truths in the "myth of the model minority" as a better starting point for analyzing the emerging Asian American racial category. We should recognize that positions such as that taken by Judge Karlin provide to the Asian American racial category racial privileging in such measurable areas as neighborhood housing, employment status and overall family income.

The difficulty comes in attempting to situate this racial category without succumbing to the "model minority" stereotype. Karlin's colloquy both reflects the "myth of the model minority" and further defines it by ascribing to a Korean grocer certain class privileges (shopkeeper status), higher social status (strong family) and moral values (law-abiding) all in contrast to the demonized Latasha Harlins who lacks all of these values. The result is that the Asian American racial category is *defined* by this narrow stereotype. Omitted is any sense of personal or social history, community or real family life, religion and spirituality, all of which would be part of any historically textured description of Asian Americans.

The destructive aspect of Karlin's colloquy can thus be seen in its contribution to the creation of the Asian American racial category by limiting the identification and understanding of that racial category. This entire effort took place in the midst of a media circus, with full broadcast and print media coverage. Karlin's efforts were therefore not limited to the courtroom or even the traditional legal texts, but rather became part of our everyday popular cultural discourse.

IV. Conclusion

In conclusion, I address two issues. The first is a question that has been posed in presentations of earlier versions of this paper: What do I think Judge Karlin should have done? Foremost, I believe that Judge Karlin should have shown genuine compassion for all parties. Karlin should have addressed the death of Latasha Harlins by examining the real Latasha Harlins, not a demonized stereotype of Harlins. Further, in so doing, Judge Karlin should have addressed squarely the questions of punishment and deterrence as they affected Du—and most importantly, as they would affect African Americans, Asian Americans, and whites in the aftermath of her sentence. While no one can be expected to predict the future, Karlin's failure to examine these crucial issues has had dire consequences.

Had Karlin addressed these issues, I do not believe that she could have come to the same conclusion regarding parole and a prison sentence. But even had she come to the same final decision, her reasoning would have been far more defensible. Karlin would have had to confront genuinely the extraordinarily difficult and intractable character of racial tensions that we face today.

Even more disturbing, however, is the legacy of this incident in two sets of media images of violence, both centered around "the Korean grocer." One set of images is the video of Du shooting Harlins, and the videos and photos of Korean grocers using guns to defend their stores. These images are linked together by Judge Karlin's defense of Du's shooting of Harlins. Karlin's colloquy ties them together as a legitimate exercise of self-defense of property and person and as well, links them to the stereotype of the Asian American "model minority." The other set of images are those which legitimize violence directed at Korean grocers, celebrated in films such as *Menace 2 Society* which begin with the shooting of a Korean grocer, and in music by various "gangster rap" artists. The acceptance of violence against Koreans as a naturalized stereotype of reality is the flipside of Karlin's use of demonized stereotypes to portray Latasha Harlins.

These images of violence portray Koreans and African Americans in direct opposition to each other, as if they were removed from our American social context. If we hope to address the manner in which these stereotyped images become embedded in social understandings and are then reproduced in our conduct, it is crucial that we recognize the full racial context in which they flourish, including the role of the judiciary and racial groups seemingly removed from the immediate conflict. Racial violence is the product of all of our conduct and it is crucial to recognize that responsibility.

Los Angeles Times November 22, 1991: the text of remarks by Los Angeles Superior Court Judge Joyce A. Karlin in the sentencing of Soon Ja Du. Edition: Home Edition Section: Metro Page: 7 Pt. B Col. 1; supplemented *Los Angeles Daily Journal,* November 22, 1991, vol. 104, p. 6, col. 3.

TEXT:

1   One thing I think both sides will agree on is that nothing I can do, nothing the judicial system can do, nothing will lessen the loss suffered by Latasha Harlins' family and friends. But the parties involved in this case and anyone truly interested in what caused this case can make sure that something positive comes out of this tragedy by having Latasha Harlins' death mark a beginning rather than an end—a beginning of a greater understanding and acceptance between two groups,

some of whose members have until now demonstrated intolerance and bigotry toward one another.

2 Latasha's death should be a catalyst to force members of the African American and Korean communities to confront an intolerable situation by creating constructive solutions. Through that process, a greater understanding and acceptance will hopefully result so that similar tragedies will not be repeated.

3 Statements by the district attorney, (which) suggest that imposing less than the maximum sentence will send a message that a black child's life is not worthy of protection, (are) dangerous rhetoric, which serves no purpose other than to pour gasoline on a fire.

4 This is not a time for revenge, and my job is not to exact revenge for those who demand it.

5 There are those in this community who have publicly demanded in the name of justice that the maximum sentence be imposed in this case.

6 But it is my opinion that justice is never served when public opinion, prejudice, revenge or unwarranted sympathy are considered by a sentencing court in resolving a case.

7 In imposing sentence I must first consider the objectives of sentencing a defendant:
1) To protect society.
2) To punish the defendant for committing a crime.
3) To encourage the defendant to lead a law-abiding life.
4) To deter others.
5) To isolate the defendant so she can't commit other crimes.
6) To secure restitution for the victim.
7) To seek uniformity in sentencing.

8 The question becomes, are any of these sentencing objectives achieved by Mrs. Du being remanded to state prison?

9 Let us start with the last objective first: uniformity in sentencing. According to statistics gathered for the Superior Courts of California, sentences imposed on defendants convicted of voluntary manslaughter last year ranged from probation with no jail time to incarceration in state prison for several years.

10 Because of the unique nature of each crime of voluntary manslaughter, and by that I mean the uniquely different factual situations resulting in that crime, uniformity in sentencing is virtually impossible to achieve.

11 Which, then, of the other sentencing objectives lead to the conclusion that state prison is warranted?

12 Does society need Mrs. Du to be incarcerated in order to be protected? I think not.

13 Is state prison needed in order to encourage the defendant to lead a law-abiding life or isolate her so she cannot commit other crimes? I think not.

14 Is state prison need to punish Mrs. Du? Perhaps.

15 There is, in this case, a presumption against probation because a firearm was used.

16 In order to overcome that presumption, the court must find this to be an unusual case, as that term is defined by law.

17 There are three reasons that I find this is an unusual case:

18 First, the basis for the presumption against probation is technically present. But it doesn't really apply. The statute is aimed at criminals who arm themselves when they go out and commit other crimes. It is not aimed at shopkeepers who lawfully possess firearms for their own protection.

19 Second, the defendant has no recent record, in fact, no record at any time of committing similar crimes or crimes of violence.

20 Third, the defendant participated in the crime under circumstances of great provocation, coercion and duress. Therefore, this is, in my opinion, an unusual case that overcomes the statutory presumption against probation.

21 Should the defendant be placed on probation?

22 One of the questions a sentencing court is required to ask in answering that question is "whether the crime was committed because of unusual circumstances, such as great provocation." I find that it was.

23 I must also determine the vulnerability of the victim in deciding whether probation is appropriate. Although Latasha Harlins was not armed with a weapon at the time of her death, she had used her fists as weapons just seconds before she was shot.

24 The district attorney argues that Latasha was justified in her assault on Mrs. Du. Our courts are filled with cases which suggest otherwise.

25 Our courts are filled with defendants who are charged with assault resulting in great bodily injury as a result of attacks on shopkeepers, including shopkeepers who have accused them of shoplifting.

26 Had Latasha Harlins not been shot and had the incident which preceded the shooting been reported, it is my opinion that the district attorney would have relied on the videotape and Mrs. Du's testimony to make a determination whether to file charges against Latasha.

27 Other questions I am required to address in determining whether probation is appropriate are "whether the carrying out of the crime suggested criminal sophistication and whether the defendant will be a danger to others if she is not imprisoned."

28 Having observed Mrs. Du on videotape at the time the crime was committed and having observed Mrs. Du during this trial, I cannot conclude that there was any degree of criminal sophistication in her offense. Nor can I conclude that she is a danger to others if she is not incarcerated.

29 Mrs. Du is a (51)-year-old woman with no criminal history and no history of violence. But for the unusual circumstances in this case, including the Du family's history of being victimized and terrorized by gang members, Mrs. Du would not be here today. Nor do I believe Mrs. Du would be here today if the gun she grabbed for protection had not been altered. This was a gun that had been stolen from the Du family and returned to them shortly before the shooting.

30 The court has been presented with no evidence, and I have no reason to believe that Mrs. Du knew that the gun had been altered in such a way as to—in effect— make it an automatic weapon with a hairpin trigger.

31 Ordinarily a .38 revolver is one of the safest guns in the world. It cannot go off accidentally. And a woman Mrs. Du's size would have to decide consciously to pull the trigger and to exert considerable strength to do so.

32 But that was not true of the gun used to shoot Latasha Harlins. I have serious questions in my mind whether this crime would have been committed at all but for a defective gun.

33 The district attorney would have this court ignore the very real terror experienced by the Du family before the shooting, and the fear Mrs. Du experienced as she worked by herself the day of the shooting. But there are things I cannot ignore. And I cannot ignore the reason Mrs. Du was working at the store that day. She went to work that Saturday to save her son from having to work. Mrs. Du's son had begged his parents to close the store. He was afraid because he had been the victim of repeated robberies and terrorism in that same store.

34 On the day of the shooting Mrs. Du volunteered to cover for her son to save him one day of fear.

35 Did Mrs. Du react inappropriately to Latasha? Absolutely.

36 Was Mrs. Du's over-reaction understandable? I think so.

37 If probation is not appropriate, and state prison time is warranted, then a short prison term would be an injustice. If Mrs. Du should be sent to prison because she is a danger to others or is likely to re-offend, then I could not justify imposing a short prison term.

38 But it is my opinion that Mrs. Du is not a danger to the community and it is my opinion that she will not re-offend. She led a crime free life until Latasha Harlins walked into her store and there is no reason to believe that this is the beginning of a life of crime for Mrs. Du. But if I am wrong, Mrs. Du will face severe consequences.

39 For all of these reasons it is hereby adjudged that: on her conviction for voluntary manslaughter, Mrs. Du is sentenced to the midterm of 6 years in state prison. On the personal use of a firearm enhancement, the defendant is sentenced to the midterm of 4 years, to run consecutive to the 6 years for a total of 10 years. Execution of this sentence is suspended.

40 Mrs. Du is placed on formal probation for five years on the following terms and conditions:

41 Mrs. Du is to perform 400 hours of community service. I strongly recommend that for the maximum impact on Mrs. Du and for the community, this service should be in connection with efforts to various groups to unite the Korean and African American communities.

42 Mrs. Du is to pay $500 to the restitution fine [sic] and pay full restitution to the victim's immediate family for all out of court expenses for Latasha Harlins' funeral and any medical expenses related to Latasha Harlins' death.

43 Mrs. Du is to obey all laws and orders of the probation department and the court.

44 If I am wrong about Mrs. Du and she re-offends, then she will go to state prison for 10 years.

Endnotes

1. Superior Court of Los Angeles County, No. BA037738; People v. Superior Court (Du) 5 Cal.App. 4th 822 (1992)

2. A search on February 21, 1993 of the Los Angeles Times Dialog database through Westlaw on the terms, Judge Joyce Karlin, Soon Ja Du or Latasha Harlins, found 258 references, including many substantial articles and major news reports.

3. The titles of the superior court case and the reported opinion use "Soon Ja Du" and place Du's surname last. In referring to defendant Du in this article, I will follow standard Korean usage of the placement of the family surname.

4. Neil Gotanda, A Critique of "Our Constitution is Color-Blind" 44 Stanford Law Review 1 (1991) at 16-23.
5. The concentrated extent and losses of Korean merchants during the civil disorders were staggering. While estimates have varied, with substantial losses among Hispanic and African American businesses, one author estimates that half of the businesses destroyed were Korean. He also charges:

    In fact, the rioters were aiming at business establishments. At the end of the fury, 1,867 Korean businesses were looted or burned. Korean businesses alone suffered an estimated $347 million in property damage—about one-half of the total loss from the riots.

    The worst damage to Korean property, however, did not occur in the African American neighborhood of South Central Los Angeles, only nine percent of all Korean businesses in LA are located there. The heaviest loss occurred north of South Central, in Koreatown, which is inhabited mostly by poor Latino immigrants. Peter Kwong, "The First Multicultural Riots," from Inside the L.A. Riots: What Really Happened—And Why It Will Happen Again 88 (1992).

    For a more detailed analysis of Korean losses, see, Paul Ong and Suzanne Hee, Losses in the Los Angeles Civil Unrest, April 29-May 1, 1992: Lists of the Damaged Properties and The LA Riot/Rebellion (1993, UCLA Center for Pacific Rim Studies).
6. Staff of the Los Angeles Times, Understanding The Riots: Los Angeles Before and After the Rodney King Case 40 (1992).
7. When I say Karlin uses harmful or demeaning stereotypes, I mean that she draws upon existing "racial identities," i.e., socially developed attributes ascribed to those identified as African Americans or Korean American or Asian American, which are either assumed to apply to Latasha Harlins and Du Soon Ja, or are at odds with the specific descriptions of them from the Court of Appeals. I am not trying to deny there exists gang activity among African Americans. What I call a stereotype is the universalization of the notion of a criminal menace from African American youth into a powerful image which can be assigned to Latasha Harlins in the face of factual evidence which directly contradicts that universalized image.

    Further, these images need not necessarily be "demonic" or universally harmful. This section explores the implications of "benign" or "favorable" stereotypical images.
8. Judge Karlin does not mention the choice by Du and her family to operate a store in a racially particularized neighborhood. The Appeals Court noted that the Du family sold one business and chose to purchase this business in a "bad neighborhood." Appeal at p. 828. Had Karlin recognized a "consenting shopkeeper" instead of an "innocent shopkeeper," Karlin could then have allowed an inference that Du understood some of the dangers of operating a small business in a poor neighborhood. Du's use of the revolver would take on a more calculated character. Instead of Du as the innocent victim of a "defective" revolver, her use of the revolver was part of the difficult and sometimes harsh environment in which the Du family had chosen to work. I am not suggesting that self-defense, including armed self-defense, is inappropriate. At issue here is Judge Karlin's understanding of the context for the use of firearms and how Karlin has characterized Du Soon Ja's use of the weapon as completely without fault.
9. The actual prevalence of gangs is much more restricted than is the popularly presented or imagined in the television, news or police attribution of a "gang related incident." The popular imagination has constructed gangness so that it is now present for all African American youth. See, e.g., the discussion in the

appellate opinion which quotes defendant Du as testifying that she told her son that "gang members in America"..."wear some pants and some jackets...wear light sneakers, wear a cap or a hairband, headband ...have some kind of satchel and wear some thick jackets...[B]e careful with those jackets sticking out." App. at 826, n. 5.

10. Appeal, fn. 7 at 829.
11. See discussion in 5 Cal. App. 4th 822, 829 (1992).
12. In the appeal, the defendant's son is quoted as describing the situation as "having to conduct business in a war zone" (app. at 828).
13. See, e.g. the photo in Los Angeles Times, Understanding the Riots: Los Angeles Before and After the Rodney King Case 77 (1992).
14. Du is positioned as unconscious victim in the Appeal in which Du testified she did not remember firing the gun and passed out after the incident (app. at 827).
15. Bob Suzuki, "Education and the Socialization of Asian Americans: A Revisionist Analysis of the "Model Minority" Thesis, 4 Amerasia Journal 23 (1977).
16. William Petersen, "Success Story: Japanese American Style," New York Times Magazine vi-20. (January 9, 1966). Similar articles included Julian Makaroff, "America's Other Racial Minority: Japanese Americans," 210 Contemporary Review 310-314 (1967); Barbara Varon, "The Japanese Americans: Comparative Occupational Status, 1960 and 1950-", 4 Demography 809-819 (1967)

     A recent article which discussed the model minority is Don T. Nakanishi, Surviving Democracy's "Mistake": Japanese Americans and the Enduring Legacy of Executive Order 9066, 19 Amerasia Journal 7-35 (1993).
17. See especially, Bob Suzuki, "Education and the Socialization of Asian Americans: A Revisionist Analysis of the "Model Minority" Thesis, 4 *Amerasia Journal* 23 (1977).
18. Lisa Lowe, Heterogeneity, Hybridity, Multiplicity, fn. 7 at 40.
19. See *generally*, The State of Asian Pacific America, A Public Policy Report: Policy Issues to the Year 2020 (1993).
20. See, e.g., Nakanishi, "Surviving Democracy's Mistake."
21. See, e.g., Chink! ed. by Cheng-Tsu Wu (1972).
22. 118 U.S. 360 (1886).
23. See, e.g., the work of Edna Bonacich, e.g., Jonathan H. Turner and Edna Bonacich, Toward a Composite Theory of Middleman Minorities, 7 Ethnicity 144 (1980).
24. More recently, the Los Angeles Times Sunday Magazine presented a photo with accompanying text of Korean grocers and African American patrons. Los Angeles Times Magazine 20, October 17, 1993, Photographed by Chang W. Lee, Article by John W. Lee, "Counter Culture: In Los Angeles, Korean-American Stores Are Sometimes the Flash Point of Racial Animosity—But They Are Also the Proving Ground For Tolerance.
25. At a 1993 statewide California meeting of civil rights activists, the question of reissuing liquor store licenses to Korean grocers in the face of African American opposition to the perceived proliferation of liquor stores was presented as a significant civil rights issue.
26. Consider the endlessly repeated story of Korean cultural reluctance to touching strangers resulting in hostile encounters when money is offered and change returned.
27. S*ee generally*, Toni Morrison, ed., Race-ing Justice, En-gendering Power, Essays on Anita Hill, Clarence Thomas, and the Construction of Social Reality (1992);

and Michael Omi and Howard Winant, Racial Formation in the United States, From the 1960s to the 1980s (1986).

28. See David Theo Goldberg, Racist Culture: Philosophy and the Politics of Meaning (1993), arguing that one way of developing "a general but open-ended theory concerning race and racism" is to explore "the discourse of race and racism." He continues by saying that while "racism is itself a discourse . . . the field of discourse at issue is made up of all racialized expressions." at 41.

29. Michael Omi and Howard Winant, Racial Formation in the United States: From the 1960s to the 1980s 68 (1986) [emphasis in original].

30. Gotanda, Critique at p. 23.

31. See Douglas S. Massey and Nancy A. Denton, American Apartheid: Segregation and the Making of the Underclass (1993) for an exploration of African American/White property distributions.

32. The difficulty in finding data on such issues was illustrated in a recent issue of the Los Angeles Times. In the October 26, 1993, Orange County edition, there were two articles which surveyed attitudes towards crime and criminal on the basis of race. The principal article which apparently ran in all of the regional editions of the Los Angeles Times, reviewed attitudes towards the verdict in the Reginald Denny beating trial—the truck driver whose televised beating at the beginning of the Los Angeles civil disturbances had become one of the visual symbols of those events. The survey answers were categorized by race into Anglo, Black, and Latino. The lack of an Asian category made comparisons between Asians and Blacks difficult (LA Times, 10/26/93, "Opinions in the Denny Case" O.C. edition, p. A18).

Another article limited to the Orange County edition was titled "As O.C. Neighborhoods Change, Tensions Build." One of the questions asked of those whose neighborhoods were experience racial change was whether Asian or Latinos moving into the neighborhood made it better or worse. The answers strongly suggested that Latinos moving into the neighborhood was perceived as worse that Asians moving in. While this is largely raw data needing analysis, the limited question supports my intuition that racially based attitudes towards Asians are more favorable than those towards other non-White racial minorities. Throughout the article, there was no analysis of Blacks because "the Orange County sample is too small for separate analysis" (Los Angeles Times, 10/26/93, "County's Neighborhoods Changing" p. A16).

I use these two surveys to illustrate that differentiation between different non-White racial groups is part of the popular culture of the Southern California area. It also illustrates the limited amount of research data available on Asians. Even in Southern California with its substantial Asian American population, the editors of the dominant metropolitan newspaper could largely ignore Asians in its surveys.

33. Two recent books illustrate these different approaches. Ronald Takaki's recent survey history accepts without comment the use of the category of Asian Americans. (Ronald Takaki, Strangers from a Different Shore: A History of Asian Americans, 1989.) By contrast, Yen Le Espiritu builds her analysis around the various immigrant groups as "ethnicities" and analyzes "Asian American" primarily as a social and political formation in which race is an important, but secondary factor. (Yen Le Espiritu, Asian American Panethnicity: Bridging Institutions and Identities, 1992.)

34. The academic examinations, I suspect, will vary depending upon the discipline and object of study. Visual media stereotypes appear to have been generalized within an Orientalist tradition at least since the end of the nineteenth century. My examination of legal materials, however, suggests that even today, there is no acceptance of Asian American as a legitimate category to be used in legal discourse.

35. Ronald Takaki, A Different Mirror: A History of Multicultural America 415 (1993).

36. Quite aside from the widely divergent histories of African Americans and Asian Americans, the simple call to the common experience of not being White has proven inadequate in current racial dynamics. Two movies reflect the gap in these differences. In Spike Lee's 1989 production, "Do The Right Thing," in the midst of Black-White violence, a Korean grocer is able to save his store by a broad appeal to racial unity. The 1993 film, "Menace 2 Society" begins with the violent shotgun murder of a Korean grocer and the videotape plays a role in the subsequent plot. Between the two films are the civil disturbances of April-May 1992 in Los Angeles in which Korean-owned businesses were often targeted for destruction.

Chapter Eight

Can We All Get Along?

Kichung Kim

Let me begin with a statement and a question. I believe our two communities—Korean American and African American—have much in common, much that should bring us together. We are natural allies by history and circumstances. Yet, we have become antagonists. Why? This is the question each one of us should ponder long and hard, and one I would like to address here.

When I think of our two communities, two images come to mind—one of a scene from my own childhood long ago in a small town in northern Korea, and the other a scene from a Langston Hughes story called "Big Meeting."

Let me begin with the image of my childhood in northern Korea. I must have been a mere child because I was still tagging behind my mother whenever she went anywhere. My mother's oldest sister was a devout Christian, and whenever she and my mother got together the two of them would start singing a particular hymn, my aunt singing loudly and carrying the tune, while my mother just followed along. The hymn would begin with the words "Going across River Jordan"—in Korean, *"Yodangang ul nomoso"*—and it would always end with the same words, *"Yodangang ul nomoso..."*: Going across River Jordan.

What made the hymn-singing so deeply affecting to me was not so much the words, for I had no understanding of what the words meant, but that my mother and aunt would always sob and cry as they sang. As they went on with the hymn, their sobbing and crying would become more intense and louder. As they came to the end of the hymn, with the words once again about "Going across River Jordan," both of them would dissolve into loud weeping and wailing, tears literally streaming down their faces.

And I too, without knowing why, would weep with them. Later, after rinsing their faces in cold water, my mother and aunt would calmly return to their trials-and-sorrow filled daily life. Such was my earliest introduction to Christianity.

My second image comes from the Langston Hughes story called "Big Meeting." There's a boy in this account, too, and he is perhaps a little older than I was at that time in northern Korea. As the story begins, the boy is watching his mother at a big camp meeting. At first he's simply a spectator with a kind of a young boy's smart-aleck superiority. But soon, despite his worldly-wise cynicism, he sees what it's all about, why his mother is clapping her hands, dancing and singing:

> I've opened up to heaven
> All de windows of ma soul
> An' I'm living on de halleluian side!

sings his mother, clapping and "dancing before the lord with her eyes closed, her mouth smiling and her head held high."[1]

As for this boy in Hughes's story, too, this is his first real introduction to the meaning of his mother's faith. For the first time he understands why his mother claps, sings, and dances before the Lord; why his mother "Working all day all (her life) for white folks, had to believe there was a 'halleluian side' "; and why all those many years "she had prayed and shouted and praised the Lord at church meetings and revivals, then came home for a few hours' sleep before getting up at dawn to go cook and scrub and clean for others."

I don't know if these two images make the same connections for you in your minds that they make for me in mine. What connects them for me is the fact of suffering and the will to rise above that suffering I see so vividly in both of them. As Richard Wright once put it so memorably, "the hunger of the human heart for that which is not and can never be, the thirst of the human spirit to conquer and transcend the implacable limitations of human life."[2] More vividly than anything else, my memories and Hughes's story help me better understand why our people—African Americans and Korean Americans—have for so long looked to Christianity not only for comfort and consolation, but also for strength to carry on their struggle.

Victimized so cruelly and for so long by so many people, alien as well as their own kinds, where else but in their faith could they look for relief from their suffering and the strength to carry on? Where else but in the promised land beyond River Jordan or in a few moments snatched from a life of toil and suffering, dancing before the Lord on the "halleluian side"?

It is often said that we Koreans are a people who harbor a great deal of what is called *han,* a Korean word meaning accumulated sorrow and bitterness from wrongs long suffered but not yet redressed. No doubt this is true, for we Koreans are a people with a long history of many wrongs done to us. Being a sort of land bridge between the continent of Asia and Japan, throughout history we have suffered repeated invasions and occupation by the Chinese, Mongols, Manch'us, Japanese. And in our own times we have suffered invasions and occupations by the Japanese, Russians, and even Americans.

According to one historical source, during the Mongol invasion and occupation of Korea in the year 1253, more than 200,000 Korean men, women, and children were abducted by the Mongols. There is no need to mention all the unspeakable horrors of murder, rape, mutilation, and abduction suffered by Koreans during the Japanese invasions of the 16th century. These were followed in less than 50 years by the Manch'u invasions. Throughout our history, we've also been hurt in other people's wars. As a well-known Korean proverb says, we have been like a shrimp that got caught between two battling whales and got its back broken.

That is how it seemed to us when our country was divided up at the 38th parallel after World War II by the USSR and USA. When the Korean War erupted in 1950, many of us thought we got caught in other people's war, that is, a war between two giant whales, the USSR and USA. And of course, millions of Koreans got killed and maimed in that war and it was our country alone that got ravaged by that war. From the Korean American point of view, therefore, what happened in Los Angeles last year seemed awfully familiar.

Now please don't think I'm trying to say Korean Americans bear no responsibility for last year's troubles in Los Angeles. I'm simply trying to give you an idea why many Korean Americans feel the way they do. Many Korean Americans felt and still feel that their businesses got burned down in the fires of racism—an economic injustice that was not really of their own making. Of course, we Korean Americans are not blameless; we have made mistakes, mistakes out of ignorance and insensitivity.

The only reason I mention all this is to make the point that as a people of *han,* we Korean Americans must see that if another people could harbor more *han* than even us, it has to be the African American people. We must not only see but also come to grips with the reality of African American suffering in this country during the last 400 years.

Kidnapped from their native land to suffer the horrors of the "Middle Passage," brought to these shores as chattel slaves, they suffered for centuries in unspeakable bondage. Even after their legal freedom at the conclusion of the Civil War, African Americans continued to suffer from the lynchings, black codes, and Jim Crow laws of the Reconstruction. They have suffered legal and de facto segregation even in our own times.

Could any people on earth have suffered more and so unjustly?

Thus not only are African Americans and Korean Americans both people of *han,* people who have long suffered wrongs done to them, we are also natural allies by history and circumstances. When we have so much in common, so much that should bring us together as brothers and sisters in Christianity and allies in our struggle to throw off oppression, why have we become antagonists? As I have said, this is the question each one of us must ponder long and hard.

Let me conclude by paying tribute to our African American brothers and sisters.

All Americans—and especially we Asian Americans—must never forget that we are deeply indebted to African Americans for the tremendous gains we have made in this country during the last 30 years in achieving equal rights in housing, employment, educational opportunities, and many other areas.

Even in the San Francisco Bay area, those of us who have lived here long enough still remember all the neighborhoods, clubs, schools, and jobs which were once closed to us simply because of our skin color. How have we achieved these gains? Mainly through the efforts of African Americans and their leaders like Martin Luther King and Rosa Parks, and their struggles and sacrifices. All Americans have literally reaped the fruits of their hard work and sacrifices.

W.E.B. Du Bois spoke words nearly a century ago that still ring true today. In response to the assertion that America was exclusively a white men's country, Du Bois said of the part that African Americans had played:

> Before the Pilgrims landed we were here. Here we have brought our three gifts and mingled with yours: a gift of story and song—soft, stirring melody in an ill-harmonized and unmelodious land; the gift of sweat and brawn to beat back the wilderness, conquer the soil and lay the foundations of this vast economic empire...; the third, a gift of the Spirit...
> ...we have woven ourselves with the very warp and woof of this nation...we fought (your) battles, shared (your) sorrow, mingled our blood with (yours), and generation after generation (we) have pleaded with a headstrong, careless people to despise not Justice, Mercy, and Truth, lest the nation be smitten with a curse. Our song, our toil, our cheer, and warning have been given to this nation in blood-brotherhood.[3]

With Du Bois, I ask all of us: Would America be the America that it is today without the contributions of African American people?

Endnotes

This is an edited version of a keynote speech at a forum sponsored by African American and Korean American Clergy of Oakland and the East Bay, May 2, 1993.

1. Langston Hughes, *The Heath Anthology of American Literature,* Lauter et al., (eds.), second edition, II, Massachussetts: D.C. Heath & Company, p. 1625.
2. Richard Wright, *Black Boy,* Harper and Row, New York, 1966, pp. 131-132.
3. W.E.B. Du Bois, *The Souls of Black Folk,* New American Library, New York, 1969, pp. 275-276.

Chapter Nine

Monologue from a Performance Piece: My Mother and the LA Riots

David Mura

I'm sitting in this Japanese restaurant with my parents,
   in Chicago,
and instead of talking about shopping or golf or tennis,
my mother for once is talking about something serious:
She can't understand why there's people in L.A. tearing
   things down.

Now you must understand, as much as I am intellectual, a
   writer, an artist,
as much as I have all the politically correct far left wacko
   socialist leanings—
I really don't—repeat really don't—want to talk about this
   with my mother.
Because I know what will happen: I will talk, I will explain
   things,
and then, she'll repeat her question as if she hasn't heard
   a word:
[*Turn to right*] "Why did they burn down their own
   neighborhood? David,
they don't have any grocery stores now, they can't buy food
   near by.
I know you say they're angry. But what good does that do?
And look at those men who pulled the white truck driver from
   his truck and threw bricks at him?
Isn't that the same thing as Rodney King?"

And I begin to explain again, and again she interrupts, and so
    I ask,
"Do you really want to know my answer, Ma, or is this a
    rhetorical question?"
only I try to phrase it so bitterly ironical,
because I don't, repeat, I don't want to get into it with
    my mother.
I mean really, I should just shut up and eat my dinner, which
    my father, of course, is paying for.

So I just gave up.
Now I know, I know. I could have told her two black men and
    two black women
who drove down to Compton and saved that white truck driver.
Or I could have told about Sun Ja Du and Latasha Harlins,
how the judge's sentence said to the black community—
    Fuck you.
A black life ain't worth shit. We've got to protect the Koreans
    and their property.
(Course, once the riots went down, you know where the police
    made their stand? Not at the Korean stores. No way. The
    cops were down at the malls of Alexander Haagan, a white
    political patron.)

Or I could have said to her: Mom, do you think only black
    people riot?
Do you think Japanese Americans don't do things like that?
But what about the riots at Heart Mountain, ma? What
    about Tule Lake?
What about the time two thousand Japanese Americans
    went on a rampage in Manzanar, wanted to tear the
    whole place down, and the guards opened up at them
    with machine guns, killed this Issei man. That man, he
    was just Rodney King.
And the good Japanese Americans?
They were burning down their prison, they had nowhere else
    to go either.
And that's what happened in L.A. mom. That's what happens
    when you keep people in cages.
Only you don't see it. Just like you didn't see how miserable I
    was all through high school,

how depressed, how I hated myself, how I hated being
    Japanese America,
how I hated *feeling* this pressure all the time to get A's and
    be a good model citizen,
and all the time inside I felt like a gook, a fucking gook, ma,
and you don't want to see it, you don't want to see anybody
    else's pain.
It's all that goddamn Nisei see no evil, speak no evil, hear no
    evil, let's be monkeys bullshit.
Ma, when are you going to wake up? When are you going to
    wake up?
[*Turns to audience.*] Oh, sorry. I guess I'm straying a bit,
    aren't I?

Anyway, what does it matter? What does it matter? My mother
    doesn't know this.
And even if she did, she'd still vote Republican.
And every time a homeboy sees a Japanese woman driving by
    in her Lincoln or Prelude,
it won't mean jack shit that she's Jap not Korean.
All he'll see is someone who got theirs before him.
Someone living off his back. Who just came yesterday.

[Get up] And if one of those homeys sees me? Well, he'll think
    the same thing.
What the fuck does he care I'm telling you this story?

Monologue from a Performance Piece: My Mother and the LA Riots was first published
in *Asian American* No. 2, Winter 1993.

Chapter Ten

August 1968

Peter Bacho

On the shaded bank I sat and stared at the narrow lagoon, its waters dark, deep, perpetually still, even when the winds came to stir the willows that covered its shores. Somewhere beyond, though not too far, were skylines and neighborhoods, cries of pain and anger. To this I'd return, but later. For now, it was just me and my special place. Secluded and safe, it served as shelter in Seattle which, in the summer of '68, was a city seeking shelter from itself.

I knew the spot well, having discovered it eight years earlier at the end of a bike ride thirty minutes from my Central District home. At ten, I was armed only with a fishing pole and a cap full of hope. That afternoon I caught a small bass, staying long enough to watch shadows from the shore stretch across the water to end yet another summer day.

Over the years, I'd return, often with friends but sometimes alone, often to fish but sometimes—as now—just to watch. And wonder at the constancy of its rhythm, especially now in a city trapped in an age full of change.

Change. To Seattle it came in '68, charging hard like a downhill train at this quiet, complacent town. I saw it in my neighborhood, a quiet mix of blacks and Filipinos, among people I'd known for a lifetime. Their anger—black anger, the fuel that drove the revolution—and the response: white fear riding three cops to a car. But what about us—neither black nor white—who lived on the same block and shared the poverty? Did the revolution spare observers?

I had no answer as I moved toward the water's edge, my gloom broken by a sudden flash of green followed by a loud splash. Distracted, I smiled, watching the ripples reach the shore; a bass was chasing its elusive meal. This meant late afternoon, when waters were cooled by a jagged blanket of shade reaching from the far bank to touch where I stood. There was a second splash, then another. Soon the surface would roil with hungry predators and frightened, elusive prey. I glanced at my watch; five-thirty it said. Aaron, one of my best childhood friends, had called to say he wanted to talk. Important, he said. He'd be here in thirty minutes, time enough to sit, relax, and enjoy the unchanging late day rhythm of this special place.

* * * * *

The lagoon quickly filled with ripples and leaps tied by memories to my heart, making it race. I could hear it pound, even as the surface, once so frenzied, turned suddenly still.

Then suddenly more leaps: powerful upward thrusts at the apex of which were midair pirouettes that mocked gravity. The performers were two of the biggest bass I'd ever seen: tail walkin', pole breakin' trophies. Aaron and I hurriedly cast our lines to the centers of the splashes. A second later we pulled them in, laughing while older fishermen glared in envy.

One of them, an old black man in faded blue coveralls, walked over to us. "Nice fish," he smiled. "Wha's you boys' secret?"

Aaron laughed. "Ain' no secret, mister. Me and my partner," he said pointing at me, "we jus' havin' fun."

As he spoke, the sky began to darken but not from the sudden movement of clouds. I scanned the horizon. To the east, where our homes were, a thin line of smoke rose lazily skyward.

Alarmed, I tried to get my friend's attention. But by then he was in full debate on fishing minutiae: live bait or artificial lures, bass or trout. I tried subtlety—not wanting to be rude—head nods and hand signs, all useless.

"Worms and stink bait, sonny," the old man said. "Works for me—been workin', too, near fifty years—and that's all that counts." He spoke solemnly, using age and a full, resonant baritone to intimidate twelve year old Aaron and win the point.

This boy, who loved the skill of lures, didn't even flinch. "Mister, maybe for you," he said nonchalantly, "and don' mean no disrespect." He then pointed to his prized fish and set one more hook. "That fish there," he said evenly, "caught it with a lure, and ain' no one can say it don' work."

That's the way he was. His carefree ways covered a mind that was always on. The old man didn't have a chance.

"Aaron," I said loudly. No reply. He was expanding the discussion, moving on to the merits of his favorite lures.

"Now, flatfish . . ."

He never finished the sentence. This time I yanked on his wrist so hard his head bobbed, and added for good measure a scream that stopped hearts.

"Aaron . . ."

* * * * *

"Damn, Buddy," said a familiar voice. "Keep it down, man. Folks'll get the wrong idea, you screamin' my name. Damn, we close'n all, but I ain' yo' bitch." I didn't even look, didn't have to. Aaron had been gone a year, courtesy of a scholarship for poor but promising tokens, at an elite eastern school. He looked the same, except for his once closely cropped hair which, now unfettered, rose to form the tallest 'fro I'd ever seen.

Same old Aaron, speaking the rude, loud patter of the street. Time in college, even a fancy one, hadn't refined him. I was glad.

Bloods spoke that way, Filipinos, too. That's how we grew up. But now we were young men, old enough to interest local draft boards. And although we'd both become bilingual—over the years we'd learned how to speak to whites—back home and together, we fell into our language of choice.

His serve, my volley. I smiled and fired back.

"Shoulda tol' me, brotha' man," I said slowly. "'For you gave it up."

We shook hands. "Same old Buddy," he laughed. "Always tryin'."

"Uhuh," I nodded. "You was good, too. Girlfriend know about this? Better tell her, man . . ." Dangerous words used only against enemies— or friends, very good ones. Heads got broken for less.

Still, I savored the score—bull's-eye. He cringed, a sure sign to press on. "Take it there ain' no barbers back east. Say you get loaded, man, drop a roach on your head, a lit one, bury it in that nappy shit." I paused. "You my friend 'n all," I sighed, "but damn, man, you' a fire hazzard."

First his manhood, then his hair. Music was next. "Whatcha think, man," I began solemnly. "I'ma put you on the spot: Beach Boys or Beatles? You gots an opinion. I know it. Surveyed the brothers on the corner, and they say the Boys 'cause they' American."

Another pause. "Who say white folk can' jam?"

He'd have to come back and break my roll. "Buddy," Aaron finally said, interrupting me. He sounded meek, and for good reason; he was holding bottom ground, in this case somewhere near the mouth of a sewer with more shit on the way. "Same ol' no fishin' Buddy," he finally said with more confidence. "Turn around, boom, you out."

* * * * *

Weak. Hangin' with rich, polite white boys got him out of practice. So I let him slide. Besides, what could I say? It was true, all true, and a source of mild childhood ridicule (mostly from him). Still, I was glad to see Aaron. We'd been friends since grade school, a bond cemented by time spent fishing these waters. Every summer, we'd walk or ride the three miles to fish our spot, sometimes five days straight. It would've stayed that way if I'd had a say. I didn't, and when his folks divorced, Aaron and his mom moved across town, disrupting prematurely a lovely summer schedule I never wanted to end.

Eventually, and like any boy reaching puberty, I found other interests. This left less time to fish, more time to navigate an awkward adolescence—complete with voice change, body hair, and overnight height that stole coordination. I liked my old self better, but knew it was gone, sloughed off and sun dried like old snake skin. I figured I was stuck for the duration, however long **that** was (until sixteen, it turned out), and decided then to endure as best I could. Tomorrow would bring answers. But when it didn't, as was often the case, I'd go to the lagoon, sit on its bank, and fish waters that never changed.

Sometimes Aaron would come with me, catching the bus across town. On those rare days, we'd renew our friendship, fishing this lagoon the ritual that kept our bond current. We'd spend hours just catching up, then push ahead to bold points too distant from who we were. Under the willows, protected by shade, we traded secrets and dreams often staying after dark. On these occasions, he'd dig in his pocket and flip me a dime. "Better call," he'd say, "we ain' done yet. Yo' mama get mad, tell her you here wit' me. We in this together."

The passing of summers also made it clear that for a while, puberty had been kinder to him than me. Only one year separated us, but during that span, it may as well have been ten. He was quickly becoming a man of the world, or at least of one grander than mine.

"Hey, blood," Aaron said on one occasion. "Got me some."

I didn't know what he meant but felt pressure to keep up, to reply and seem wiser than I was. "Yeah?"

"Fine bitch, too," he said. "Right there in her mama's house. She's older, three years or so. Ain' nothin' better'n older woman." He paused, smiling at the thought. "Hey, Buddy, ever get an older woman?"

His question presupposed prior experience, nonexistent at fourteen. I was caught in the grip of manchild stagnation, all pustules and the first sparse strands of facial hair. An older woman? Any woman. I was lucky my mom still claimed me.

My face flushed as his inquiry dangled, unanswered. I just stared at the water.

Fortunately, the lagoon granted a reprieve that lasted the rest of the day. "Damn," he shouted, as a hungry bass rose to take his plug. After five minutes of spirited leaps and dives, Aaron landed his fish and, by day's end, three others.

I was less successful, which was usually the case, but didn't care. Unlike Aaron, who skillfully deceived fish, I preferred a less taxing approach: worms or marshmallows and eggs. That way I could bait a hook, drop it in the water, and forget about it until the bobber dipped or the pole twitched.

While waiting on the bank, my attention would drift toward conversations, laughter, daydreams; an inevitable nap also filled each afternoon. "Man," Aaron once scolded, waking me, "you here to catch fish."

"Uhuh."

For me, being at the lagoon was reward enough; catching fish was incidental. Aaron was right. When I fished I napped, and saw nothing wrong with pairing the two.

* * * * *

"Hey, man," Aaron said, interrupting my stream of memories. Emboldened by my silence, he was again on the move. "I remember . . ."

But not too far before I cut him at the knees. "Needs my sleep, blood," I said. "It enhances my beauty which, when I gets enough, I will donate to yo' needy ass." Another score. Didn't even have to look. Faking a yawn, I rolled over on my side. It was too easy. Aaron had been away too long, but he'd keep trying, and I'd keep shutting him down. It was time to change.

"'Sides, man," I said, breaking the cycle, "wha's so important you gotta wake me in the first place?"

The shift surprised him. "Nuthin'," he said.

"Then, sucka', what we doin' here?" I stared at him and spoke with a tone that said more abuse was on its way. "Man, I coulda been wit' yo' . . ."

"All right," he said evenly.

" . . . girlfriend."

Aaron sighed. "God's truth, man, no more bullshit," he said.

I smiled and nodded.

"Two nights ago I was hangin' wit' some brothers from the old neighborhood. You know, Marcus'n them. Not doin' nuthin', just hangin' down on Cherry near the school. It was hot, hot as the devil, but we was cool, just sippin' wine, mindin' our own business. When all of a sudden—boom—cops was goin' crazy. So many pigs, man, I ain' never seen. Flyin' by, I mean **flyin' by**. So me and my partners, we go check it out."

I knew the scene. Night before last, violence had erupted along 23rd Avenue, the heart of the city's ghetto. From my house, about two miles away, I heard the sirens, saw the smoke.

"Uhuh," I nodded. "Heard talk, blood. So I stayed home, caught it on the news."

"Madness, man," Aaron said softly. "Street was packed, nuthin' but black on black, and all this blue comin' down. Some of the young bloods, man—hotheads—was stoppin' cars, pullin' folk out." He paused and slowly shook his head. "White mostly, 'ceptin' one."

Although no one had died, all of the victims had been beaten. Some badly. The news said that one young man (identity withheld) was in a coma and near death. I stared at my friend.

He ignored me and continued to speak, mumbling, averting his eyes. "There was one dude. They threw 'im on the ground, whupped 'im like a dog. He curled like a baby, and they was kickin' 'im. He was beggin', and they was still kickin' 'im. Cavin' 'im in, too. Eff'd 'im up good." He paused and took a long breath. "It was wrong, man."

"What'd you do?" I asked.

"Nuthin', not a damn thing," he said, his voice a near-whisper. "There was too many, man. Even my partners—Marcus'n them—jumped in. Madness. Then when the cops come, they back off and split. Then the dude gets on his hands and knees—I don't know how—and he look dead at me. I knew 'im, Buddy. Damn, I knew 'im from school. Chinese dude named Ron."

"Damn," I said quietly.

"Caught up wit' Marcus the next day. Act like nuthin's wrong. Then I ask 'im why he beat that boy, and he jus' shrug and say, 'That punk Chinaman? Ain' one'a us, no big deal.' "

Stunned, I just looked at the ground, losing myself in a world of small circular patterns drawn by my finger, hoping that words I'd heard I hadn't. In our neighborhood, blacks and Filipinos had shared a bond formed by poverty and bad attitude. We'd always run together—a natural match, or so I'd assumed. Reflexively, I touched the corners of my eyes and traced the contours. Chinese, no doubt, as was my pale (for a Filipino) complexion. "Damn," I repeated.

Just who was "us"? Had I been expelled? Were my traits now targets—entries stamped in a passport to a beating? Or worse?

Aaron continued quietly. "Marcus don' even flinch, man, don' even worry. He say that killin' that boy was no big deal."

"He's dead?" News reports hadn't confirmed his death.

Aaron looked at me. "Man," he said quietly, "Jesus couldn't rise from that whuppin'."

I was trying to sort through thoughts now jumbled by anger, confusion, and fear. I looked up at Aaron, studying a face I knew well, and saw colors—blacks and browns, discordant for the first time. I sighed. A friend, I thought, or was he? I didn't know. "So what you' sayin'," I finally said, "is that stuff's changin' . . ."

Aaron shrugged. "Guess so."

Maddening nonchalance. "Like I was sayin', man," I said slowly, and paused to ponder and load each word to follow, deadly and primed. Just aim and squeeze, smoothly not jerked, to hit the heart of a friendship stuck in the clammy grip of an early August night. On such nights, rare for this town, heat lingered far beyond welcome, like a stubborn houseguest. It taxed civility, induced strokes, corroded restraint.

"Some ignorant blood, like that fool Marcus, your friend, he's gonna take me out and it's cool 'cause the revolution's on and I ain' black, and it's payback for oppression I had nothin' to do with." I was screaming, almost spitting the words.

Inside my head, unseen mallets beat a rhythm, pounding on walls. At my temples, the most frequent point of percussion, beads of sweat started to form, pausing to gather and grow before the fall. I wiped them all with the palm of my hand. More appeared, but these were left alone as I glared at Aaron.

"Answer me, man," I demanded.

"You didn' ask no question," he said calmly, and turned away. My eyes tightened, becoming slits—furrowed and focused, the not quite human gateway to a heart filling with rage. The mallets slammed louder, faster. I exploded.

"Nigger," I hissed, using **that** word for the first time. Surprised, I wondered what lay at the end of the bridge I was about to cross. But on that night, with the heat still thick, anger was my fuel. It alone drove me, and came quickly to a boil, seeking pores, finding fissures, forming words full of venom. I gathered for the kill.

"You go to college" (aim and squeeze), I said coldly, "you still just a nigger" (smoothly not jerked).

Fight or flight, either one, I was ready for both, but not his reply.

"It's **nigga**," he scolded as he turned toward me. "Listen to yo'sef talk, man," he said evenly, "can' even say it right. You soun' like a damn white man."

Sound like a white man?

This time I turned away, only to turn back to the sounds of movement. A rustling of grass and soft footfalls moving slowly away. I blinked, adjusting my sight in time to watch Aaron walk slowly up a narrow trail that led to this place.

He stopped in a cluster of evergreens. There, in the distance and the fast fading light, he became a silhouette that turned to face the water. To face me.

"I'da backed you, man, the silhouette said, its words sounding like the first notes of a dirge. "Come down to it, I'da backed you, my brother. Against Marcus. Against anyone."

The silhouette paused before speaking again. "Brother mine," it began slowly, sadly. Then slower, sadder: "Brother, no more."

The silhouette then retreated into shadows that merged with the night. I wanted to call out, but held back, knowing it was too late to heal with words wounds that words had caused.

I stared at the water and whispered another curse heard only by the dark. For me there'd be no shelter, not even here. At least not tonight. Maybe never again.

Chapter Eleven

Harmony

R. A. Sasaki

Mrs. Igarashi, my piano teacher, lived in a Victorian flat on Octavia Street. From our house on Pine Street on the edge of Japantown, it was only a five-block walk. Nevertheless, Mama would always make sure that someone escorted me there and came to pick me up when I went for my lesson.

The dangers then seemed more moral than physical. Next door, an unassuming fellow named Toda quietly brewed moonshine sake in his bathtub. As we passed my friend Chieko's house, I would eye the upstairs floor of the neighboring house with avid curiosity. A bad woman lived there, we knew. From Chieko's room, we could see the woman's coffee-colored face in the window. She would lift her hand and tap on the pane when young men walked past. We sometimes saw young Japanese fellows go into the house, to emerge a while later, straightening their collars. Another bad woman lived over O'Malley's stable on the next block. I sometimes played with her red-haired daughter, who would tell me about the men who came to see her mommy.

I was an *ojōsan*, the eldest daughter of a prosperous businessman. Papa's store next to the City of Paris Department Store downtown was a showplace of Oriental goods. It was 1922. Papa had been in this country for twenty-five years, and after hard work and careful saving, his business was doing well. When I needed a new coat for school, the City of Paris would send someone to our house with three or four coats my size. I would try them on, pick one, and they would take the others back to the store.

If we had been in Japan, I would have gotten lessons in flower arranging and *koto*. Instead, we were in San Francisco. I had piano lessons.

My piano teacher was a white lady who was married to a Japanese. Mama heard about her from Murata-san, who worked as a chauffeur for some *hakujin* people in Pacific Heights and was always coming around to our place. We didn't know of any Japanese piano teachers, and not all *hakujin* piano teachers would take Japanese students. In Japantown, if you needed a doctor, you couldn't just look in the phone book. You asked your neighbor who their doctor was. That's how Mrs. Igarashi, being married to a Japanese, ended up teaching almost all the aspiring pianists in Japantown.

Among Mrs. Igarashi's prodigies, Emiko Otani was the only Japanese. Thus it was to her that I was constantly compared and invariably found wanting.

"Emiko Otani mastered this in just two weeks," Mrs. Igarashi would sigh as my copy of *Everybody's Favorite Piano Pieces* fell open, as if on command, to "Für Elise." I had been laboring over the piece for several months. If only my fingers were as well-trained as my piano book! After playing the refrain one too many times and puffing to a halt, I took a deep breath and sat with my hands in my lap, only to hear Mrs. Igarashi say, "*Emiko* has such a wonderful ear." Then we would both sigh.

"How many hours did you practice this week?" Mrs. Igarashi always asked me, before anything else. Impossibly honest, I always replied, "One." Then I'd have to listen to a lecture about the importance of practicing at least two hours *every single day*.

Having decided that no amount of instruction was going to get me onstage at Carnegie Hall, Mrs. Igarashi decided that I might as well prove myself useful. She would have me do errands for her—errands that my own mother didn't ask me to do.

"Oh, Keiko, you're here," she would greet me at the door. Then, handing me a dollar bill, she would say, "Would you run down to McAllister Street and pick me up a pound of chuck steak?"

McAllister Street was a few blocks south of Geary, which formed the southern border of Japantown. It was definitely outside of our neighborhood. I would hurry past the Chinese restaurant on Geary and cross over to avoid the billiard parlor on Eddy. There were usually two or three black men lounging outside, talking. I kept my eyes straight ahead and walked faster.

I knew almost all the shopkeepers on Post Street, in the heart of Japantown, but I didn't know any on McAllister Street. They had names like Karp and Heineman. The smells emanating from their open doorways were of sausage, pickles, freshly baked bread.

When I got back to Mrs. Igarashi's, I would hand her the meat and her change. Then we would sit down at the piano, and in the remaining thirty minutes or so, she would mention Emiko Otani at least twice.

Mama often came to meet me and walk home with me, sometimes bringing my sister Sachi, who was four, and the baby, Kazuo. When Mama was busy cooking for Papa and his workers, she sent Uncle Takeyan's wife, or Murata-san, or some other visitor who was staying at Pine. She would never let me go to McAllister Street alone. I was only nine. Mrs. Igarashi didn't seem to think about things like that.

"*Doo?*" Mama would ask after each lesson.

"Okay," I would say.

But finally one day, after a particularly brutal lesson in which Mrs. Igarashi mentioned Emiko Otani not twice but five times, I was mad enough to tell.

"I don't like Mrs. Igarashi," I said. "She makes me go to McAllister Street to buy her meat."

"*Nani??*" Mama was outraged.

And that was the end of lessons at Mrs. Igarashi's.

Mama was a very broad-minded and forgiving person; but when people violated her sense of decency and common sense, she acted quickly. I was not really keen on piano lessons, and for a while I hoped she might forget all about them. I wanted to be an actress.

My girlfriends from Kinmon Gakuen, the Japanese language school we had to attend every day after regular school, always came over on weekends, and we would dress up in Mama's coats and hats and play like we were ladies. We gave each other glamorous names like Gloria—that was me. Chieko was Clara. Fumi was Dorothy. In our fantasies, we were society ladies, grown up and beautiful—with curly blonde hair and blue eyes. With a name like Gloria I could almost forget about my straight black hair and solemn brown eyes. With a name like Keiko, they only seemed to stand out.

As it happened, I was the only Japanese student in my class at school. My classmates were mostly the sons and daughters of wealthy white businesspeople who lived in mansions in Pacific Heights, an opulent neighborhood which loomed above Japantown like the very unscalable heights of the American Dream itself. Our house on Pine Street was on the border between the two neighborhoods. Most of the Japantown children went to Henry Durant or Raphael Weill, schools located west and south of Japantown. But our across-the-street neighbor, an Irish lady with three daughters, had urged Mama to send us to Pacific Heights Elementary School instead.

At the start of every school year, I had to suffer through the humiliation of being seated with all the boys, because the teacher had not realized that "Keiko" was a girl's name. "Kee-ko Morawacky," the teacher would hazard, a note of barely suppressed outrage creeping into her voice, and she would peer sternly at me as if to reprimand the bearer of such an outlandish and unpronounceable name. The other children would snicker. Some of the boys started calling me "Cuckoo." Boys were horrid.

I asked Mama one day if I could have an American name. She said better not to change it, since someday we would all go back to Japan. I wondered what kind of a place Japan must be, if one needed to have a name like Keiko there. I must have looked disappointed, and in an attempt to divert me, Mama suddenly announced that she had found me a new piano teacher. Mrs. Williams, who lived around the block from us, had recommended a Mr. Johnson, who gave lessons to her daughter. Mr. Johnson would come to our house and conduct the lessons there.

Resolutely, I dusted off *Everybody's Favorite Piano Pieces* and waited for my first lesson with Mr. Johnson.

"Kei-chan," Mama called. "Johnson-*sensei ga kimashita yo.*"

I came into the hallway. The blackest black man I had ever seen was standing next to Mama, hat in hand. I stopped short, staring.

"How do you do, Miss Moriwaki," Mr. Johnson said, holding out his hand.

I looked at Mama, who nodded her head at me in unmistakeable command.

I shook his hand. "How do you do," I said, but my voice was so faint I wasn't sure if he heard me.

"Take Johnson-*sensei no* hat," Mama instructed.

I took his hat and ran to hang it on the coat rack as Mama showed him into the living room, where our piano was.

I waited a while until I caught Mama's eye and beckoned her out into the hall.

"*Nani, Kei-chan?*"

"He's *kurombo,*" I whispered.

Kurombo meant "nigger," as I was to learn later. Some Japanese said the word as if they were spitting; others, like me, used it because it was the only word we knew to describe black people. I didn't know many *kurombo*. There was the mail man Mama sometimes invited into the kitchen for coffee. Then there was Mrs. Williams, our around-the-corner neighbor, who would stop to chat with Mama on her way to church. There was a boy in my class at school, but I never spoke to him. The only others I knew were the bad woman next door to Chieko and the men who hung around outside the billiard parlor on Eddy Street. I had never seen a black teacher before, much less a black piano teacher.

"Mama," I said, "I don't want to take lessons from him."

Mama patted me encouragingly on the back.

"Mr. Johnson is a very good teacher," she said to me in Japanese. "Mrs. Williams said so." Then she nudged me into the living room.

I seated myself on the piano stool and waited.

"Why don't you play me your favorite piece?" Mr. Johnson said.

I didn't really have a favorite piece, but I figured I knew "Für Elise" about as well as I was ever going to know any single piece of music, so I opened my music and struggled through it.

"It isn't my favorite piece," I explained quickly when I had finished. "But I've been practicing it forever."

"Well then," Mr. Johnson said gravely, "I guess you must be ready to try something new." He pulled Schumann's "Scenes From Childhood" from his satchel. "Listen," he said.

He played the first piece, then turned to me.

"Well, what do you think? Would you like to learn how to play that?"

Mrs. Igarashi had never asked me if I wanted to learn something. She just made me.

"All right," I said.

I won't say that I suddenly decided that I wanted to be a concert pianist; but I did begin to approach my piano lessons without that sense of escalating dread. For one thing, Mr. Johnson did not know Emiko Otani and could not prod me with images of her superior talent. For another, he never asked me how many hours I had practiced; but I had a feeling he knew, just by the way I played. And when I played badly, he felt no need to humiliate me by calling it to my attention—I humiliated myself.

Mama and I ran into Mrs. Otani, Emiko's mother, at the American Fish Market on Buchanan Street one Saturday morning. After many polite murmurings back and forth, Mrs. Otani referred to Mrs. Igarashi, and Emiko's struggle with the piano. Of course she was being modest. Among Japanese it was a cardinal sin to brag. Emiko's mother was proud of her daughter and showed it by disparaging her talent. If Emiko had been a mediocre pianist, she would have avoided the subject entirely. I noticed that it was she and not Mama who brought up the subject of piano lessons.

Mrs. Otani sighed and said that Mrs. Igarashi had been inquiring after me. This I doubted.

Mrs. Otani waited expectantly for information; it was all over the community that I was taking lessons from a *kurombo*. But Mama refused to take the bait. Finally, Mrs. Otani was driven to directness.

"*Sorede, Keiko-chan wa gambarimasuka?*" She asked if I was still playing.

"*Mmm*," Mama replied.

Mrs. Otani circled closer. She asked how my new piano teacher was. I squirmed, and gave Mama's hand a gentle tug.

Mama replied that my new piano teacher was quite satisfactory.

"*Kurombo, deshyo,*" Mrs. Otani said.

Mama said, yes, Mr. Johnson was a Negro.

Mrs. Otani asked if he really came into our house.

Mama said, well, yes, that's where our piano was—inside the house. Then she went on to say that Mr. Johnson (emphasizing his name) gave full value for the dollar, and had been highly recommended by the organist of the First Baptist Church.

"Johnson-*sensei,*" Mama concluded emphatically, "*wa* best teacher *desu.*" Then, explaining that she had twenty people coming for lunch, she excused us and we left.

"Mama," I said as we climbed the Buchanan Street hill toward home, "I didn't know Mrs. Williams was the organist at the First Baptist Church."

"Mmm," Mama said.

After a couple of months of lessons with Mr. Johnson, I realized that I had stopped noticing all the things that made him different: how black his hands looked on the ivory piano keys; how, unlike Mrs. Igarashi, who had doused herself with an overpowering perfume that made me want to sneeze, Mr. Johnson smelled faintly of sweat and pipe tobacco. On rainy days he smelled of wet wool. I no longer noticed how the sleeves of his suit jacket were a good two inches short of his wrists. He just became Mr. Johnson.

At the end of each lesson, Mama would bring him a cup of Japanese tea. He accepted graciously, feeling perhaps that it would be rude to refuse. Hearing Tad Hirose shout, "Iceman's coming!" from the street, I would dash out to join the other kids in scrambling for ice shavings that flew up in the air as the Ice Man chipped off big blocks for our ice boxes.

Mama would stay to see Mr. Johnson through his tea. I don't know how they communicated; Mama's English was usually liberally flavored with Japanese words and sounds; or rather, her Japanese was occasionally punctuated with English. But maybe there was something in the music of her language that Mr. Johnson understood.

One day the Ice Man must have been late, for I lingered.

"Wouldn't you rather have coffee?" I asked Mr. Johnson, noticing for the first time what it was that my mother served him every week: Japanese green tea in a Japanese teacup.

"Oh no, not at all," Mr. Johnson said. "I can drink coffee anywhere. But this is the only place I can drink Japanese tea."

I found this amusing.

"We drink that all the time," I said.

"Well then I guess you don't appreciate how special it is," he said. "But there is one thing you can do for me," he added.

I leaned closer.

"You can explain to me how to pick up this teacup without scalding my hand."

I laughed.

"I'll tell Mama to put it in a cup with a handle," I said, jumping up.

"No, no," Mr. Johnson said. "You all use these little cups without handles. I want to do this the right way."

"Pick it up towards the top, where it isn't as hot," I instructed shyly. I had to think for a minute, trying to recall how I'd seen Japanese people lift their teacups every day of my life. "Then put your left hand underneath, like this." I showed him.

Mr. Johnson tried this.

"Amazing," he said. "Thank you, Kei-chan."

I was surprised. Usually only family or very close friends called me "Kei-chan." It was like saying "Jimmy" instead of "James." *Yoso no hito*, people who were not closely related, would call me "Keiko-san." Mr. Johnson probably did not know this; he had heard Mama using this name for me, and was doing the same. I wondered if I should explain this; but then, I didn't want to hurt his feelings by implying that he was a *yoso no hito*.

"What do you think of the name 'Gloria'?" I asked him, on an impulse.

"Gloria?" he said. "I think it's a very nice name."

"I wish I could change my name," I said. "Nobody at school can pronounce 'Keiko.' They call me 'Cuckoo.' " I hadn't meant to say this last part, but it came out.

Mr. Johnson looked at me gravely.

"It sounds like they need more practice," he said. "I once wanted to change my name. I'm called Obediah—Lord, if that isn't a mouthful. Obediah Johnson. My daddy was a minister, picked that name from the Bible. I wanted something easy, like Bob, or John."

"What happened?" I asked.

"When I was in the Army, I got stationed in the South—Alabama. That's where my daddy was born, you know. I found out that in Alabama there were other folks with names like 'Zachariah' and 'Ezekiel'—all names from the Good Book. And 'Obediah' just started sounding right."

"Don't you want to go and live in Alabama?" I asked.

"No, ma'am," he said emphatically. "Going to Alabama was good, 'cause I found out where I come from. But I also found out where I belong. I was born in California, and here I'll stay."

"I was born here, too," I said. "I've never been to Japan."

"I'll bet if you went to Japan, you'd find that all the prettiest girls are named 'Keiko'," Mr. Johnson said. "The world is full of Glorias—I have five other students named Gloria. What do you want to go calling yourself 'Gloria' for?"

I wondered if it was true about the Keikos.

As Christmas approached, preparations began for the annual Christmas pageant at school. I dreamed of being an angel in a white robe, filmy wings, and a silver halo. But every year when I raised my hand, the teacher didn't seem to see it, and the angel parts always went to *hakujin* girls with golden curls. I always watched from the audience.

So I celebrated Christmas at home. Mama and Papa were Buddhists, but Christmas was one of those irresistible American customs, like fresh-baked bread. We always had a tree.

When Mr. Johnson came for our lesson in early December, I had a surprise for him. I was already at the piano when he arrived, playing the melody to "Silent Night," which I had figured out myself.

Mr. Johnson paused in the doorway and listened. Then he came and sat down next to me.

"Try this," he said, playing three bass notes in stately succession, several times.

"What is that?" I asked.

"Just try it," he said.

I tried it. "That's boring," I said.

"Okay," he said, "you go on and keep playing 'Silent Night,' and I'll play my part."

I looked at him skeptically, but proceeded to play.

Our notes fit together perfectly, making sense where there had been none.

"Oh," I said.

"If there were only one part to play," Mr. Johnson said, "life would be mighty boring. We could all play the melody, but we'd just be tinkling tunes. Or we could all play the bass and drive each other crazy." He chuckled.

"But when the melody, the harmony, the bass, and a little bit of percussion, all come together—," here he smiled, "—well, then you have *music*."

"You want to learn some Christmas carols?" he asked.

I nodded, and told him about never getting to be in the Christmas pageant at school. Maybe there was no such thing as a Japanese angel.

"We'll ask your Mama," he said, "and if she says it's all right, we'll learn some Christmas carols. And don't you fret about the school pageant," he added. "We're going to have a piano recital the Saturday before Christmas."

I asked if I could come.

"Come?" he hooted. "You're going to be in it."

This was my chance. I had never performed in public before. At home I indulged a fantasy about becoming an actress, but at school even the thought of speaking up in front of the other children was daunting. Now that I had the chance to be the one the audience watched—I was petrified.

"Mama, do I have to?" I whined.

Mama told me to think of Mr. Johnson. I should do it for him. What if, after all his hard work, his students refused to perform? How would he feel?

For the next three weeks I put Emiko Otani to shame. I practiced every day after Japanese school and on weekends. It got so that my little sister Sachi, who at first had hovered reverently at my elbow at the novelty of my fevered practicing, would run about with her fingers in her ears, yelling, "Kei-chan, stop!"

"Mama, do I have to?" I asked again as the date neared. The piece I had chosen to play sounded better, but I was no less terrified at the prospect of performing in front of total strangers.

Mama surprised me.

"*Ne,* Kei-chan," she said. She told me that if I really didn't want to, I didn't have to. It wasn't worth getting sick about. I considered the prospect of backing out.

"Johnson-*sensei,*" she sighed. "He'll be so disappointed."

The recital was to be held at the Church of Jesus Christ on Gough and Golden Gate. I had a new dress for the occasion—pale blue. Uncle Takeyan brought over a corsage and pinned it to my dress, whispering encouragement into my ear.

Takeyan *no obasan* was going to watch Sachi and Kazuo so that both Mama and Papa could attend. Murata-san offered to drive us in his employer's Franklin. He was outside warming it up as Papa and I waited for Mama to finish dressing. It didn't take her long, but she always waited until the last minute. Papa, meticulous and punctual as usual, stood at the foot of the circular mahogany stairway, making impatient scolding noises as Mama rushed around upstairs; but he looked fine indeed.

When we got to the church, there was no one else outside. Perhaps the recital had already begun. Papa swung open the heavy door, and we heard a multitude of voices. We went inside.

A hundred eyes met ours. A hush fell. As we walked down the aisle, fifty faces turned to watch our progress.

Mama, Papa and I were the only people in the church who were not black.

The church was warm. I followed Papa's stiff back, feeling Mama's reassuring hand on my shoulder. I passed a lady in a red dress and a bright red hat. I had never seen such a red hat. The eyes below it were watching me curiously. I looked away.

A murmur started in the church and grew.

A figure detached itself from the others seated in the front pew and came to greet us. It was Mr. Johnson.

"Mr. and Mrs. Moriwaki, thank you so much for coming," he said. "Won't you have a seat? We're about to get started."

He directed Mama and Papa right to the front row and gave them a program. Mama nodded to the couple next to them, who nodded back.

"Kei-chan," Mr. Johnson said. "You come sit up front."

Mr. Johnson's other students, about twenty of them, sat in folding chairs facing the audience. As we approached, they regarded me with unabashed curiosity.

"Right here," he said, giving me a program and a reassuring pat on the shoulder, and I found myself sitting next to a skinny girl in a pink dress who looked about my age. I lowered my eyes and folded my hands in my lap.

I was so overcome by self-consciousness that two children got up and played before I became aware of what was going on around me. I looked at the program and saw that I was seventh, right after a girl named Gloria. She was the only Gloria on the program; I wondered what had happened to the other four.

After each child performed, there was polite applause. You could tell who the parents were because they clapped the loudest and smiled the most. I peeked up to see Mama and Papa politely applauding with the others. I couldn't imagine them smiling and clapping loudly for me; Papa would rather die than make such a vulgar display of pride. Suddenly, I was dismayed. When it came my turn, no one would clap for me. We were strangers here, and Mama and Papa would be on their best Japanese behavior; they would behave with restraint and humility. My heart sank.

I noticed that the skinny girl next to me was wiping her hands on her dress. I looked up and caught her eye. She opened her eyes wide in mock fright, and I smiled.

"Gloria Williams," Mr. Johnson was saying, "playing Beethoven's 'Moonlight Sonata'."

The skinny girl rose and went to the piano. I was next.

From what seemed like a great distance, I heard my name called.

"Playing 'Of Other Lands and Other People,' from Schumann's 'Scenes From Childhood'."

My mouth went dry. As I got up and went to the piano, the silence that followed me was curious, expectant.

My first notes were tentative. Then, in my nervousness, I began to play faster. And faster.

It was over before I realized it. I had probably set a world's record, but I'd hit all the right notes. I breathed. There was an awful silence.

Then it started. The applause. I looked up; a sea of black faces smiled at me, nodding approval. I recognized Mrs. Williams, our neighbor. She must be Gloria's mother. She waved. I waved back. Mr. Johnson caught my eye and winked.

Mama was smiling, too, in harmony with the faces around her. Papa was nodding solemnly, acknowledging the audience's tribute to me with humility, and I knew he was proud.

I was in a church filled with people. They were kindly giving me an ovation. It lifted me up, filled me, carried me back to my seat. And as I floated on the warm tide of their applause, I felt that the world, like music, was much bigger than I had thought, and I could begin to imagine that there might be a part for me somewhere in it.

"Harmony" originally appeared in *Story Magazine,* summer 1993.

Chapter Twelve

Different Silence(s): The Poetics and Politics of Location

Traise Yamamoto

1.

Last night, dinner with friends. At some point, we decide to go for a walk because it is a beautiful evening, and because the rhythms of walking bring out the rhythms of talk; speech syncopated between steps. There are four of us. We are all dressed in the easy sloppiness of the middle class. There is a baby strapped to the stomach of one of the two men.

We walk through a neighborhood where poverty is nonexistent, then through one where Hondas and fancy import cars, flower gardens and freshly painted house-fronts give way to older American cars, low-maintenance shrubs, shabby window casings and faded brown front doors.

Paired off and talking movies, the four of us move slowly down the street. As we approach a yard in which three young boys are playing, I hear, "Look!" (the long drawn out "oooo" of childish fascination), "A Chinese Lady!" The boy who has spoken, the youngest of the three, is about nine. And he is African American. The other two stare dutifully; they are also African American.

To speak or not to speak? How many times have similar things been said within my hearing, shortly followed by the yo-yo-ed vowels parodying "Oriental" speech? How many times has the next question been, "When did you get off the boat?" To be silent is to give in, to not-face and so to lose face; to be silent is what is expected of "a Chinese lady." But to speak is to risk intensified "chink talk." To speak is to risk losing my temper and having to see the satisfied grins, the mean pleasure of having gotten a reaction. It hardly matters that I am twenty years older than the boy who has spoken. The space into which I have suddenly been flung—keenly conscious that I am not simply one of four friends, but one Asian American with three white friends—is non-temporal: it could be a scene from anywhere between the time I was five to now. The neighborhood resembles the one I grew up in; the boys are the boys that were inevitably part of every school year, the boys that have become the men fascinated by the erotic exotic.

We are not yet past the house. To speak or not to speak? The boy is young. Is it simply a statement that he has noticed my difference? Just one of those things kids bravely call out from the safety of their own front yard, an honest inquiry? Or is there an Asian kid at school whom he picks on, whom he is identifying with me? "Not Chinese," I say, "Japanese. I am Japanese American."

I have to say it twice because he asks again; this is a new angle on the universe. "I am Japanese American." Then: "What are you?" "Oh," he answers, surprised, "I'm Black." I say, "Yes. You are not Chinese either, I take it." "Oh no," he giggles. Suddenly, he is just a child again. "Not me," he says as we—finally—pass by. My friends, silent this whole time, wait the space of a two-beat pause. Then, movie-talk.

***

You ask me to speak. You tell me at parties how lucky I am to be Japanese (always forgetting "American"), how you wish you could be Japanese so you too could "be so graceful," or so you could have straight black hair, or because you always have liked kimonos. You tell me in classes you are glad I talk because when I do, you learn something—about yourself. You tell me in clothes stores that I should get the red blouse because "Orientals look so nice in red," that I should get the A-line dress because it makes me look "so doll-like." You suggest that housecleaning is a good way to make extra summer money, then say I'm a snob when I tell you that my grandmothers did not clean other women's toilets, other women's children, other women's dirtiness so I could grow up and do the same thing. You ask me to speak. Sometimes, I do. And sometimes when I do, you say, "You're so unlike most Japanese women. You are very articulate (funny, loud, strident, etc.)." And if I speak in anger, you are surprised, call me bitter, tell me I'm lucky I'm not Black, Chicana, Native American; or, worse, you apologize for all whites of all time, want me to forgive and absolve for all Asians of all time. Or you tell me you feel you can talk to me (the comparative implicit) because I am not threatening.

***

But there are other things besides frustration and fear that keep me silent, that keep me stuck between speaking and not speaking. If you grow up Japanese American, you grow up with the intense insider/outsider mentality that the Isseis brought from a country where therapy is still not widely practiced or participated in. The boundaries begin with oneself, then ring gradually outward: the family ("This is family business," my Nisei mother would say, "and you are not to go blabbing it around outside"), the Japanese American community, the Asian American community. What belongs within must stay within: don't lose face, don't spill your guts, don't wear your heart on your sleeve. Fifty years after the war, most of those interned in the "relocation camps" will not speak of it. Boundaries. Self-containment: don't bother other people. *Shikata ga nai*. It can't be helped. There is nothing to be done. Its goodness lies in a certain acceptance, a giving of oneself to the world as it is. But it can modulate into resignation, passivity. So one doesn't speak because there is no use in it, *shikata ga nai*, no use to calling so much attention to oneself, to one's family; no use to shame others, both inside and outside.

***

I begin with these anecdotes because I think it is too easy, and ultimately dishonest, to talk about the signification of silence in literary or theoretical terms only. We must understand how these silences move and move in our own lives, our own psyches. Otherwise, a solely theoretical account of the multivalence of silence risks objectifying it as a mere trope or theme—risks objectifying our very selves. We are silenced, we are silent, we silence, and if we cannot talk about those acts with complexity, simplification will tell us that to be silent is to be non-existent, self-hating, somehow less-than. We must listen to our own silences so that we may speak and speak through silence.

2.

"I am weary," writes Mitsuye Yamada, "of starting from scratch each time I speak or write, as if there were no history behind us, of hearing that among the women of color, Asian women are the least political, or the least oppressed, or the most polite" (Yamada 1981, 71). Endless repetition is not simply to say, and then to say again. It is language circling round its own opacity. To say and not be heard, to say and have to say again is to be silenced, to be spoken, to be made invisible in a skein of language not one's own. Who has access to the what and wherefores of articulation also has the power to separate, make distinctions, make selves and others. And with the power to name and shape speech comes the power to name and shape silence.

The twinned themes of speech and silence occur repeatedly in the writings of Asian Americans, particularly in the novels, memoirs, poetry and essays by Asian American women. For them, silence is something to be broken, shattered, shredded; it is something solid through which one must pass in order to join one's voice to the voices on the other side. Or it is something that sits stone-heavy in the body, or it is a stifling enclosure within which the body suffocates. "The strongest prisons are built / with walls of silence," writes poet Janice Mirikitani (Mirikitani 1987, 5). These are the images of imposed silence, of a silence either repressive (imposed from within the culture) or oppressive (imposed from outside the culture).

But the complexity of Asian American women's relationship to silence does not stem solely from this dynamic of resistance and rejection, for there is also an understanding of and feeling for silence as a positive force, as something in and of itself, not simply the absence left when speech is non-existent; there is a chosen silence which, no less than speech, carries the power of signification, holds the doublenesses of meaning. Asian Americans must continually attempt to negotiate between two disjunctive signifying systems and from that negotiation construct a sense of their own subjectivity. The problematics of doing so, however, involve the extent to which they are constructed by what is essentially a double-bind: the silence through which dominant culture constructs Asian Americans is so powerful that neither speech nor silence seems able to reappropriate subjectivity. Because Asian American women, in particular, are seen through the double veils of racism and sexism by a culture that does not assign silence an active role, they find themselves objectified by a silence that is misunderstood and with which they are identified to the point of synonymity. What they perceive as the multivalence of silence is reduced and simplified to the flatness of a stereotype, and thus turned against them. This is especially true in situations where Asian American women attempt to use silence as an act of refusal or resistance. "Silence as a refusal to take part in the story," writes Trinh Minh-ha, "does sometimes provide us with a means to gain a hearing. It is voice, a mode of uttering, and a response in its own right. Without other silences, however, my silence goes unheard, unnoticed; it is simply one voice less, (one) more point given to the silencers" (Trinh 1989, 83).

3.

I have been teaching Maxine Hong Kingston's *The Woman Warrior* for the past week. It has been, as always during the years I have taught this book, an uphill climb, though the students like it, like the accessibility of the voice speaking to them. "God," one woman says in a paroxysm of relief, "I'm glad I'm not Chinese. No wonder Maxine hated being Chinese, no wonder she rejected it. Chinese girls just had to be silent all the time." She supports herself by pointing to the crucial scene in which a young Kingston torments a schoolmate in the girl's bathroom. It's a disturbing and powerful account of how internalized dominant culture stereotypes result in acts of projected self-hatred. There are many who agree with my student's analysis, though some in more sophisticated ways. It is easy, though reductively inaccurate, to read this passage simply as Kingston's realization that silence, emblematic of Chinese culture, is bad and must be eradicated before she can attain any kind of control over her own subjectivity. It is equally problematic to separate silence from the culture, as though it were an undesirable aberration to be excused and then ignored. Kingston's text shows the ways in which silence articulates subjectivity, and it shows how Asian Americans can begin to doubt the viability of that articulation when the syntax of their silence is not understood. "It was when I found out that I had to talk," writes Kingston, "that school became a misery, that the silence became a misery." Before that, she says, "I enjoyed the silence" (Kingston [1975] 1989, 166). Because Asian and Asian American women are seen as non-lingual—whether represented as stoically, obediently silent or as smiling ninnies tripping through mangled sentences—and therefore as other, rejecting silence becomes an act of rejecting the self as other, rejecting the raced and gendered self that is so inextricably tied to silence. In such a dynamic, speech itself becomes the medium of alienation, and in Kingston's narrative the result of her encounter is a psychological lapse into silence. What this suggests, I think, is that the silent self cannot be the scapegoat, cannot act as the magnetizing locus for the negativized stereotypes of dominant culture to be conveniently repressed and extricated without fundamentally displacing the sense of self.

I try to explain this to my class. I point out the many ways in which silence signifies in Kingston's book—as protection, as preserver of singularity, as complete attentiveness, as marker for who is identified with the group and who is not—argue for looking at it as a narrative that grapples with trying to reconcile two cultural systems, one of which is privileged and which privileges speech, the other which values speech but which also articulates itself in silences.

Another student shakes his head in a way that suggests I have made no sense at all, and says, ignoring Kingston's Stockton roots, "With all that, of course she wanted to be an American." A pause, "Who wouldn't?"

4.

In her book *Desert Run*, Nisei poet Mitsuye Yamada opens with a poem that represents a coming to terms with silence:

> Everything is done in silence here:
> the wind fingers fluted stripes
> over mounds and mounds of sand
> the swinging grasses sweep
> patterns on the slopes
> the sidewinder passes out of sight.
> I was too young to hear silence before (Yamada 1988, 1).

In dominant culture constructions, silence is often configured in visual and spatial terms; in such an equation, silence equals invisibility or the position of outsider. Strikingly, Asian American women's writing reflects a sense of the silent self as invisible. But in these lines, Yamada's descriptions of the silence around her are rendered in visual, not auditory, terms. She realigns silence with visibility, reclaiming it from absence. Silence is healer here, signifies not the absence of self but the complete presence of it.

In much the same way, Joy Kogawa's Obasan uses silence to signify the healing and redemption that have finally come to the main character, Naomi Nakane, at the end of the novel. Though she both begins and ends in silence, the nature of those silences is fundamentally different. Naomi begins in a stasis within which even words do not signify: "there is in my life no living word. The sound I hear is only sound. White sound." In contrast, her silence at the novel's close is sensate, full; water and stone dance "a quiet ballet, soundless as breath" (Kogawa 1981, 247). Gayle Fujita has traced what she calls the sensibility of silence in Kogawa's novel. Its essence, she writes, "is Naomi's nonverbal mode of apprehension summarized by the term 'attendance' " (Fujita 1985, 34). Kogawa's novel is, in many ways, an exploration into how Naomi Nakane resists the role of the Asian American woman as the site in and around which the discourses of silence are formulated and inscribed. It is significant that while her mother's and Obasan's silence have scarred her, she rejects the searing volubility of her Aunt Emily. Instead, in much the same way that she understands the truth to be "murky, shadowy and grey" (Kogawa 1981, 32), Naomi comes to understand that the "powerful voicelessness" (Kogawa 1981, 241) that has sealed the past and projected it, missile-like, through her life can also be the silence that dances, moves, listens, speaks, as it has throughout her life, though she may not always have recognized it.

5.

In a society that does not expect articulate speech, let alone articulate silences, from Asian American women, the act of writing becomes the broadest stroke towards speech. But sometimes that stroke is too difficult against the current of self-doubt, the belief that what one has to say isn't important or "universal" enough.

It took me years to discover that there was such a thing as a Japanese American writer. I had begun to believe what I had been told and retold: Asian Americans are non-verbal, unimaginative and, above all, too quiet to be writers and poets. "Of course there aren't any," a white friend informed me, "they're all engineers or social workers." I had begun to believe that we had nothing to say and no way of saying it.

But when I finally began to find and read the writing of Asian Americans, I myself became one of the silencers. It wasn't good enough or complex enough; it wasn't metaphysical, lyrical, memorable enough. That there seemed to be little of Eliot's extinction of personality seemed proof positive that this was writing of a lesser order. After all, how could a literature be great that was so imbued with the historical, experiential and personal? If good, was it as good as Shakespeare, Donne, Auden, Stevens? In short, did the work of Asian Americans meet up to the literary standards of academia and *The Norton Anthology*?

Inevitably, the answer was no. What I saw when I read the work of Asian Americans was myself. My experience was suddenly reflected back to me: I saw rooms in which I could see myself walking, heard conversations in whose accents and timbres I could hear my family's voices. Instead of Virginia Woolf's Boeuf en Daube and Proust's madeleine, there were tofu and takuan, sashimi and sake. But this couldn't be the stuff of literature. In devaluing the worth of my own experience I dismissed Asian American literature, assuming it to be simple rendering without the subtlety of art.

Even now, it is difficult for me to silence the one-eyed critic I hear in my head: *not good enough no one will be interested not universal dull minor literature self-indulgent simplistic not really art hack writing no good only about yourself.*

***

It seems significant to me that Sansei writers to an extraordinary degree choose poetry, the art of shaping silences, as their medium. I think it's a way of recuperating silence, its complexity and richness, the ways in which it can speak what speech cannot, create presence by the merest stroke, by what it implies. It is also an act of claiming visibility in what is often perceived as the most privileged form of articulation. Silence is thus simultaneously broken through and reappropriated in a form that relies on silences.

Mine is not the individual talent Eliot had in mind when he spoke of its relation to literary tradition, and I sometimes wonder whether Whitman addresses me when he calls out to the poets of the future to look for him under their boot-soles. I do know that when I tell people I write poetry, they often go on to tell me how much they like haiku, as if it were inconceivable that I might write in Homeric dactyls or Dantean *terza rima*. I know that I don't like it when a poem or manuscript is rejected with what is thought to be a helpful bit of advice: more poems on "the Asian American experience." I think of Paul Laurence Dunbar: when he was invited to read his poetry, the audience wanted to hear only his dialect poems— poems of the "Negro experience" in "Negro tones"—and drowned him out when he attempted to read his non-dialect poetry. It's not that I don't write about and out of my experience as a third-generation Japanese American woman, but that I don't feel compelled to trot out the particulars of "Asian stuff" on demand and for display.

And yet, those particulars are what I respond to when I read Asian American writers. There is always for me a pleasant thrum of recognition; I feel a sense of a shared past, that we share the language of our grandparents. Every internment camp poem speaks my parents' and grandparents' past, speaks their silence. Every short story, novel, memoir guides me and tells me what I could not know enough: we have something to say and we have ways to say it.

***

Every poem I write silences those who assume my aptitude in non-verbal fields (I first came to understand the use of the collective "you" when math teacher after puzzled math teacher would say, "But you're usually so good at this kind of thing") or my limited abilities in what must surely be my second language.

But every poem I write also testifies to what has increasingly become the uneasy relationship between the desire to speak the invisible mysteries that move my inner life, and the desire to speak what Blake called "the minute particulars" of which my daily life is comprised. I suppose it is much the same for every writer, the struggle to balance the timeless and the temporal. But for me, whose experience of daily life is inseparable from my identity as an Asian American woman, there is always the question of whether gender and ethnicity will become the filtering lenses through which my work will be judged, by which my work will be obscured. Yet, to write out of some "universal" mode in an attempt to avoid those lenses would be to erase myself with each stroke of the pen. "She who 'happens to be,'" writes Trinh Minh-ha, "a (non-white) Third World member, a woman, and a writer is bound to go through the ordeal of exposing her work to the abuse of praises and criticisms that either ignore, dispense with, or overemphasize her racial and sexual attributes" (Trinh 1989, 6).

For me, none of this can dampen the pleasure of articulation, the sensual satisfaction of words on the page and, most of all, the sense that to speak is necessary—because the alternative is the silence that comes from without, the silence that cannot speak through fear, frustration, doubt, and the words of the other. But I must also remember that speech for the sake of speech only works to keep me tied to those who would assume my silence. It means forgetting, too, that mine is a heritage that knows the beauty of silence, its many and varied inflections, the ways in which it creates spaces and openings. There is a silence that comes from within, what the famous Zen koan calls the soundless sound of one hand clapping. There are silences of difference, different silences.

References

Fujita, Gayle K. 1985. " 'To Attend the Sound of Stone': The Sensibility of Silence in *Obasan.*" *MELUS* 12 (3): 33-42.

Kingston, Maxine Hong. 1989. *The Woman Warrior: Memoirs of a Girlhood Among Ghosts.* New York: Vintage International. (Originally published 1975.)

Kogawa, Joy. 1981. *Obasan.* Boston: David R. Godine.

Mirikitani, Janice. 1987. *Shedding Silence.* Berkeley: Celestial Arts.

Trinh, Minh-ha. 1989. *Woman, Native, Other: Writing Post-coloniality and Feminism.* Bloomington: Indiana University Press.

Yamada, Mitsuye. 1981. "Asian Pacific American Women and Feminism." In Cherrie Moraga and Gloria Anzaldua, eds., *This Bridge Called My Back: Writings By Radical Women of Color.* Watertown: Persephone Press.

———. 1988. *Desert Run: Poems and Stories.* Latham: Kitchen Table Women of Color Press.

Chapter Thirteen

Claiming Land, Claiming Voice, Claiming Canon: Institutionalized Challenges in Kingston's *China Men* and *The Woman Warrior*

Rachel Lee

Maxine Hong Kingston's *The Woman Warrior* and *China Men* present a literary puzzle for their critics: on the one hand, they compose a companion set of autobiographical "talk story"[1]; on the other, the two books, published four years apart, not only portray distinct gendered subjects, but also differ in their degree of narrational intimacy. As Amy Ling notes, "*China Men* seems to spring more from an intellectual rather than a gut/ heart source . . . the author seems somewhat less personally engaged with her material than she was in *The Woman Warrior*" (Ling 1990, 144). This paper focuses on the thematic and programmatic differences in these two works. While in *China Men* Kingston attempts to restore the place of Chinese American men in history (and, correlatively, in the literary canon), in *The Woman Warrior*, she focuses upon a female subject who struggles to find an appropriate language in which to frame her identity. Interestingly, although these two books shared comparable market popularity (both achieving *New York Times* best-seller list status), *The Woman Warrior* (over ten years after publication) overshadows *China Men* in the general literary vocabulary of academics.[2] This phenomenon, I wish to suggest, results directly from the two books' thematic differences. Whereas *China Men* originates from an impulse to claim America, *The*

Woman Warrior focuses upon an Asian American woman's self-definition. To pursue this line of argument, I first offer a reading of *China Men*'s claims on America, then re-evaluate these claims in light of *The Woman Warrior*'s emphasis on voicing and intra-ethnic conflict. Finally, I return to the question of the two works' differing degrees of popularity. What are the institutional implications of Kingston's female-centered text as more frequently read than the "male," race-centered one? [3]

China Men

In a 1980 interview with Timothy Pfaff, Kingston makes clear that her purpose in *China Men* is to claim America: "What I am doing in this new book is claiming America . . . which goes all the way from one character saying that a Chinese explorer found this place before Leif Eriksson did to another one buying a house here" (Pfaff 1980, 1). Kingston portrays the various routes to claiming America, from actual physical harnessing acts performed upon the land to claiming as proclaiming—a non-violent option for the marginal wo/man. As her brief examples indicate, however, Kingston begins her exploration into Chinese American claims by revealing her male protagonists' tendency to claim the materiality of America through the land; that is, the Eriksson predecessor claims through first property rights, while the characters who buy houses put down roots by economically investing in the land. This notion of buying into America—and the correlative notion of America as real estate (not as ideal of liberty, democracy, racial plurality)—becomes a central problem for Chinese Americans in looking at their sojourner fathers whose goals were to venture to the Gold Mountain, achieve financial success, and return to China.

For Kingston, gender enters uncannily into this economic terrain, as seen in her two-page, introductory tale entitled "On Discovery." North America, a land of "no taxes and no wars," is also the "Land of Women" or "Women's Land." Yet, Kingston does not merely show this virgin America as an unfallen paradise: in the beginning, she seems to say, was violence; and, thus, Tang Ao, the male Chinese explorer who discovers America, crosses to Women's Land only to be captured by the female inhabitants and forcibly feminized (they sew his mouth together, bind his feet, and cross-dress him to make him suitable for serving a meal at the Queen's court). Crossing boundaries to establish claims involves the violent restructuring of both settlers and the soil.

In America or Women's Land, the encroaching Chinese man becomes silenced and forced into labor. Clearly, Kingston alludes to the Chinese male's larger heritage of emasculation and oppressive working conditions in America, a legacy which resurfaces in the depiction of her earliest American ancestor, Bak Goong (or great Grandfather). In "The Great Grandfather of the Sandalwood Mountains," Kingston describes the severe conditions under which Bak Goong toils. Most oppressive is the contractors' injunction against laborers' speaking while working. The China Men must "hack a farm out of the wilderness" (98) yet neither proclaim their victories nor encourage their fellows. Kingston, however, refuses to deliver a purely heroic rendering of these male ancestors. She portrays both their striving against oppression, as well as their own conspiracy in the destruction of the land to serve economic purposes:

> [The China Men] were the first human beings to dig into this part of the island and see the meat and bones of the red earth. After rain, the mud ran like blood . . . .The wagoners, who had a good job, drove the cane to the sugar mill on a route along the sea. It was crushed into molasses and boiled into sugar, for which the world was developing an insatiable hunger as for opium (103).

Kingston appears to be straining under contradictory impulses: she wishes to show a Chinese American first-endeavor in cultivating the land (and thus first right to proprietary claims), but she also struggles with a disapproving attitude toward the violence involved in harnessing the earth to trade interests. Her metaphors are telling: one hacks at the earth's flesh, making the soil bleed, in order to service a highly profitable trade which, like opium, remains inimical to the Chinese.

The land as sugarcane farm contrasts greatly to the land which Bak Goong wishes to praise initially in song:

> The sights of the day unreeled behind his eyelids—the ocean jumping with silver daggers, fronds shredding in wind, twin rainbows, spinning flowers, the gray mass of the maze tree like all the roads of many lives. How was he to marvel adequately, voiceless? (100)

The scenery of America astounds in its vitality—spinning, shredding, jumping. Yet instead of realizing in voice a vibration of equal vigor, Bak Goong can only reflect upon his forced voicelessness. Additionally, the figure of the monk—both silent and celibate—cojoins the prohibition on words with the prohibition on sexuality. " 'If I knew I had to take a vow of silence,' [Bak Goong] added 'I would have shaved off my hair and become a monk. Apparently we've taken a vow of chastity too. Nothing but roosters in this flock' " (100). The Chinese laborers can neither create families nor speak (both activities which would imprint a Chinese American trace upon an American cultural terrain). Furthermore, both restrictions serve capitalism, the code of silence preventing organized uprisings, while sexual prohibitions not only increase work efficiency but also prevent the possibility of American born progeny who might claim their "native" rights.

Proceeding a generation further, Kingston likewise portrays Grandfather's, or Ah Goong's, part in building the transcontinental railroad as both valiant and violent. At Central Pacific's command, he fells a redwood:

> The trunk lay like a long red torso; sap ran from its cuts like crying blind eyes. At last it stopped fighting. . . . The men measured themselves against the upturned white roots. . . . A hundred men stood or sat on the trunk. They lifted a wagon on it and took a photograph. The demons [white men] also had their photograph taken (128-129).

Again, Kingston anthropomorphizes the land, empathetically aligning herself with it; the men, at least, wait until the redwood "stop[s] fighting" before mounting it for posterity. The photograph, supposedly recording the workers' measured superiority (over the land), ironically symbolizes the powerlessness of China Men to receive historical recognition. That is, the photograph (record of deeds) which becomes incorporated in official documentation remains the white men's photograph, which Kingston intentionally adds as afterthought.

While rectifying a warped historical record and underscoring Chinese Americans' legitimate place in U.S. labor history, Kingston complicates her own endeavor by adopting a contradictory attitude toward male heroism as defined through violent, civilizing acts. Part of the endeavor to bind America "with crisscrossing steel" (146) involves using dynamite and gunpowder to rip holes through mountains. Thus, Ah Goong is "hired . . . on sight [because] chinamen had a natural talent for explosions" (128). Kingston makes clear that the explosions in this country are not innocuous: the year is 1863 when "some of the banging came from the war to decide whether or not black people would continue to work for nothing" (128). For Kingston, the current use of gunpowder to build railroads cannot be divorced from either its history as a tool of oppression (as well as liberation) or its link to America's most divisive economic war. Furthermore, Kingston's open admission of her anti-draft politics at the time of *China Men*'s writing, render her military metaphors particularly acute.[4] Ah Goong's "[running] up the ledge road . . . watch[ing] the explosions, which banged almost synchronously, *echoes booming like war*" (131, emphasis added) thus suggests a negative portrait of heroic behavior[5]—a forced or commissioned violence upon the land, but nevertheless a complicit act of violence. From her grandfather to her brother in Vietnam, Kingston depicts Chinese Americans as having earned their citizenship through war-like engagement and endangerment, for this is the only sanctioned means of proving one's citizenship.

Kingston turns from this physical claiming of the land through labor/sacrifice to alternative means of claiming America. Ah Goong attempts to imprint a trace of himself through urinating and then ejaculating into open space:

> One beautiful day . . . sexual desire clutched him so hard he bent over in the basket. He tried to rub himself calm. Suddenly he stood up tall and squirted into space. "I am fucking the world," he said. The world's vagina was big, big as the sky, big as the valley. He grew a habit: whenever he was lowered in the basket, his blood rushed to his penis, and he fucked the world (133).

Unable to legally define his place in America, Ah Goong ejaculates into open space—attempting to "fuck the world" or control space by feminizing and subsequently raping it. Kingston alludes here not only to an American tradition of frontier expansion construed as sexual aggression (which Annette Kolodny's *The Lay of the Land* suggests), but also to a tradition of Asian American writing focused upon male impotence.[6] David Leiwei Li suggests that although Ah Goong shares in a "lay of the land" discourse, that his fucking the world remains a substitutive gesture for the lack of any real "political or economic mastery over the land" (Li 1990, 491). He contends that Kingston, even while celebrating China Men's devotion to westward expansion, "sees that they are not victors but victims" (Li 1990, 490). Yet, while portraying her China Men as victims of society, Kingston also shows their participation in and tacit approval of a patriarchal code which mandates women's subjection. The question becomes "Is an oppressive act of violence mitigated by the oppressor's prior victimization by another's hand?"

Kingston finds no easy resolution to this question. She attributes to her father "wordless male screams" (13), since he cannot effectively defend himself against a customer's false accusations. Though verbally impotent with the American police, Baba has the power to oppress within his household, making his narrator-daughter "sicken at being female" (14). While ostensibly vindicating her male ancestors, Kingston portrays an uneasy relationship between the male subjects of her book and her narrator-self, oftentimes employing buffering techniques when portraying paternal brutality. For instance, the narrator conveys a beating, possibly inflicted on herself, through third-person narration:

> He chased my sister, who locked herself in a bedroom. "Come out," he shouted. But, of course, she wouldn't, he having a coat hanger in hand and angry. I watched him kick the door; the round mirror fell off the wall and crashed. The door broke open, and he beat her. Only, my sister remembers that it was she who watched my father's shoe against the door . . . and I who was beaten (253).

The beating construed as violence to another effectively distances the victim and the reader from any direct impact with the remembered incident; the strategy also deflects narrative focus away from any condemnation of Baba toward reflections upon memory retrieval. Again, Kingston remains precariously situated as a female author who wishes to rectify the racist historical erasure of China Men, yet plays upon an uneasy tension between men and women of the Asian American community.

To Kingston's credit, she refuses to offer an idealized vision of China Men's claims. Both material claiming and domination through feminization remain less than satisfactory means for placing oneself and one's people in the American terrain. Yet, China Men did not merely bind the land nor speculate on its material wealth and then leave; they have also marked the land, by burying their dead along the transcontinental tracks. Although Kingston indicates that "there is no record of how many died building the railroad" (138), she stresses that China Men have indeed made America their home, despite historical and political non-recognition. Both physically and discursively they have imprinted themselves upon the land:

> The men plowed, working purposefully, but they dug a circle instead of straight furrows. . . . They had dug an ear into the world, and were telling the earth their secrets. "I want home," Bak Goong yelled, pressed against the soil, and smelling the earth. "I want my home," the men yelled together. "I want home. Home. Home. Home. Home" (117).

Although many of the men direct their thoughts of home to China, the transformation of the desire "I want home" into the definitive "Home. Home. Home. Home" effects a declarative naming of the new land as home. The China Men achieve a home built not upon labor spent, nor life sacrificed, but upon a mental commitment to the new land. As Kingston makes clear, this proclaiming remains unsanctioned by U.S. authorities, the China Men having to bury their words. Yet, this unsanctioned *proclaiming* represents an alternative means of *claiming* America, one which has not been co-opted by American economic interests.

The Woman Warrior

Likewise, in *The Woman Warrior*, Kingston uses the Fa Mu Lan tale to rewrite heroism and vindication in terms of voicing rather than violence. In "White Tigers," the heroine disguises herself as a man, takes her father's place in the army, and rectifies the wrongs against her family by cutting off the heads of her enemies. Motivating Fa Mu Lan are the "words [carved] at [her] back" (63)—a list of grievances which her parents have literally etched onto her skin (41). When the narrator brings the warrior tale into the present, she makes clear that though she shares with Fa Mu Lan the "words at our backs," it is "the reporting [that] is the vengeance— not the beheading, not the gutting, but the words" (63). Kingston replaces Fa Mu Lan's warrior deeds with writing as vengeance and trades "manthropomorphic" heroism for articulation.[7]

In *The Woman Warrior*, the narrator struggles with what are true stories or false stories. For instance, the narrator makes explicit her confusion over her mother's tales:

> I don't want to listen to any more of your stories; they have no logic. They scramble me up. You lie with stories. You won't tell me a story and then say, "This is a true story," or, "This is just a story." I can't tell the difference. . . . I can't tell what's real and what you make up (235).

In this one instance, the narrator rejects these Chinese myths because of their indeterminate truth value. However, in other narrative moments, the narrator capitalizes on the ambiguity between "what's real and what['s] made up" to create a perception of the world which is both Western and Eastern, logical and imaginative. In "White Tigers," for example, the narrator prepares for her role as an avenging warrior-writer by learning "to make my mind large, as the universe is large, so that there is room for paradoxes. Pearls are bone marrow; pearls come from oysters . . ." (35). Both metaphoric and scientific characterizations of "pearls" present a version of "truth."

Thus, the narrator's dilemma over her mother's stories, while couched in terms of truth and falsity, really concerns how one should interpret each fiction. That is, what is the appropriate "Western" response to an "Eastern" truth, and vice versa? Kingston's reparation candy story illustrates this point well. After a pharmacy employee mistakenly delivers a drug prescription to the narrator's household, Brave Orchid (the narrator's mother) insists that the pharmacy has cast a sickness taint over her home. She commands her daughter to ask the drug store to "rectify their crime," to give her "reparation candy," and thus dispel the curse of "sick medicine" with "sweetness" (197-198). Though illogical (false) from an American perspective, the mother's perception of "sick medicine" remains true within her belief system. The "superstition," neither essentially true nor false, presents the dilemma of the Chinese American daughter unsure of which belief system should inform her actions.

In contrast, China Men's narrator has foregone overtly questioning the truth value of Chinese tales rather to sit back and "listen." Comparing narrative techniques of the two works, Kingston states, "In *China Men* the person who 'talks story' is not so intrusive. I bring myself in and out of the stories, but in effect, I'm more distant. . . . [I was more interested in] writ[ing] from their point of view and . . . less interested . . . in relating how I felt about them" (Pfaff 1980, 26). Clearly, *China Men*'s narrative focuses less on the truth values of stories and chooses instead to adopt her subjects' point of view. Though the narrator does question the validity of the official historical record (for instance, in questioning the newspaper account of "The Wild Man of the Green Swamp"), she predominantly records the deeds of her protagonists, rather than focusing upon her narrator-self in relation to these familial connections, as she does in *The Woman Warrior*. In addition, *China Men*'s lessened preoccupation with the slipperiness of words allows the narrator to rectify historical omissions. Instead of wondering whether the story of Tang Ao or Bak Goong is "true," the narrator listens and metaphorically transcribes her ancestors' stories providing alternate narratives to that privileged tale known as "history."

Concerning itself with voicing rather than claiming, *The Woman Warrior* emphasizes verbal over physical exchange as the preferred method of resistance. For instance, the book begins with the injunction "You must not tell anyone . . . what I am about to tell you" (3), which Kingston violates by narrating the tale of her "No Name" Aunt, who becomes extra-maritally pregnant and kills herself. Kingston's opening chapter thus enacts a vengeance through words against a patriarchal silence which has both rendered her aunt's story unspeakable and sought to erase her existence.

The text also concerns itself with the quality, not just the content, of one's voice: how one can speak—the process of articulation—becomes as important as what finally emerges verbalized. In her last chapter, "Song for a Barbarian Reed Pipe," the narrator reflects upon social prescriptions for female verbal behavior from both the Chinese and American communities. Although Chinese sayings equate "feeding girls" with "feeding cowbirds" (54), the strength of these women's voices in Chinese communities belies the belittling suggestions of the traditional aphorisms: "Normal Chinese women's voices are strong and bossy. We American-Chinese girls had to whisper to make ourselves American-feminine. We invented an American-feminine speaking personality . . . ." (200).

Not all Chinese American girls find this speaking personality, as Kingston indicates in her portrait of "one girl that could not speak up even in Chinese school" (200). In telling the tale of the narrator's wordless twin, Kingston dramatizes the struggle with silence, and the Western notion of speaking as the index to individuation and hence personality. In this tale, Kingston's first-person narrator appears a girl of twelve years old who describes her burgeoning sense of individualism in the sixth grade as "that year I was arrogant with talk" (202). Her struggle with an alter-ego silent Chinese girl stages a battle against voicelessness, with the narrator trying to force words from the stoic girl by, in turns, threatening and cajoling her. Ironically, words fail to produce the narrator's desired effect, so she begins torturing the silent girl, pinching her cheeks, pulling her hair, all the while accompanied by the command, "Talk . . . Just say 'Ow. . . . Say 'Leave me alone,' and I'll let you go" (207). The child-torturing scene evokes divided sympathies from the reader. On the one hand, the tortured girl's silent tears speak for a stoic resistance and heritage of silence inspired by the fear of speaking incorrectly (and as a consequence getting deported). On the other, the narrator's insistent pleas urge the little girl to function practically in accordance with a Western world view, to gain a personality and individualize herself through a mastery of language. In the end, the young Maxine falls sick for the next eighteen months, seemingly punished for abusing her cohort. She admits upon returning to school that "[she] was wrong [about the silent Chinese girl]," that not talking does not translate into an inability to survive in America: "I was wrong about nobody taking care of her. . . . She did not have to leave the house except to go to movies. She was supported. She was protected by her family, as they would normally have done in China . . . " (212). Kingston's dramatizing the struggle to overcome silence thus results in a contradictory message—that while voicing is important it is not necessarily the only way to define oneself.

In addition to contesting the conventional connection of voicing with individualism, the narrator's encounter with the silent Chinese girl also sheds light on the heterogeneity of the Chinese American community (even more specifically the female, adolescent Chinese American community). On a symbolic level, these two girls adhere to and represent widely differing notions of community and self. For Maxine's silent twin, assimilating to Western paradigms of individuality and verbal assertiveness remains a non-necessity for she can survive through her familial and communal networks. For the narrator, however, community remains a more variegated entity: it can be a repressive and intolerant body which stones the village crazy lady for her extremes of individuality, her lack of participation in the common language, and her inability to access shared meanings (111-112).[8] Community may also be a source of rich "mythic" vision, as it can also provide a network for survival, support and unification for labor protest, as *China Men*'s railroad workers' strike illustrates (140-44).

Whereas in *The Woman Warrior*, Kingston highlights communities' internal conflicts and often oppressive power, *China Men*'s communities rarely receive a negative portrayal; the movement in this latter book seems to be an embracing and celebrating of racial lineage and communal claims to America. The individual rifts which show the community's intraracial tensions (where the narrator addresses her father) seem quieted and smoothed over, subordinated to the priority task of celebrating Chinese American male subjects from their point of view. This positive and harmonious conception of community in *China Men* and the contrasting ambivalent characterization of heterogeneous communities in *The Woman Warrior* indirectly lead to their disparate claiming techniques. Built upon a notion of cooperative strength, *China Men* seeks to place its early male immigrants within a community of pioneering Americans. The China Men participate in an already authenticated set of gestures (e.g., the cultivating and taming of the wilderness) and by this shared ritual are initiated into the community of Americans who can trace their American-born ancestors back for several generations. *The Woman Warrior*, on the other hand, appears to adopt a more individualist stance. Its narrator remains in tension with various communities and their intolerant by-laws (which often lend communities cohesiveness but which sacrifice deviant members for the community's greater strength). Ironically, *The Woman Warrior*'s unease with community has resulted in its celebration by an institutionalized (academic) community, while *China Men*'s proofs and claims have been less enthusiastically embraced by this same group. In fact, one might argue that *China Men* remains slighted because of its enabling stance toward hegemonic structures. That is, if the challenge in *China Men* is to incite official recognition of China Men's place in America, one wishes to subvert only to the extent to which one wishes to be accepted into the public record.

Kingston metaphorically portrays the gradual process of official acceptance in her vision of soil-sprouting tales. Though China Men of the past have been forced to bury words, Kingston predicts that their implanted stories will push to the topsoil and demand recognition: "Soon the new green shoots would rise, and when in two years the cane grew gold tassels, what stories the wind would tell" (118). Though the proclaiming aloud of stories does not constitute canonical recognition, the gesture toward claiming a place in American tradition or claiming legitimacy in the canon ultimately reinforces the authority of that official body and its power to exclude.

In contrast, *The Woman Warrior* concludes with the image of a woman thoroughly dispossessed of home and community: she is the exile Ts'ai Yen whose singing voice is compared to an "icicle in the desert" (243), achieved but not quite legitimate and certainly precarious. Her claim to the land remains incomplete, and the establishment of Ts'ai Yen as a foremother is not the highlighted agenda, but rather her impulse to song and the quality of this song comes into narrative focus.

Conclusion: Kingston and the Canon

How, then, does the wider readership of *The Woman Warrior* over *China Men* reflect on the academic institutions which embrace them? Conversely, how does one assess the two books in light of their qualitatively different institutional incorporation? To begin with, I wish to suggest that *The Woman Warrior* has been validated through its successful incorporation into Women's Studies programs, while *China Men* sits uncomfortably between English literature and Ethnic Studies programs. Portraying a female subject shaping an identity, *The Woman Warrior* appears non-threatening to Women's Studies departments, which can easily embrace it as a young progeny, and luckily, one which might deflect accusations of white feminist dominance. On the other hand, *China Men*, with its male protagonists, presents a less tantalizing or obvious teaching option for feminist critics (although I must add that reducing appeal to gender correspondence between the reader and textual protagonists seems to me an altogether unsatisfactory critical approach). Its highlighting of racial oppression over intraracial sexism leaves Women's Studies departments baffled, for how can one equate gender oppression with racial oppression? Thus, *China Men* makes its claims on American literature departments and appears an alien and demanding challenge to the traditions of history and the canon. Less comfortable than Women's Studies with embracing non-canonical works, literature departments shuffle *China Men* off to Ethnic Studies programs *where they exist*, or leave it for the few Asian American English professors to teach in a seminar. If, however, *China Men* is a text ostensibly about male characters but told through a female narrator's point of view, why has it not been embraced by Women's Studies for subverting white, male hegemony? Perhaps, as Audre Lorde suggested twelve years ago, Women's Studies and gender criticism today still remain dominated by white feminism and have not truly taken into account issues of race and class beyond token provisos (Lorde 1983, 98-101). [9]

By way of conclusion then, if the success of *The Woman Warrior* relies on its flouting of canonical/hegemonic norms, this phenomenon reflects a logical knot of our times—that we value texts based upon the degree to which they remain marginal. The argument, being circular, leads us back to the suggestion that *China Men* may be the more radical of the two texts, precisely because of its lesser degree of institutional success. *The Woman Warrior*, because of the fact that it celebrates marginality, has been legitimated by the institution, which ironically wishes to posit its critical endeavors as a champion of marginality, even when the institution itself is a legitimating discourse.

Endnotes

1. Kingston originally conceived of the two books as one large volume, with several stories from the separate volumes being composed contemporaneously (Pfaff 1980, 25).

2. The MLA Bibliography (1981-90) lists more than three times as many scholarly citations for work pertaining to *The Woman Warrior* than it does for *China Men* (39 cites to 11).

3. Though hesitant to label *The Woman Warrior* "female-centered" and *China Men* "race-centered," I do so because of their already institutional assignments as such. But as Kingston revises male claims in *China Men* and asserts a gendered racial program in *The Woman Warrior*, perhaps one needs to debunk the binary opposition which disallows these books to be concerned with both gender and race.

4. See Pfaff 1980, 27. Kingston's overt preoccupation with the war and her pacifist stance come to light most clearly in the Li Sao section where Peace abandons the world and in "The Brother in Vietnam" chapter.

5. In "The Woman Warrior versus the Chinaman Pacific," King-Kok Cheung discusses Frank Chin's brand of Asian American heroism which "endors[es] violence as a positive expression of masculinity"; she further suggests that an alternative to the "masculist orientation of the heroic tradition" is needed (Cheung 1990, 244, 242).

6. In Louis Chu's *Eat a Bowl of Tea* (1961), for instance, losing one's volition becomes synonymous with losing control over one's penis, the phallus representing the power to dominate. Is Kingston conducting a metacommentary on previous Asian American fiction which concerns itself with male impotence and its intersection with the loss of Chinese patriarchal tradition and the correlative loss of an obedient wife?

7. In " 'Don't Tell:' Imposed Silences in *The Color Purple* and *The Woman Warrior*," Cheung reads the Fa Mu Lan warrior legend as liberating even as it binds Kingston in male discourse: "While the warrior legend opens Maxine to an unconventional way of asserting herself—both fighting and writing being traditionally male preoccupations—it still sanctions patriarchal values . . . .[Fa Mu Lan] distinguishes herself by excelling in manly exploits. Internalizing the communal denigration of women, the protagonist begin[s] by assuming that only 'manthropomorphic' beings can offer guidance, inspiration, salvation" (Cheung 1988, 166).

8. Ironically, one can view Maxine as an intolerant community member verbally "stoning" the silent girl for her failure to share in a common speakerly language.

9. *China Men* appears a less tantalizing choice for feminist programs only when the latter are predicated on an uncritical and undifferentiated exclusion of "male discourse." As King-Kok Cheung suggests,

> Lest feminist criticism remain in the wilderness, white scholars must reckon with race and class as integral experiences for both men and

women, and acknowledge that not only female voices but the voices of many men of color have been historically silenced or dismissed . . . .Women of color should not have to undergo a self-division resulting from having to choose between female and ethnic identities (Cheung 1990, 246).

References

Cheung, King-Kok. " 'Don't Tell:' Imposed Silences in *The Color Purple* and *The Woman Warrior.*" *PMLA* 103: 2 (March 1988): 162-174.

——. "The Woman Warrior versus The Chinaman Pacific: Must a Chinese American Critic Choose between Feminism and Heroism?" In *Conflicts in Feminism*, edited by Marianne Hirsch and Evelyn Fox Keller. New York: Routledge, 1990.

Chu, Louis. *Eat a Bowl of Tea.* New York: Lyle Stuart, 1961. Reprint, Seattle: University of Washingston Press, 1979.

Kingston, Maxine Hong. *China Men.* 1980. New York: Knopf. Reprint, New York: Vintage Books, 1989.

——. *The Woman Warrior.* New York: Knopf, 1976. Reprint, New York: Vintage Books, 1977.

Kolodny, Annette. *The Lay of the Land.* Chapel Hill: University of North Carolina Press, 1975.

Li, David Leiwei. "*China Men*: Maxine Hong Kingston and the American Canon." *American Literary History* 2:3 (Fall 1990): 482-502.

Ling, Amy. *Between Worlds: Women Writers of Chinese Ancestry.* New York: Pergamon Press, 1990.

Lorde, Audre. "The Master's Tools Will Never Dismantle the Master's House." In *This Bridge Called My Back: Writings by Radical Women of Color*, edited by Gloria Anzaldúa and Cherríe Moraga. Latham, New York: Kitchen Table Women of Color Press, 1983.

Pfaff, Timothy. "Talk With Mrs. Kingston." *New York Times Book Review*, June 15, 1980: 1+.

Chapter Fourteen

Trickster Strategies: Challenging American Identity, Community, and Art in Kingston's *Tripmaster Monkey*

Sharon Suzuki-Martinez

Fearlessly swinging from chandeliers and trickster lines, transgressing all boundaries, Maxine Hong Kingston's *Tripmaster Monkey: His Fake Book* challenges the constructions of American identity, community, and art. More specifically, Kingston challenges one of her most vociferous critics, the writer Frank Chin. Chin and the fellow editors of *Aiiieeeee!* and *The Big Aiiieeeee!* (Jeffery Chan, Lawson Inada, and Shawn Wong) regard Kingston as a "fake" Asian American writer and accuse her of having sold out to white supremacism.[1] Unwittingly, they also create a narrow, prescriptive aesthetic whereby the Asian American literary tradition must be based predominantly on a few Chinese classics which have the main theme of: "all life is war and all behavior is tactics and strategy."[2]

In this essay I will show how Kingston challenges the editors of *Aiiieeeee!* and the hegemony through *Tripmaster Monkey*. She does this by journeying through anomaly and by using various trickster strategies to dismantle these two value systems and to construct a pluralist, community-based aesthetic and identity.

Tripmaster Monkey can be read as a celebration of the anomalous. It explores the worlds of anomalous people—those who escape the system, who are either ignored or treated as a living form of dirt. As Mary Douglas asserts in *Purity and Danger*, "Dirt is the by-product of a systematic ordering and classification of matter, in so far as ordering involves rejecting inappropriate elements" (Douglas 1989, 35). In short, dirt is matter out of place. Kingston shows American minorities as people out of place, but only so because of the faultiness of the American system.[3]

Kingston explores anomalous people who elude the mainstream. More specifically, it is the Asian Americans who have never been simply "American" because as Wittman Ah Sing comments, "It has to do with looks, doesn't it? They use 'American' interchangeably with 'white' " (329). Asian Americans can only be foreignly "inscrutable" and "exotic." In order to criticize the exclusivity of the American system, Kingston has her marginalized characters engage in subversive trickster strategies.

Trickster Strategies

Carnivalesque hybridization, postmodernism, and Chinese American theater could all be called "trickster strategies" because all share some of the basic traits of the mythic con artist, a favorite trope among many writers and theorists of the marginalized. This is because as Wittman, "the present-day U.S.A. incarnation of the King of the Monkeys" knows, the trickster is the ancestral prototype and role model of the marginalized. The trickster is a marginalized being by definition: one whose actions break down categories and oppositions. The trickster "embodies all possibilities—the most positive and the most negative—and is paradox personified" (Babcock 1985, 154). Inspired by the unnamed, untamed energy of the marginal wilderness, it brings changes and creative energy, as well as destruction and chaos. In short, the trickster points out faults in the system, and scoops out the hidden "dirt"—the system's contradictions and weaknesses—thereby keeping the whole structure unstable. Likewise, many minority writers and theorists seek to shake up, reinvigorate, and reconstruct American culture. To this end, *Tripmaster Monkey* deploys the three trickster strategies briefly defined here.

Carnivalesque Hybridization

In *The Politics and Poetics of Transgression*, Stallybrass and White (1986) use Bakhtin's idea of the "carnivalesque" to deconstruct the bourgeois construction of classification and identity by looking at sites of transgression.[4] A site of transgression occurs where there is a breakdown of the binary extremes of high and low that make up a hierarchical order.

The carnivalesque, as the word suggests, is connected to the energies of the carnival. In literature, it can be recognized in scenes dominated by the heterogeneity of the crowd, disproportion, excess, chaos, physical needs and pleasures, impurity, and the body imaged as "multiple, bulging, over- or under-sized, ...mobile and hybrid" (9). While associated with the low, the carnivalesque actually "mediates" between center and margin or high and low (25). While Stallybrass and White break down the carnivalesque into three symbolic processes, only one of them—hybridization—is radically transgressive. Hybridization "produces new combinations and strange instabilities in a given semiotic system. It therefore generates the possibility of shifting the very terms of the system itself." (Stallybrass and White 1986, 58). Hybridization creates an instable, anomalous zone where self and other are disturbingly enmeshed. I will talk about this concept especially in terms of Wittman and the narrator.

Chinese American Theater

One way of looking at *Tripmaster Monkey* is as a narrative about the mythic history of Chinese American theater. As the narrator recounts:

> A company of one hundred great-great-grandparents came over to San Francisco during the Gold Rush, and put on epic kung-fu opera and horse shows. . . . theater for a century, then dark" (249-250).

It is Wittman Ah Sing's goal to revive this nearly lost American tradition.

Chinese American theater (like *Tripmaster Monkey*) follows Chinese theater in its wide range of drama, motivations, and simultaneous activities. Both forms of drama encourage what would be considered in America unrelated genres and happenings. Chinese "Theater may combine any of a variety of arts; including literature, music, acting, singing, costume, make-up, dance or acrobatics" (Mackerras 1983, 1). In similar heterogeneous fashion, one critic characterizes Chinese American theater as drama and music along with "numerous exhibitions and competitions by kung fu and martial arts schools; festivals, parades; dance concerts; street fairs and bazaars" (Wong 1976, 14).

Kingston seems aware of the intersections between the traditions and calls for Chinese American theater to be an integral part of its community.[5] This will be discussed primarily in the section on carnivalesque events and Wittman's performance.

Postmodernism

Postmodernism is difficult to define because of its variety. On one hand, it is an incorporation and subversion of literary modernism and its aesthetic of difficulty, individualism, and western, masculinist elitism.[6] On the other hand, it has an aesthetic (if certainly a rhetoric) of plurality, dialogue, difference, indeterminacy, and deconstruction. Linda Hutcheon defines postmodernism as "fundamentally contradictory, resolutely historical and inescapably political . . . Because it is contradictory and works within the very systems it attempts to subvert, postmodernism can probably not be considered a new paradigm. . . . it may mark however, the site of the struggle of the emergence of something new" (Hutcheon 1989, 11). She goes on to describe the enabling context of the possible sites of struggle and emergence: "The political, social and intellectual experience of the sixties helped make it possible for postmodernism to be seen as what Kristeva calls 'writing-as-experience-of-limits' . . . limits of language, of subjectivity, of systematization and uniformization" (Hutcheon 1989, 15). Emerging out of these limits is what had earlier in modernism been excluded from serious consideration: popular culture and the views and values of minorities. This "articulation of the marginal" is also one of the main concerns of postmodernism.

The articulation of the marginal does not entail speaking from the margin, which would retain the hierarchical structure of high/low and center/margin; rather, it means to speak from the center and thus to destroy the structure from within. *Tripmaster Monkey* does this by implicitly raising three important questions:

1) What has it meant to be Chinese American (the "oriental" stereotype represented in literature and popular culture)?
2) What is the hegemony that creates such representations?
3) Fully aware of the historical and present situation, how might Chinese Americans create themselves?

These questions move the Chinese American through positions of increasing power: as the object in question, to the questioning subject, and lastly, to the creating subject.[7] This process is accomplished by the application of the trickster strategies of hybridization, Chinese American theater and postmodernism as analytical frameworks to *Tripmaster Monkey*'s protagonist, narrator and carnivalesque events.

Wittman Ah Sing—Postmodern Monkey

While seeming to be modeled after the writer-critic Frank Chin, Wittman Ah Sing goes beyond Chin. Amy Ling has already pointed out their similarities:

Both Wittman and Chin are . . . playwrights, whose literary style is hip, energetic, scintillating, sometimes bombastic, often angry, aggressively masculinist, fervently espousing "yellow power" while simultaneously lapsing into self-contempt and bitterness against the Chinese American community (Ling 1990, 149).

However, in other ways, they are very different. By the end of his own story, Wittman has lost all the alienating traits he initially shared with Chin. One reason for this is that Kingston does not model Wittman after Chin, but rather parodies Chin. According to Hutcheon, parody is not just a mocking representation, but rather, "a perfect postmodernist form . . . for it paradoxically both incorporates and challenges that which it parodies" (Hutcheon 1989, 17). Kingston isn't trying to mock or destroy Chin; in fact at times she echos and celebrates his striking language: "Where's our jazz? Where's our blues? Where's our ain't-taking-no-shit-from-nobody street-strutting language? I want so bad to be the first bad-jazz China Man bluesman of America" (27). Her book also addresses the three Chinese literary classics that Chin prescribes for the Asian American tradition. But Kingston does challenge Chin's emphasis on war by transforming his literary twin: "Studying the mightiest war epic of all time, Wittman changed—beeen!—into a pacifist" at the end of the book (340).

Another perhaps more important reason why Wittman transcends Chin is because Wittman is also the trickster Monkey King. His name, Sun Wu Kong, means "Aware of Emptiness," which allows him to be free of the subjection of classification because he is aware of its emptiness (or nonreality). Perhaps because of this the Monkey King is able to go through seventy-two transformations. Likewise, Wittman's is an instable identity made up of multiple selves that arise to fit (and disrupt) the occasion. One example is his transformation into "a working stiff on his way to his paying job":

> He put on the suit that he had bought for five bucks at the Salvation Army— the Brooks Brothers three-piece navy-blue pinstripe of some dead business-man. Wittman's suited body and hairy head didn't go together. Nor did the green shirt and greener tie . . . match each other or the suit. . . . His appearance was an affront to anybody who looked at him, he hoped (44).

Thus armored, he gets himself fired from his job for creating a pornographic scene with a Barbie doll and a wind-up monkey.

Even his everyday appearance, a carnivalesque, postmodern motley of startling juxtapositions, suggests multiple meanings. He can be read as a "Chinatown Cowboy," a "Chinese Beatnik" Hamlet, a "hippy dippy" zen soldier, all at once.

This physical appearance also suggests the wide range of influences that make up the text and Asian American identity. Wittman's "trip" is always to be "aware of the run of his mind" by being conscious of how texts create cultural and personal worldviews. Texts can be literary, musical, cinematic, from ads, newspapers, cartoons, and so on. He connects texts to texts and texts to contexts (and what is a con/text but a "fake book"?). In Walt Whitmanesque style, Wittman figuratively sings a new "Song of Myself" by claiming an identity and subjectivity created by a wide variety of texts and contexts. But before doing so, Wittman must ask first: what has it meant to be Chinese American? The answer lies in American popular culture. Specifically, he condemns *"Flower Drum Song . . .* a bunch off A.J.A.s and 'Eurasians' playing weird Chinese"(23); Kerouac's poem with the line " 'twinkling little Chinese.' Refute 'little.' Gainsay 'twinkling.' A man does not twinkle. A man with balls is not little" (69); as well as "Hop Sing" and Charlie Chan (320). However, in order to go beyond mere disgust for stereotypes, Wittman needs the help of the narrator.

The Narrator—Androgynous Hybridity

The narrator helps Wittman reach the second question, which puts him in the position of the questioning subject and not the subject in question. The question is: what is the hegemony that creates such representations of Chinese Americans? Or, how is racist Euramerican culture constructed? To answer this, collaboration is needed between Wittman and the anonymous omniscient narrator who are so much alike in voice and concerns that it is often difficult to tell them apart.[8] Indeed, even if Kingston has identified the narrator as "a Chinese American woman, . . . Kwan Yin (the Goddess of Mercy)" and Kingston herself, the voice is generally impossible to distinguish from Wittman's (Ling 1990, 150). The plural female narrator and Wittman (a plural male himself) have the same energetically mischievous, mocking, and often ironic tone:

> "Conservative like F.O.B.? Like Fresh Off the Boat?" He insulted her with translation; she was so banana, she needed a translation. "Conservative like engineering major from Fresno with a slide rule on his belt? Like dental student from Stockton? . . . But I'm an artist, an artist of all the Far Out West. Feh-see-no. Soo-dock-dun," he said, like an old Chinese guy bopping out a list poem (19).

Wittman's quotations and first-person thoughts sound just like the narrator's third-person statements. This is no accident; as Ling says, "Kingston, skilled in ambivalence and paradox is always crossing boundaries" (152). Likewise, Wittman and the plural female narrator cross each other's identity boundaries to form an androgynous hybrid. This community of selves provides a complete voice and thought able to critique the American system from multiple angles.

The plural female narrator—a Chinese American, Kwan Yin, and Kingston herself—is simultaneously general and specific, historical and immortal, limited and unlimited in scope and knowledge. The narrator needs this kind of complexity to parallel the contradictory energies of Wittman, who is also Chin, the Monkey King, and the artistic men in Kingston's family (Ling 1990, 149). Pairing them creates a balance of power between male and female and other categories as well. For instance, the high and low are brought together and given equal power in the pairing of Kwan Yin and the Monkey King. Kwan Yin is the goddess of compassion and one of the most highly evolved and unselfish of beings. As a trickster, the Monkey King is subversive, primitive and one of the most selfish of all beings. By having them speak in one nearly indistinguishable voice, the reader is made to realize that these two powers may be like the upper and lower parts of the same body or the same culture.[9]

What Kingston seems to be suggesting in this pairing is that compassion and subversion both spring from the same human drive for freedom. We have a deep yearning to experience the world without the boundaries imposed by classificatory systems. Hierarchy and individualism blind us to the fact that we are all equally important and interdependent for survival. The compassion and subversion, the high and low that Kwan Yin and Monkey represent, cut through illusions generated by the American system that have caused divisions between Asian Americans. Believing illusions like beauty is only blue-eyed and blond creates self-hatred and shame, not a strong community. Going beyond illusions is possible only with the combination of compassion and subversion characteristic of the plural narrator and Wittman.

Only through male and female collaboration can the work of deconstructing the racism of American culture begin. And only at this point can the last question be raised.

Carnivalesque Events—Converging and Emerging Theater of Identity

The last question is: fully aware of the historical and present situation, how might Chinese Americans create themselves? The answer lies in the hybrid narrator investigating scenes of carnivalesque hybridization and their aftermaths. The first scene, Lance Kaniyama's party, foreshadows the second event, Wittman's production of Chinese American theater.

Not surprisingly, one of the main themes that runs through this party is the crossing of boundaries. The narrator comments on "that trip where the margins between human beings, and between human beings and other creatures, disappear" and about "things that cross over" from "hallucination or a story or on another planet or in a thought or dream . . . into the real world" (88, 104). The party is a dizzying combination of different worlds or different "trips" that Wittman is able to cross into and cross out of, at will. He discovers people tripping out on drugs, health food, storytelling, war, and more. However, what Wittman absolutely cannot tolerate is Lance's mixing of business and party. Wittman challenges his best friend to a fight and brings in war, another opposing principle to party. He does so mainly because (as the narrator comments): "The best parties end in a free-for-all," and perhaps because in the traditional story, the Monkey King goes "off to war and party" (115, 138). This action is inspired partly by Lance's earlier party surprise attack: a full-blast stereo reconstruction of World War II.

This conjunction of party and war allows Lance and Wittman to confront hostile tensions between Japanese Americans and Chinese Americans. Wittman tells Lance:

> You A.J.A.s are really good at belonging . . . .That's why they locked you up, man. They don't like you taking over the dances and getting elected Most Popular. (While we Chinese-Americans are sweating Most Likely to Succeed, and don't spend money on clothes, or on anything.) (118).

This confrontation further allows the two friends to become closer friends. Here Kingston confirms what many American Third World feminists argue—that confrontation over differences is the first step in building group unity and resisting the masks of stereotypes. Only then can the project of self-representation begin.[10]

The second part of this scene begins in the next chapter and forms a bridge between the two main carnivalesque events. It is during the party's aftermath that Wittman describes his vision of Chinese American theater. He presents the spirit of this theater as a carnivalesque "fat dancer [who] has unbound feet and unbound tits and unbound hair. She busts through stereotypes" (147). He wants his theater to offer freedom in an aesthetic that "busts through" western standards of beauty and embraces the beauty, sexuality, and humanity of all marginalized people.

The second major carnivalesque event is the performance of Wittman's theater of "spontaneity," hybridity, and community, where "everyone came" bringing "chicken scraps and dog scraps" of "what a Chinese-American is made up of" (277). The play appropriately opens on halloween night, the carnivalesque time when the boundaries disappear between worlds, and the humanscape becomes a "world upside down" where children rule and the marginalized become centrally represented in the costumes of the revelers. Wittman's Chinese American theater is a combination of freak show, vaudeville, and improvised drama involving traditional Chinese characters and historical Chinese Americans. The climax of this play echoes the earlier party that unified party and war. This time there is an even greater spectacle of fireworks where "Night mirages filled the windows, reflecting and magnifying—a city at war and carnival" (301). And most powerful is the narrator's reading of a long list of Chinese stereotypes, while Wittman simultaneously erases these with Chinese fireworks: the traditional sound of war and celebration.

Constructing identity and community is like a perpetual artwork in progress. The narrator tells us that Wittman finds out "that one big bang-up show has to be followed up. . . . He was defining a community. . . . Community is not built once-and-for-all; people have to imagine, practice, and re-create it" (306). Interestingly, although this last chapter is called "One-Man Show," by this time Wittman has been transformed from the western styled, isolated artist to a community artist. Trinh T. Minh-ha sees the latter as a Third World form of artist, an artist who functions as "a neighborhood scribe" and "Inspirer inspired by his people" (13). In other words, an artist who can never separate art and identity from community.[11]

So back to the final question: how shall Chinese Americans construct their own identities? *Tripmaster Monkey* suggests keeping all options open, artistic traditions alive, and "writ[ing] the play ahead of them to include everyone and everything" (277). It means that Chinese Americans should theorize and create unity for their dynamic, heterogeneous community. For the individual it means developing a self that is an expression of the community and is a community of selves able to work within, and yet able to question the larger American community. In the end, *Tripmaster Monkey* says that being Chinese American requires being a tripmaster/trickster—one who is able to transform self and world, to transgress and trip through worlds, and to seek to go further than what a *Big Aiiieeeee!*, or Chinese, or Euramerican culture have offered.

Endnotes

1. The editors of *Aiiieeeee!* reject most Chinese American woman writers as well as men sympathetic to feminism as "fake." Read Chin's "Come all Ye Asian American writers of the Real and Fake" in *The Big Aiiieeeee!* (New York: Meridian Press, 1991) 1-92.

2. The Chinese classics Chin names as the foundation of the "real" Asian American literary tradition are Lo Kuan Chung's *Romance of the Three Kingdoms*, Shi Na'an's *The Water Margin*, and Wu Cheng-En's *Journey to the West (Monkey)*. Interestingly, all of these play a big role in *Tripmaster Monkey* and yet the book was still attacked by the *Big Aiiieeeee!* editors.

3. Or more precisely, the plural systems of culture, economics, politics, etc. Kingston is also simultaneously critiquing the treatment of the lumpenproletariat as well.

4. Since American forms of classification have been directly derivative of European models, Stallybrass and White's ideas are still highly applicable for this discussion.

5. For more information, See Stallybrass and White (1986); Jo Humphrey's *Monkey King: A Celestial Heritage* (all publication information undisclosed); and Mackerras (1983).
6. Arnold Krupat's *Voice in the Margin* (Berkeley: University of California Press, 1989), has been highly influential on my views of modernism.
7. I must give credit to Gayatri Spivak who first said that the question is not "what is woman?" but "what is man that the itinerary of his desire creates such a text?" In *The Post-Colonial Critic*, Sarah Harasym, ed. (New York: Routledge, 1990), 42. I see Kingston as making a similar shift in her representation of Asian Americans and the hegemony.
8. In fact, many reviewers have missed the distinction between Wittman and the narrator. See Herbert Gold's "Far-Out West," *Chicago Tribune*—Books, Apr. 16, 1989: 1, 10; Anne Tyler's "Manic Monologue," *The New Republic*, 200 (16), Apr. 17, 1989: 44-6; LeAnne Schreiber, "The Big, Big Show of Wittman Ah Sing," *New York Times Book Review*, Apr. 23, 1989: 9.
9. This goes back to Stallybrass and White's (1986) analysis of hierarchy.
10. These ideas run throughout Gloria Anzaldua's *Making Face, Making Soul Haciendo Caras* (San Francisco: Aunt Lute Foundation, 1990). I was especially influenced by Anzaldua's introduction (xv-xxviii) and Lynet Uttal's "Nods that Silence" (317-320).

References

Babcock, B. 1985. " 'A Tolerated Margin of Mess': The Trickster and His Tales Reconsidered." In Andrew Wiget (ed.), *Critical Essays on Native American Literature*. Boston: Hall: 153-185.

Chin, Frank, Jeffery Chan, Lawson Inada, and Shawn Wong, eds. 1974. *Aiiieeeee! An Anthology of Asian American Writers*. Washington, D.C.: Howard University Press. Reprint, 1983, Penguin.

———. 1991. *The Big Aiiieeeee!* New York: Meridian Press.

Douglas, Mary Tew. 1966. *Purity and Danger: An Analysis of Concepts of Pollution and Taboo*. New York: Praeger. Reprint, 1989. London: Ark Paperbacks.

Hutcheon, L. 1989. "Beginning to Theorize Postmodernism." *Textual Practice* 1 (1): 1031.

Kingston, Maxine Hong. 1989. *Tripmaster Monkey: His Fake Book*. New York: Knopf.

Ling, Amy. 1990. *Between Worlds: Women Writers of Chinese Ancestry*. New York: Pergamon Press.

Mackerras, Colin, ed. 1983. *Chinese Theater: From its Origins to the Present Day*. Honolulu: University of Hawaii Press.

Stallybrass Peter, and Allon White. 1986. *The Politics and Poetics of Transgression*. Ithaca, New York: Cornell University Press.

Trinh, T. Minh-ha. 1989. *Woman, Native, Other: Writing Postcoloniality and Feminism*. Bloomington: Indiana University Press.

Wong, Yen Lu. 1976. "Chinese American Theatre." *Drama Review* 20 (2): 13-18.

Chapter Fifteen

The Margins at the Center, the Center at the Margins: Acknowledging the Diversity of Asian American Poetry

David Mura

You see, whites want black artists to mostly deliver something as if it were the official version of the black experience. But the vocabulary won't hold it, simply. No true account really of black life can be held, can be contained in the American vocabulary. As it is, the only way that you can deal with it is by doing great violence to the assumptions on which the vocabulary is based. But they won't let you do that. And when you go along, you find yourself very quickly painted into a corner; you've written yourself into a corner.
—James Baldwin, *James Baldwin: The Legacy*

For any poet, the act of writing involves a struggle between the past of the language and the present, between the social and the individual, the general and the particular. In certain periods, there may be more emphasis on tradition and continuity; at others, on the disjunctive and the new. For each poet, the dialectics of this struggle are obviously affected both by the poet's training and by the poet's life experience—for instance, how widely she has traversed across class lines or, in our society, racial lines. The latter demarcation brings us to the dilemma James Baldwin alluded to when he remarked, "No true account really of black life can be held, can be contained in the American vocabulary."[1] Any poet who wants to describe that experience must somehow violate the accepted practice of the language, must bring into the language an alien vocabulary and syntax, rhythms that disrupt, images which jar, ideas which require a totally new relationship to the language and the reality it contains.

The same dilemma holds true for Asian American poets. But how does this general dilemma affect our reading of particular Asian American poets? How can we remain aware of social exigencies and group experience and still honor a particular poet's individual vision and language? Unfortunately, certain critics, influenced perhaps by an ethnic studies model, tend to view Asian American poetry solely from a social/historical model and they often insist that it delineate a representative reality or experience. For example, in the introduction to *Forbidden Stitch*, Mayumi Tsutakawa writes that she and co-editor Shirley Geok-lin Lim "had to bypass some manuscripts reflecting experimental forms, some by very young writers, and some which did not carry a recognizable Asian voice."[2] Why this prejudice against experimental poetics? How do we decide what is a "recognizable Asian voice" and that this voice must somehow subscribe to certain aesthetic assumptions?

Such models and thinking reduce the complexity of language and our experience; they are also inimical to the singularity of poets, their ability to escape categorization, to entangle us in contradiction, and to discover a language which moves us beyond the languages we have been using. To recognize the singularity of a particular poet does not mean that certain social experiences are not shared; certainly Baldwin presumes this when he speaks of a black writer's struggle to describe black life, when he links racism with the very constructions of our language. Likewise, the issues of race are very much present in Asian American poets. But it is a mistake for critics or readers to insist that those issues be investigated within a prescribed set of linguistic codes, particularly one which privileges either the notion of presence and some socially constructed ideal of the "typical" speaking voice, or the assumptions of realism or traditional narrative. It is a mistake to look for poetry as a mere tool to illustrate certain historical experiences or events which are deemed essential to a social/historical understanding of a particular ethnic group.

I am not arguing here against the necessity of attempting to define or delineate key historical experiences or events; I don't want to deconstruct history or meaning into mere language games or nihilistic illusions. I am arguing that poetry functions as more than a mere illustration of social experience; oftentimes, the relationship between a poetic text and such experience may be more wayward and contradictory than a realistic representation. We need to realize that the way we speak or write of history or society are linguistic constructs, with their own limitations. At the same time, there is a real history and a real social experience which always eludes articulation. Poetry, by expanding our articulation of experience, provides us with a more complex view of experience. It makes us aware of the inadequacies of previous articulations; it challenges us to investigate our experiences more deeply than before.

What does all this mean on a practical level? It means that in order to understand Asian American poetry, we need to fight against reductive or prescriptive tendencies, against urges to simplify the field. A gross example, of course, is *The Big Aiiieeeee!,* where the only two contemporary Asian American poets presented are Lawson Inada and Wing Tek Lum. Another example is a syllabus from a current Asian American Studies course at a major university where the three poetry books taught were Wing Tek Lum, Eric Chock, and Juliet S. Kono, all poets from Hawaii. I don't want to go into here whatever political considerations went into the choosing of these poets, nor do I want to go into the individual merits of each of these poets. I do want to point out that all these poets share a similar aesthetic approach to language—a belief in some "typical" speaking voice; a unified lyrical "I"; a straight declamatory syntax; an absence of traditional forms of the Anglo-American tradition; a refusal to use certain levels of diction, such as words that might be deemed too Latinate or intellectual. When these poets do use narrative, the narratives generally do not question their premises or their ability to capture experience. There is a tendency to look at language as a clear vessel which carries a clear and true story.

My outline of these aesthetic assumptions is rather truncated, and my intention is not to invalidate these assumptions (although I do want to complicate them). I have seen the ways certain white critics or poets have characterized the aesthetics of poets of color as naive; in this way, postmodernist deconstructions of narrative or the lyric "I" are often used as tools to silence or marginalize unruly voices, to keep the disenfranchised from speaking. I am very aware that there are other orthodoxies outside that of the Ethnic Studies departments, orthodoxies which are bent on destroying the attempt to make Asian American Studies or African American Studies or Chicano Studies an integral part of the university curriculum. Nor do I harbor the illusion that wherever we stand we can escape the urge to create an orthodoxy, to designate a canon. But if such urges are always present, we must constantly be on guard and strive to complicate and question our formulations.

One way of doing this would be to understand that Asian American poets and the Asian American poetic text function in many different worlds. There is the world of Asian American Studies, and the various schools or groups or individuals within that world. There is the world of the MFA departments and the English departments. There are the worlds of arts organizations, in various regions of the country, from Kearny Street (San Francisco) to the Academy of American Poets (New York) to the Loft (Minnesota) to the Guild Complex (Chicago) to local writing groups. There is the world of the small presses and the New York publishing houses, of "establishment" journals like *The New Yorker* and *APR,* of regional journals like *Bamboo Ridge* or *Zzzzyva,* of avant-garde journals like *Sulphur,* of community journals like the *Rafu Shimpo* or *A* or *Asian Week.* There are the community centers or colleges or high schools or churches where poets read. There are the various worlds of the media, from a Bill Moyers PBS special to the local university radio. There are the various ways the works of these poets enter other countries, from Hong Kong to Singapore to England to Iran. Each of these worlds has its own orthodoxies and canons, its own aesthetics. One can put a particular work or a particular poet in each of these different contexts, and they are both the same and somehow different. In a certain setting, they may seem part of the dominant group, in others they may appear marginal or irrelevant.

One problem is that often people set up binary oppositions in describing the world of American literature or Asian American literature. There are the "ins" and the "outs," the "real" and the "fake," the academics and the street, etc. This is not to say that literary or cultural power in this country is equally distributed; certain poets do seem to achieve more recognition than others. Nor do I want to slip into a place where a liberal pluralism reigns, where we don't discriminate or judge but simply "celebrate" diversity. But our investigations of the field, our anthologies, our course lists, should try to cast as wide a net as possible. I am also cautioning against the tendency for convenient labels to get in the way of a real study of the poetry. At a panel on Asian American poetics in New York, John Yau recently remarked that on the West Coast or in Asian American Studies departments, he is rarely considered an Asian American poet and his work is seldom taught. At the same time, when he tells New York white literary friends that he's an Asian American poet, they tell him, "No you're not. You're a New York neo-surrealist." Through such insistence on restrictive categorizing and a singular identity, some readers refuse to recognize the complex way language and identities function.

A more adequate approach to Asian American poetry would honor the individual idiosyncrasies of particular poets. At the same time, we should look both for jarring contrasts and hidden similarities between a particular poet and other poets. We also need to put that poet not just in the context of Asian American literature but also in the context of American literature and world literature. This is a tall order, requiring a wideranging background and a willingness to question accepted categories.

But often the work of certain writers seems to demand that such multiple perspectives become involved in any reading of their work. Take for instance the work of Theresa Hak Kyung Cha, a poet who has, until recently, been generally neglected both by Asian American Studies and by mainstream literary institutions.[3] In many ways, Cha's *Dictee* resists categorization through its mixture of art forms, its range of languages, its movement between genres, its movements to the bounds of intelligibility. It is a work that is intellectual and post-modernist, and therefore, assumes a highly literate and, implicitly, elitist audience. Yet hers is a deeply committed political work, not eschewing the language of agit prop but skirting it, placing it within a complicating context. It attempts to retrieve history at the same time it questions the whole concept of history.

In the work of Cha or Trinh T. Minh-ha or Walter Lew's performance piece, *The Movieteller*, elements which might be labeled "poetry" do appear, but the works as a whole resist such isolation and demand that whatever looks like poetry in the work cannot be ripped from the work. Such writers give testament to the breakdown of genres alluded to by Roland Barthes in "From Work to Text": ". . . the Text does not stop at (good) Literature; it cannot be contained in a hierarchy, even in a simple division of genres. What constitutes the Text is, on the contrary (or precisely), its subversive force in respect of the old classifications."[4] Writers like Cha problematize the whole notion of a traditionally accepted set of linguistic rules which are designated—by whom? for whom?—as constituting poetry.

Some of these maneuvers can be seen as analogous to, say, the work of the Language Poets. This school of contemporary poetry is characterized by elliptical texts which question referentiality and narrative and which explore the process of signification rather than language's use as, for example, description or poetry's tradition as a personal, lyric utterance. One significant difference, though, is that the work of Cha always assumes history and actual events; she both acknowledges the need and uses of narrative at the same time that she questions narrative and the fictionality of any purportedly objective language of history. She will also employ direct speech of the first person; and while she places such language in a context unfamiliar to traditional lyric utterances, she is unwilling to let theoretical strictures or questions cut off the urgency and necessity of such language. In one section the "I" addresses her mother:

You traveled to this village on the train with your father. You are dressed in western clothes. At the station the villagers innocently stare at you and some follow you, especially the children. It is Sunday.

You are the first woman teacher to come to this village in six years. A male teacher greets you, he addresses you in Japanese. Japan had already occupied Korea and is attempting the occupation of China. Even in the small village the signs of their presence is felt by the Japanese language that is being spoke. The Japanese flag is hanging at the entry of the office. And below it, the educational message of the Meiji emperor framed in purple cloth. It is read at special functions by the principal of the school to all students.

The teachers speak in Japanese to each other. You are Korean. All the teachers are Korean. You are assigned to teach the first grade. Fifty children to your class. They must speak their name in Korean as well as how they should be called in Japanese. You speak to them in Korean since they are too young yet to speak Japanese.[5]

Two pages after this passage are two Chinese characters, then more text, a photo, the words "URANIA" and "ASTRONOMY" in capital letters; a chart which looks like accupressure or acupuncture points in Chinese characters. More text. Then a poem in both French and English on opposite pages:

I heard the swans
in the rain I heard
I listened to the spoken true
or not true
not possible to say.

There. Years after
no more possible to distinguish the rain.
No more. Which was heard.
Swans. Speech. Memory. Already said.
Will just say. Having just said.
Remembered. Not certain.
Heard, not at all.[6]

The passage questions the ability of language to encompass or describe experience, to delineate truth. It alludes to the distortions of memory, the instability of language. It marks a spot of both bewilderment and freedom, and forces us to read or re-read in memory the address to the Mother in a different way. In this re-reading the reader may see the arbitrariness of language, how there is no "natural" way of speaking, how the decisions to use a certain language are formed by political forces and have political ramifications. A code is imposed. Of words. Behavior. Belief. A code is questioned. Of words. Behavior. Belief. What is missing becomes as important as what is mentioned—"I heard the signs. Remnants. Missing."[7]

In many ways, Cha's work presents a challenge to the accessibility of a poet like Janice Mirikitani. And yet, there is language in Cha as forthright and clear as any in Mirikitani: "It is the husband who touches. Not as husband. He touches her as he touches all the others. But he touches her with his rank. By his knowledge of his own rank. By the claim of his rank."[8] Of course, even here, in a way that is generally absent from Mirikitani's work, there's a pointing to how the use of language determines behavior. But juxtaposing the two writers reveals an unexpected similarity and, at the same time, prompts a string of questions concerning their differences. Does the language of Cha resist certain open statements that are present in Mirikitani's work? Does it assume certain questions about language Mirikitani does not? Does it make us aware of a certain sentimentality in Mirikitani's work? Does Mirikitani's work force us to see the intellectual background of Cha's poetry as not only a plus but as problematic? Does it make Cha's use of language seem to be sometimes evasive? Or lacking in feeling? Just how are feelings conveyed in language? Mirikitani's work can be read publicly at large gatherings to a general audience, has been accompanied by jazz, has made her a public figure. Even if Cha were still alive, it's hard to see her doing readings like Mirikitani's. Does Mirikitani's poetry serve certain social functions that Cha's does not?

Obviously, we can set up various contexts and hierarchies where each of these poets comes out on top. Is this useful or necessary? How?

Beyond comparisons with a writer like Mirikitani, how should we place the work of an "experimental" writer like Cha within the context of contemporary American poetry or world literature? What do these various contexts say about the way we read contemporary Asian American poetry?

As evidenced by the plethora of new talented writers of color, we are now undergoing a vast shift within American culture. Clearly, mainstream notions of a traditional Anglo-American canon are being challenged. And yet, I think it's not quite clear how this challenge is being presented by individual poets. On the one hand there are now strong poets of color whose relationship to traditional Anglo-American poetics is fairly minimal. The work of such poets does not make use of traditional European forms; it also does not necessarily allude to predecessors within the Anglo-American tradition in terms of imagery or language or even in the use of the free verse line. Poets like Joy Harjo or Leslie Marmon Silko not only eschew traditional meters or stanzas but many of the current conventions of contemporary American poetry, which still tends to rely on the structure of the poetic line, a singular, identifiable first person, and a division between poetry and prose. Harjo and Silko, then, are quite different from a more traditional poet like Louise Erdrich, whose work resembles that of white mainstream contemporaries and alludes specifically to a Christian tradition of mythology rather than the strictly Native American tradition of Harjo's and Silko's work. Similarly, a more resolutely colloquial poet like African American Lucille Clifton is quite different from Rita Dove, where the rhythms and usages of African American speech tend to be a bit more muted and adapted to a more recognizably "literary" language. The same sort of differences arise when we compare the more "street" Jimmy Santiago Baca with Gary Soto or Alberto Rios, or the more performance-oriented poetry of Jessica Hagedorn or Nellie Wong with the poetry of Marilyn Chin or Garrett Hongo, which, though at times quite colloquial, seems more rooted in literary traditions both of the West and the East.

Within the world of the MFA writing programs, poets such as Harjo or Baca or Clifton were seen, until recently, as marginal; they were somehow examples of ethnic poets who did not attain the rigorous literary standards and craft of those who write more directly out of the Anglo/ American tradition. But this state of affairs is quickly changing. The growth of multiculturalism has placed poets like Harjo, Baca or Clifton at the forefront of today's cultural changes; and their work constitutes a major challenge to any belief in a unitary set of literary standards. Such poets are also helping to give poetry an audience that goes beyond the academy, one rooted in ethnic communities. In short, they represent a movement towards decentralization of literary power within the culture.

On the other hand, there are poets of color who have a more direct relationship to the Anglo-American tradition. But in part because the Anglo-American tradition has functioned and continues to function as a tool of exclusion, these poets of color are sometimes criticized for their relationship to the tradition, particularly by those in Ethnic Studies departments or those who feel themselves to be outside the "academy." Thus, an Erdrich or Dove or Soto or Hongo may be viewed as somehow having sold out to the academy, as having shed part of their perspective as poets of color. When such poets become associated with a mainstream critic or poet—often, the accounts of such associations are apocryphal— this is seen as further proof that something is suspect with their poetics. Thus, Helen Vendler's championing of Rita Dove has engendered a certain negative fallout within Dove's own community. I've heard poets from Hawaii condemn Garrett Hongo for dedicating too many poems to white poets. In such a climate, political positions are quickly elided into ad hominem attacks, and keep people from actually investigating an individual poet's work with an open mind.

Underlying such critiques is a basic assumption that any evidence of the Anglo-American tradition or European traditional forms in one's work invariably means one must adapt a conservative political position. It is, of course, understandable why some make this assumption. After all, the New Formalists, the leading proponents of traditional forms in contemporary poetry, generally take political positions that are fairly conservative. But the New Formalists, as do some critics of color, also hold a rather narrow and distorted viewpoint of the Anglo/American or European tradition. The New Formalists tend to posit a view of tradition which emphasizes a poet like Herbert rather than Blake; they ignore the radical stances of Shelley, or Wordsworth's relationship to the French revolution. They fail to mention formalist poets like Villon or Brecht or Pasolini or Langston Hughes or Gwendolyn Brooks. Moreover, the introduction of new poets and new critical insights into the tradition changes the ways we read older poets. For instance, after I read the essay of Edward Said that views Yeats as a post-colonial poet (rather than as an English poet), this seemingly conservative modernist took on a slightly different caste, one whose purpose of decolonization and nationalism can help instruct contemporary poets of color in a quite different way than he instructed poets such as Berryman or Lowell.[9] Because of Said's essay, I suddenly saw Yeats's obsession with history and his political involvement in the context of the history and literature of the Third World. I realized an odd link could be made between Yeats and Latin American figures like Paz, Fuentes, Vargas Llosa or Neruda, whom I viewed as embodying a very different role for the writer than that available in the MFA programs, a role which saw a conjunction between politics and literature and which viewed the writer as involved with civic concerns rather than simply as an alienated and isolated individual. On a personal level, I saw how Yeats could serve as an example for my building my own "new pantheon of heroes, myths, and religions"—not because of his particular politics but because he could be understood as writing out of a position of marginality, within the history of imperialism. After all, the Irish population was not that much larger than that of Japanese Americans. If Yeats could make mythical figures of Lady Gregory or her son or Maude Gonne, I could fashion a new mythos out of such figures as Min Yasui and Gordon Hirabayashi in my own community.

As Trinh T. Minh-ha has pointed out, there are margins within the center and centers within the margins.[10] We must be careful not to construct monoliths where they do not exist. Within the context of contemporary poetry, it's clear that Adrienne Rich both traveled far from her earlier poetical alignment with Frost and Auden and yet, at the same, is still more grounded in the Anglo-American tradition than a poet like Nellie Wong or Jessica Hagedorn. But would these Asian American feminist poets view Rich's work as conservative or regressive? I think not.

Yet in the world of Asian American literature, the use of binary critical oppositions such as "real" and "fake," ethnic and non-ethnic, marginal or mainstream, Asian or Western, often obscures the multiple sources for the work of Asian American poets who are sometimes deemed more "mainstream." Marilyn Chin finds her sources in the lines of both Donald Justice and Tu Fu; Garrett Hongo's work must be viewed against the palimpsest of Wordsworth and Malvern (through Derek Walcott) and of the *haibun* of Basho. At the same time, Chin works riffs off of American pop culture, and Hongo off of Hawaiian pigeon and African American speech. Indeed, Chin's and Hongo's linguistic fluidity and multiplicity, and the dazzling array of registers in their work, challenge the view of any central tradition, any singular or isolated view of culture. Such work attests to a mixed or hybrid cultural history and experience; it embodies a postmodern sense of language, where dictions and dialects mix and influence each other.

It is just such mixtures which a more binary approach cannot explain or countenance. There has been a tendency, for instance, to associate the work of Li-Young Lee with the academy, a tendency caused more by social associations—whom the poet is perceived to be friends with—than the poetry itself. Lee's poetry is certainly influenced by a Western metaphysical tradition, and by figures such as Heidegger or Rilke. Yet in a poem like "The Furious Versions," Lee's vision of history and human suffering takes into account a colonialist history completely at odds with contemporary American reality or with a high modernist vision.[11] His poetics has a rather tangential relationship both to the Anglo/American line and to the American free verse line; moreover, his use of the line is quite different, for instance, than Hongo's or Chin's. While at times, one can detect the influence of Whitman and Biblical prose in Lee's work, there is a fluidity to the movement of the poems, as well as a fight against syntactical regularity or clarity, that seems in the end very much at odds with the contemporary American voice. In its straining against the bounds of intelligibility and the visible, against a socially constructed language, Lee's work has certain affinities to, say, Beckett's. But Lee's sensibility is entirely different, partly perhaps because of its roots in Li Po and Tu Fu and the Chinese language. Lee's work, then, points to a margin in western literary practices which finds its source in Asian traditions.

Such an observation asks us to reconsider our notions of what we mean by traditional and experimental. As I mentioned above, there is a tendency to view an "experimental" writer like Theresa Cha as being even more elitist than poets like Hongo or Chin, much less Mirikitani or Wong. The so-called experimental writings of Cha or Mei-mei Berssenbrugge or John Yau are seen as insufficiently "ethnic" or "Asian." Yet, in the work of "experimental" poets like Kimiko Hahn or Walter Lew, the experimental or postmodern viewpoint, as a Western invention, becomes suspect. For it is precisely the importation of Japanese or Korean cultural practices that makes the work of Hahn or Lew seem so radical and new, such a break from the norm. In "Izu Dancer," Hahn centers the poem on the process of reading and translating a story of Kawabata; among other things, the poem explores the roots of Japanese characters, and thus points to a visual nature of the symbolic that is generally absent in the western tradition.[12] Lew's performance piece, "The Movieteller," revives and parodies the Korean tradition of the *pyonsa*, the narrator of silent movies. These narrators were an important vehicle for Koreans, colonized by the Japanese, to express political dissent through the subterfuge of allegory. Lew uses the tradition of the *pyonsa* in conjunction with Korean and Western film, poetry, music, and dance. In the piece, which is a tour de force of technical reproduction and postmodern intelligence, he combines multiple screen images from three films: a color version of a traditional Korean tale about a young woman; a black and white grade-B fifties science fiction film about a mermaid; and a Submariner cartoon. Through his narration, Lew leaps from film to film, often employing metaphoric connections. At the same time, other images, such as footage of demonstrations by Korean students, show up on video or slides, and become part of the narration. In both his poems and performance, Lew insists that his sources come from the radical or marginal spaces of Korean culture, that his work attempts to extend the linguistic possibilities in English through an examination, for instance, of the Korean modernists.

On a more general level, one might argue that the closer Asian American poets move to certain Asian traditions, the more unrecognizable and indigestible, at least from an American standpoint, they become. In this way, a poet like Mirikitani, with her aesthetics deriving from contemporary feminism, the Beats and the protest poems of the sixties, seems much more mainstream than Kimiko Hahn. And Yau's work and critical essays, with their search for alternative traditions and their critique of the Western notion of a centered "ego" or "I," may place him at a further remove from the American mainstream than the work of a poet like Nellie Wong.

What I am arguing is that Asian American poets need to be read against the backdrop of a multiplicity of contexts. In doing so, we need to understand how such contexts affect our reading and evaluations of these poets, how they let us see certain things in a poet's work while allowing us to ignore others. A poet like Garrett Hongo, when placed in the context of the *Morrow Anthology of Younger Poets*, can seem more mainstream than he actually is. But if you place Hongo's work within the context of other poets of color, even less "academic" ones such as Baca or Harjo, the work finds a place that a white poet like Edward Hirsch or Charles Wright does not. And if you place Hongo's work within the history of colonialism or race, or if you place him within the context of Third World writers like

Achebe, Jamaica Kincaid, Garcia Marquez, Aimee Cesaire, Derek Walcott or Pablo Neruda, you are able to see the strength and validity of his historical and political vision in contrast to that of his white contemporaries like Dana Gioa or Jorie Graham. Hongo's Volcano, Hawaii has more connections with Marquez's Macando than it does with Linda Gregg's Greek island or Richard Hugo's Montana. Similarly, Hongo's L.A. is more like the multicultural melange of Jessica Hagedorn's New York or Rushdie's or Kureshi's London than the Boston of Robert Lowell, the New York of John Ashberry, or the Detroit of Philip Levine.

We need then to recognize a real diversity in our reading practices, a reading which acknowledges our living within a multicultural and postmodern world, where the centers are illusory—though occasionally useful—fictions, and where margins exist everywhere we look. We need to see that poetry is indeed "equipment for living," but that living is a more complex task than our cultural constructions would make out. We need to see that our reading of Asian American literature, and indeed Asian America itself, must constantly question notions of the typical or the real or the authentic or the correct. To repeat, I am not arguing that we should eschew political questioning or critiques. But such questioning and critiques must start not from ideology or from formulations of the ideal or general, but from an assessment of what actually exists, from the contradictions and particulars of reality, from as wide and multiple a vision as we can possibly entertain. Such a sweep may make the whole field seem impossibly unwieldy, especially as we take in the increasing visibility of Asian Indian American poets and the poetry now just arising from the recent wave of immigration from Southeast Asia. But such a bewildering array of languages and realities and lives is what characterizes this moment in history, and if we are going to be adequate to contending with the problems of that moment, we must attempt to understand it in its totality, and not in simple, cookie-cutter parts. In this task, the irreducibility of poetic language, its ability to outbound and deconstruct our formulations, can keep us humble, flexible and aware, can make us pay attention more closely to the world.

Endnotes

1.   James Baldwin, "The Last Interview," in James Baldwin: The Legacy, ed. Quincy Troupe (New York: Simon and Schuster/Touchstone, 1989), 204.
2.   Tsutakawa, Mayumi, "Introduction," in *Forbidden Stitch: An Asian American Women's Anthology*, ed. Mayumi Tsutakawa and Shirley Geok-lin Lim (Corvallis, Oregon: Calyx, Books, 1989), 14.
3.   For all its radical departures, Cha's work is undergoing a recent wave of acceptance, both within Asian American Studies and in the world of post-modern

feminist studies, as witnessed by her recent inclusion in the seminal anthology, *Blasted Allegories: An Anthology of Writings by Contemporary Artists,* ed. Brian Wallis (New York: The New Museum of Contemporary Art and Cambridge: MIT Press, 1987).

4. Roland Barthes, *Image, Music, Text* (New York: Hill and Wang, 1977), 157.

5. Theresa Hak Kyung Cha, *Dictee* (New York: Tanam Press, 1982), 48-49.

6. Ibid., 66-67.

7. Ibid., 69.

8. Ibid., 112.

9. See Edward W. Said, *Nationalism, Colonialism and Literature: Yeats and Decolonization* (Lawrence Hill, Derry, Ireland: Field Day Theatre Company Limited, 1988).

10. Trinh T. Minh-ha, *When the Moon Waxes Red: Representation, Gender and Cultural Politics* (New York: Routledge, 1991), 16-17.

11. Li-Young Lee, *the city in which i love you* (Brockport, NY: Boa Editions, 1990), 2.

12. Kimiko Hahn, *Earshot* (New York: Hanging Loose Press, 1992).

Chapter Sixteen

The Representation of Asian American Poetry in *The Heath Anthology of American Literature*

George Uba

As an area of critical investigation, the "representation" of Asian American poetry in *The Heath Anthology of American Literature* affords several inviting paths to pursue. However, this essay does not propose to explicate the individual poems in the anthology or to analyze the poetic project each set of poems collectively represents. Nor shall it offer anything but the most cursory treatment of the respective poets or expatiate at length on those who—for whatever reasons—are excluded from the text. Instead, it seeks to examine the more primary issues of diversity, representation, and empowerment that the poetry selections raise. These are issues pertaining to canon, to literary anthologies as a species, and to the practical consequences of teaching Asian American poets in American literature classes. In addition, I want to hazard a new metaphor for the reception of Asian American poetry both in Ethnic Studies departments and in departments of literature.

First, some background for those unfamiliar with the *Heath Anthology*. The *Heath*, as it is called, is a groundbreaking anthology of American literature; first published in 1990 under the general editorship of Paul Lauter, it includes an ethnically diverse set of editors and contributing editors, many of them renowned in their various areas of scholarship.[1] In its commitment to introduce the writings of people of color into existing courses in American literature and in its determination to contest received notions of literature and canon, *The Heath Anthology* sets a new standard in its field.[2]

For these very reasons the *Heath* also has found itself at the center of controversy. It has been widely praised for its efforts to decanonize American literature, to promote diversity, and to inspire a profound reevaluation of traditional Eurocentric notions of literature. In this, it has participated in a much larger effort toward the same multicultural ends. The anthology also has been specially targeted for criticism by some reviewers, who sometimes willfully, sometimes ignorantly, reassert the priority of Western literary aesthetics.[3]

There are three contemporary Asian American poets included in *The Heath Anthology*, Volume 2 (Volume 1 stops at 1865)—Janice Mirikitani, Garrett Hongo, and Cathy Song—as well as a selection of poetry from immigrants detained at Angel Island. In addition, there are prose selections by Sui Sin Far, Younghill Kang, Carlos Bulosan, Hisaye Yamamoto, John Okada, and Maxine Hong Kingston. To convey some idea of how far-ranging the changes in the *Heath* are relative to other standard American literary anthologies, we may compare its selections in Asian American poetry, for example, to comparable offerings in the most commonly taught texts: McMichael's 1985 *American Literature* (Macmillan): none; the 1989 *Norton Anthology of American Literature*: Cathy Song; Perkins' 1990 *The American Tradition in Literature* (McGraw-Hill): none; the 1991 *Prentice Hall American Literature*: Lawson Inada; the 1987 *Harper American Literature* (which otherwise prides itself on its multicultural focus): none; the 1991 HBJ *Heritage of American Literature*: none. The Norton *New Worlds of Literature* includes a number of Asian Americans since it is predicated on the notion of ethnic American writing; for the same reason, though, it would enjoy at best only a supplementary rather than primary status in American literature classrooms.

Not only does the *Heath* include more Asian American literature than do other anthologies, but within publishing constraints it makes an effort to achieve a measure of diversity: Mirikitani emerges from and to some degree helps galvanize a tradition of political activism dating from the 1960s and retains strong ties to "protest and oral poetry" traditions of the same era.[4] Hongo serves as a sociohistorical chronicler who at once " 'searches for origins of various kinds' "[5] and investigates and helps dignify the "ordinary" lives of his fellow Asian Americans; and Song reveals strong ties to pictorial art and domestic experience. Authorial headnotes in the anthology and the *Instructor's Guide for the Heath Anthology* further contextualize the offerings: Mirikitani's tendency toward the "didactic"[6] is balanced by Hongo, who is "concerned as much with his craft as with his message" and who combines "the consciousness of the late twentieth-century ethnic nationalist with the early twentieth-century imagist's concern for the most precise, the most resonant image."[7] Both writers, in turn, are counterpointed by Song's Hawaii regionalism and by her primary concentration on private rather than public life.[8] The Angel Island poets, in contrast, are described as "non-professional" writers whose poems tend to "bemoan the writer's own situation" and whose "literary quality varies greatly" but who also perform the invaluable service of having "unconsciously introduced a new sensibility, a Chinese-American sensibility."[9]

Obviously, there remain gaps within this selection of Asian American poets. Where are the nationally respected Marilyn Chin and David Mura? Where are the avowed pioneering poets Lawson Inada, Nellie Wong, and Mitsuye Yamada? Or, for that matter, the pre-pioneering legends—Jose Garcia Villa and Carlos Bulosan? Where are Eric Chock, Carolyn Lau, Jeff Tagami, and Arthur Sze? Widely published and winners of numerous prestigious literary awards, these poets and others have earned equal rights to attendance in the anthologies of American literature. In all fairness it must be added that these are gaps of which the editors of the anthology are acutely aware. Nevertheless, among the three contemporary *Heath* poets a degree of overlap materializes when they are viewed against the broader canvas of Asian American poetry. This canvas would include, but is not limited to, the postmodern linguistic experiments of a Mei-mei Berssenbrugge or John Yau, the serious playfulness and keen urban wit of a Cyn Zarco or Jessica Hagedorn, and the Rilke-like intensities of a Li-Young Lee. As it happens, all three *Heath* poets give voice to the oppressed or the dispossessed, most often in tones of protest or elegy; all write from within a kind of representational poetics, which remains the dominant mode in Asian American poetry; all use English as their first language; all are three generations removed from the immigrant experience; and all are either from California or Hawaii. Furthermore, all are accessible as poets in the sense that each generally trusts the representational qualities of language and pursues a more or less unproblematized linear narrative. Each eschews linguistic play, self-reflexiveness, and other modes of poetic "difficulty." This hint of sameness among the three selected poets and the rich, untapped heterogeneity among so many of the unselected ones highlight the crucial difference between the terms "representation" and "diversity." In their introduction to their section on "Contemporary [Literature]: 1945 to the Present," the *Heath* editors assert that "In assembling writers of the 1980s and 1990s one cannot be comprehensive but representative."[10] As we have seen, this appears to have been the operating principle—only partially successful—upon which the selecting of Asian American poets took place. The editors go on to assert that "The danger is that this representational approach may appear to offer a miscellany, unified by little but the happenstance of the writers' dates of birth"[11] or, it might be added, by their "shared" physical traits.

I would contend, however, that in the context of literary anthologies the notion of "representative" becomes not the antithesis of the "comprehensive" but *the practical substitute* for it. In place of representativeness, then, it is more desirable to speak of diversity. And the danger is not that diverse writings may appear "to offer a miscellany"—but that they may fail to do so. The truer the spirit with which anthologies approach this idea of the miscellaneous or the diverse the better able they will be to re-examine and enlarge existing conceptions of Asian American poetry.

But it must be noted too that when the editors of the *Heath* speak of the "representative," they construe the term in a way that is different from and more complex than that which many teachers trained in, say, the traditional canon of American literature may conceive. For the former, the term "representative" is also a marker for absence, a signifier of the inevitable gaps in their selection process. Properly regarded, the poets included in the *Heath* alert us to all those that are not present there, as well as to all those absent from other, more traditional anthologies of American literature. At some level the *Heath* selections disturb us into the recognition of those poets who remain excluded rather than comfort us with those few that do not. The lesson of the *Heath*, then, is not the illusion of adequate representation but rather a stiff reminder of how adequate representation is a continuing illusion.

But while I believe that the editors impute these additional levels of meaning to the term "representative," teachers of American literature who may adopt the *Heath* in their age and survey courses are likely to receive the term, and hence the poetry, quite differently. Likely, they will be tempted to read these few "representative" writers as their entree into "knowing" and "evaluating" Asian American poetry rather than as an initial step in confronting what they don't yet know and have yet to learn. We must recall the historical context of reception for the *Heath*, i.e., that it appeared at just that moment when Asian American poetry had begun to enjoy the fruits of a truly national presence but nevertheless was still widely unsampled by professors of literature, and during just that historical period when the desire for an identifiable canon of multicultural writings had peaked. For these relative newcomers, the *Heath* poets are more likely to be seen as *representative* almost in the antiquated Arnoldian sense of literary "touchstones."

Exactly what is at stake when the term "representative" is construed in this second manner? The first and most obvious answer is that a limited number of writers become identified as *the* highwater marks of Asian

American poetry. Contributing to the problem is the paradoxical tendency in the departments of English and American literature to re-canonize rather than de-canonize American literature. This tendency may be due to a lack of awareness of the sheer numbers of writers available for consideration, but it is also inherent in the way Americans have traditionally sought to construct and receive a national literature. Writing in a recent issue of the MLA journal *Profession*, Arnold Rampersad goes even farther: "I regard canonization in itself as virtually instinctive; memory is surely the mother of all canons."[12] Perhaps. But hand in hand with recanonization will go the tendency to attach Asian American poetry to a continuous or master narrative of American literature.[13]

Clearly, something greater is at stake, then, than the repute of individual Asian American poets; the more insidious threat is that of the appropriation, absorption, assimilation, co-option of Asian American poetry itself. Practically speaking, to the degree that the selections in the *Heath* are received as representative and ultimately as canonical, Asian American poetry itself is threatened by assimilation into existing paradigms of American poetry. The marketplace pressures of the anthology industry contribute to this tendency by reducing the number of possible differences among texts of all sorts. It is easy to imagine a professor, versed in American literature and attached to a department of English, approaching Janice Mirikitani wholly in the context of traditional American protest poetry; of viewing Garrett Hongo as simply an Asian American variety of the "blue-collar" poet from Whitman to Philip Levine; of situating Cathy Song in the context of familiar domestic verse.[14] The issue goes beyond the reduction of a particular poet's work and beyond the indignity of noninclusion. It is a matter of Asian American poetry itself becoming a mere appendage—and by the publication evidence in anthologies a minor appendage—of a "mainstream" American literature. In the practical politics of the classroom, representation spells co-option.

Since the market pressures of the anthology industry contribute mightily to this tendency to trivialize varieties of literature, it is relevant to speak of Asian American poetry vis-a-vis Hispanic, African American, and American Indian poetry. Even if one resists the temptation to tally the number of poets of one ethnic group relative to another that gain inclusion in an anthology, one still need not shy away from the fact that any anthology necessarily reflects an implicit competition for limited publication space. It is, after all, part of the strategy of the anthology industry to divert attention from the necessary gaps in its fiction of inclusiveness, even to the point where the larger absences are lost sight of in the face of more immediate jostlings for position. Referring to the marginalization of language poets, Ron Silliman complains that experimental poetry is subjected to the "hegemonic strategy of divide and conquer via token incorporation."[15] That familiar refrain applies as well to Asian American poetry—when it comes to the practical politics of anthology-making.

While I am by no means prepared to concede that Asian American literature should be taught only through an Ethnic Studies department rather than an English or literature department, I will certainly agree that the problems of reception I have outlined are more likely to be avoided in the former than in the latter. On the other hand, a danger of another sort arises in the Ethnic Studies department if and when it is maintained that Asian American poets should be valorized according to their degree of accessibility or the ideological contents of their poems. To apply such criteria singlemindedly not only conjures distasteful images of censorship but actually annuls the variety of ways in which Asian American poetry successfully challenges dominant modes and achieves political expression.

Since the writings of Asian America—some of them—will be taught in literature departments anyway, the larger issue is actually this: how can we support and maintain the idea of a decanonical, or at least a perpetually renegotiable, Asian American literature while still maintaining the currency of such literature in the marketplace of the university? The answer is to start by reconstructing the way we receive literary anthologies themselves. Given a practical need for such anthologies, we must ask what we gain and what we lose by "representing" diverse literatures in such necessarily reduced forms. What existing problems do we address, and what new problems do we create? What, exactly, is the relationship between literary anthologies and canon formation? And how do we deter that relationship when it threatens to become fixed?

And beyond such reconstitution we also need a new paradigm that accommodates the fragmentary way in which varieties of literature, including Asian American, are increasingly received. In reconsidering her own earlier formulations on American literary history and in adapting from Gloria Anzaldua's *Borderlands/La Frontera*, Annette Kolodny has recently argued for the creation of a "frontier literary history" based not on geographic or chronological considerations but on successive intersectings—physical, cultural, linguistic, etc.—which necessarily invoke a plurality of cultural experiences.[16] Anzaldua uses borderlands or *fronteras* as negatives; she argues, however, for the congruent idea of "frontiers" when she urges the individual to "be a crossroads."[17] According to Kolodny's refiguration, we need to thematize the "frontier" as "a multiplicity of ongoing first encounters."[18]

Adapting Kolodny's idea for our own purposes, we may say that each anthology-inspired encounter with, say, an Asian American poet should be regarded not as the appropriating of an additional piece of a grand but amorphous puzzle but as the experiencing of another frontier that serves to remind us that no such overarching puzzle exists and that the body of literature under discussion remains situated on perpetually shifting ground. Moreover, it may serve to remind all who would teach the writings of Asian Americans that the cultural and linguistic intersectings of these literatures are not limited to the contacts between the non-Asian American and the Asian American but include multiple meetings within Asian America itself. A fourth-generation Chinese American and an immigrant Hmong have much to learn from and teach one another. The suburban-raised, Chicago-born Sansei, David Mura, and the urban-wise, Manila-born Jessica Hagedorn must be continuously attentive to their differences, even as they seek to name their poetic commonalities. The nostalgic Stephen Shu Ning Liu and the anti-nostalgic Carolyn Lau must continuously negotiate, even as they cross in opposite directions, the meanings of Chinese American poetry.

Likewise, we need to approach the selections in the *Heath* as a frontier (which they are) but not as *the* frontier or rather not as *the* representation of that frontier. As a whole the selections must remain a site of open contestation, not a closed settlement. Just as Kolodny's idea is that rather than "defining a frontier as a site of primitive or disparate technologies, it might prove more useful to think in terms of competing appropriate technologies and rapid technological exchange,"[19] the trope of the frontier enables us to approach the anthologized Asian American poets synergistically but without the double burden of (a) an implied subordination to a dominant model of American literature and (b) an implied representation of each particular, putative "whole" of Asian America that the happenstance of name, ethnic origin, gender, poetic style, and so on may seem, at first glance, to invite.

Situated in a recognizable, if fluid, geographic, cultural, and psychological locale, these writers necessarily will constitute diverse—and often oppositional—voices; they will be liberated from the shackles of a master narrative of American literature, yet at the same time be permitted their full range of differences not only from one another but from those who choose not to write at all. Thus, a Janice Mirikitani, for example, can be historically situated—even linked to that aforementioned protest tradition of American poetry—but without being absorbed by that narrative and without bearing the additional burden of serving as the spokesperson for Asian American radicalism, which neither she nor any other one person can do. Nor is a poet not immediately recognizable as "ethnic" or "political" to be disclaimed: for she or he too constitutes a frontier. Just as tellingly, the immigrant poets at Angel Island need not be defended on the primary grounds of historical relevance. As another frontier, these poems instruct us not only in history but in literature as well: they redefine for us what literature was at a particular place and time (and to an extent what literature continues to be)—which is to say multicultural, multilingual, often interdisciplinary, and always a succession of encounters from a variety of cultural sites.

Endnotes

1. *The Heath Anthology of American Literature,* Vols. 1-2 (Lexington, MA: D. C. Heath and Company, 1990). Cited hereafter as *Heath.* Amy Ling is one of fourteen primary editors of the anthology. Contributing editors include Oscar Campomanes, King-Kok Cheung, Elaine Kim, Him Mark Lai, Genny Lim, Shirley Lim, and Judy Yung.
2. I have used both the *Heath* and other anthologies in my own courses in American literature. The response on the part of my students has been very positive and leads me to believe that the *Heath* is indeed superior to any other standard American literary anthology.
3. See, for example, Lillian S. Robinson, *The Nation,* 2 July 1990, 22; and Mark Edmundson, *The Times Literary Supplement,* 19 October 1990, 1133.
4. Judith A. Stanford, ed., *Instructor's Guide for The Heath Anthology of American Literature* (Lexington, MA: D. C. Heath and Company, 1990), 700. Cited hereafter as *IG.*
5. *Heath,* 2551.
6. *IG,* 700.
7. Ibid., 718, 714.
8. *Heath,* 2584. Elaine H. Kim rightly points out that Song's "most effective poems" in her award-winning *Picture Bride* are "the ones that explore the relationship between the persona and her family." In "Defining Asian American Realities Through Literature," in *The Nature and Context of Minority Discourse,* Abdul R. JanMohamed and David Lloyd, eds. (New York: Oxford Univ. Press, 1990), 169.
9. *Heath,* 1755.
10. *Heath,* 1768.
11. Ibid., 1768.
12. "Values Old and New," in *Profession 91* ([New York]: The Modern Language Association of America, 1991), 10.
13. In one version of this narrative, the "development" of Asian American poetry begins with the oral poetry of the Angel Island Chinese, proceeds to the orally-based protest poetry of Mirikitani, and "culminates" first in Hongo's efforts at cultural retrieval and then in Song's concentration on the family, in which the vexed process of assimilation continues.
14. Such classifying need not be even remotely accurate. Witness the egregious error Richard Hugo commits in his foreword to *Picture Bride,* when he associates Song with Asian exoticism, specifically with a "sensibility strengthened by a patience that is centuries old, ancestral, tribal, a gift passed down." In *Picture Bride* (New Haven: Yale Univ. Press, 1983), x.

15. Quoted in "Poetics as Politics," a review of *The Politics of Poetic Form*, Charles Bernstein, ed., in *American Book Review*, April-May 1991, 5.
16. "Letting Go Our Grand Obsessions: Notes Toward a New Literary History of the American Frontiers," *American Literature* 61 (March 1992): 1-18.
17. "Arriba, mi gente," *Borderlands/La Frontera* (San Francisco: Spinsters/Aunt Lute Press, 1987), 195.
18. Kolodny, "Letting Go," 13.
19. Ibid, 11.

Chapter Seventeen

The State of Asian American Studies in Wisconsin

Amy Ling

In April 1991, when offered the directorship of the brand new Asian American Studies Program at one of the Big Ten universities, I accepted with joy—exhilarated and excited by the challenge. However, uprooting my entire family for the move from the East to the Midwest included what may prove to be the sacrifice of my husband's career. After much agonizing, he agreed to go, and I began my work at the University of Wisconsin in August 1991, only to make several stunning discoveries. First, I learned that the relationship between the state legislature and the university is often more adversarial than supportive; second, that the university is facing a period of downsizing and financial cutbacks; third, that the university's reputation for progressive even radical politics may have been deserved three decades ago but more recently, a member of the Department of History has founded on campus a vocal local branch of the reactionary National Association of Scholars. There's nothing like sailing to the middle of a large lake and having the wind suddenly die on you. There you are—all rigged up with no power of locomotion.

On the other hand, as one administrator assures me, it may be taken as a mark of special favor and particular interest on the university administration's part that *despite* a time of fiscal constraint, an Asian American Studies Program has been begun. An associate dean has reasoned in this way: "If we've just begun this program, we're committed to developing it; so we're not about to cut it." Toward the end of my first semester, the Dean of Letters and Science managed to scrape the bottom of the barrel and find enough funds to offer us one additional faculty line (to be used by halves of two people since the program can make only joint appointments with established departments), one full clerical line, half a graduate assistant, some student hourly help, and a reasonably generous supplies and expenses budget. I was heartened. It wasn't a dead calm in this lake.

Certainly, the presence of Donna Shalala, a chancellor who has been strong in her support for minority faculty recruitment and retention, and for Ethnic Studies programs, made it possible for our program to be created. A few racially inflammatory incidents on campus in 1988—when some fraternities decided a simulated slave auction would be fun—provided the impetus for the university to take action in sensitizing and educating students about racism. A collaboration of activist Asian American undergraduates, graduate students, faculty and staff wrote an excellent proposal for the establishment of an Asian American Studies Program, which, with the backing of the chancellor, was passed and is slowly being implemented. Despite the subsequent departure of this chancellor and three deans in three years, the administration continues to remain supportive; however, a recent poll showed that only 32 percent of the faculty supports Ethnic Studies.

Being given the green light to search for candidates and filling these lines, however, are two very different matters. Finding candidates whose interests and qualifications suit both the Asian American Studies program and also satisfy a traditional department's requirements is no easy matter. The more time goes by, the more I realize the near-impossibility of this task. Our first year, we had a few superb candidates; one with degrees in several different disciplines and a Ph.D. in Ethnic Studies. Unfortunately, Ethnic Studies does not exist as a department at the University of Wisconsin. When I tried to place this candidate, each department in turn found some rationale or vague explanation as to why she wouldn't do. "We don't have enough enrollment" or "She doesn't seem to be enough of a sociologist or political scientist." "She's not quite right for our department." "Her speciality is not high on our priority list." Was I being stonewalled? Or did all five departments have legitimate reasons for not making this hire? Two department chairs told me outright that they did not believe any lines or even half-lines were "free." They reasoned that if they went in with Asian American Studies in a joint hire this year, a few years down the road, this line would be counted "against them." In a time of financial constraint, their own priorities had to come first, and Asian American Studies was a luxury they couldn't afford. One professor actually told me he didn't understand why the university needed an Asian American Studies program; he was Irish and wasn't fighting for the establishment of Irish American Studies. There was no point in seeking help from the administration to push through an appointment that did not have the support of the department in which the candidate would eventually be seeking tenure.

Frustrated and discouraged, I turned to the directors of the programs in American Indian Studies and Chicano Studies, wondering how they had managed to make any joint hires at all. American Indian Studies has a faculty FTE count of 2.5; Chicano Studies has 2.5 FTE; African American Studies (8.3 FTE) was established twenty years ago as a department but is not interested in any joint hires. They counselled patience. This was only my first year; it had taken them many years to make successful hires. All interdisciplinary programs have the same difficulty. When the right person comes along, they assured me, then things will click into place. It is now three years, and we have still not been able to make a hire.

Recent research analyzing the success and "non-success" of Black Studies Programs may be applicable and instructive to Asian American Studies Programs. The results of Jo Ann Cunningham's survey of seven Black Studies Programs in New Jersey cited seven variables as critical to their success:[1]

1. Commitment and longevity of a pro-Black Studies central administration.
2. Having allies at the central administrative level.
3. Longevity, charisma, and strong leadership of the director or chairperson.
4. Faculty retention and promotion.
5. Publications and academic awards of members of the program or department.
6. Student enrollment.
7. Curriculum development.

What is missing from this list is faculty support, for, as I have learned the hard way, administrative support without faculty support will not bring about the desired results. Hiring, retention, and promotion all begin at the faculty level; higher administrators usually rubberstamp candidates that have been recommended by the faculty. Decisions in all these critical areas—hiring, retention and promotion—are judgments about a person's quality and desirability. And such judgments depend a great deal, much as we'd like to think we're all "rational" and "objective," on the personal perspectives and political stances of those doing the evaluations. For example, faculty holding the views of the National Association of Scholars, who are opposed on principle to Women's Studies and Ethnic Studies as quota fillers, will judge as inferior any research in these areas because, in their view, the *areas themselves* are not respectable academic pursuits. The success of any Ethnic Studies program then boils down to the prevailing institutional attitude of administrators *and* faculty. If diversity and a just and equitable society is valued, ethnic studies will flourish. If a reactionary backlash, a longing-to-return-to-the-"good-old-days," prevails, then Ethnic Studies will be fighting a losing battle.

At the University of Wisconsin, in the wake of the creation of the Asian American Studies Program, a small but vocal group has been asking for the establishment of a Puerto Rican Studies Program. Not surprisingly, in a time of financial constraint, the reactionary elements in the faculty see the "proliferation" of individual ethnic studies programs as a threat to traditional departments. Some recent university history has made this attitude all too visible.

In December 1991, the Letters and Sciences dean put us all through an exercise euphemistically named "Quality Reinvestment," a means of involving all the faculty in the necessary downsizing of the university. Each department and program was asked to write a detailed self-evaluation including its present offerings, its national standing, its future needs and plans. The dean appointed faculty committees in the three divisions (Humanities, Natural Sciences and Social Sciences) charging each committee to evaluate the reports in its division and to make recommendations to him as to where the "quality" of a program or department demanded "reinvestment" and, obviously, the corollary and the real purpose of the exercise, where cuts should be made. These committees' reports were released in late spring 1992.

The Social Sciences Committee targeted Women's Studies, all Ethnic Studies (that is African American, American Indian, Chicano, and Asian American), Environmental, and International Studies for partial cuts, baldly stating, "We find the growth of these new instructional units (NIUs) as posing possible serious problems for the University." By coincidence, in eight out of nine cases, this committee recommended continued funding for those departments and programs with which its own committee members are affiliated. That a Jewish Studies Program was also created in 1991 was not an issue brought up in this report because this fortunate program has its own million dollar grant and does not make competing claims on the communal pot. That the university already has in place a profusion of Ethnic Studies programs (Southeast Asian Studies, South Asian Studies, East Asian Studies, Slavic and East European Studies, Scandinavian Studies, Latin American Studies) was not an issue either because these programs are not "new." (African American Studies, though twenty years old, was, however, considered "new.") The basic premise of this disturbing report thus seems very clear: that which is new and that which has to do with women and racial minorities cannot, at the same time, have anything to do with quality and should be eliminated. That which is old and established is obviously good and should be preserved. The NIUs (the new) were spoken of as though they were cancer cells seeking to grow and overtake the healthy cells (the old).

Fortunately two successive deans have disregarded the recommendations of this committee. In the fall of 1993, no departments were allowed to search except Ethnic Studies programs. Once again, we have had excellent candidates, but the tenure-based departments have been slow to evaluate candidates' materials. In the meantime, we have lost potential faculty members to other universities.

I personally have received a warm welcome at the university, but it is altogether possible that this welcome was extended only by those supportive of an Asian American Studies Program, and that those opposed have not come forth. How large their numbers or how deep their silent resentment, I have no way of knowing. I do know that in my first year here, several conservative national leaders have been invited to speak on campus, including Lynne Cheney and Dinesh D'Souza, and that their audiences have numbered in the hundreds. I also know that though the Ethnic Studies graduation requirement has swelled my classes in Asian American literature, at least two of the students in my class of sixty at the end of this semester were still resentful and unconvinced that the texts we studied had any literary merit. One student told me that these were the best books she had read in her four years as an English major; another student considered them "smarmy" and could not relate to them at all.

We're all aware that the political climate of the country for the past decade has become increasingly conservative. However, the events of late spring 1992 may be a catalyst for change. In wake of the Rodney King trial, the eruptions on the battlefield of Los Angeles, and the demonstrations of displeasure in other urban centers; in the light of census figures and predictions of increasing numbers of so-called minorities in these United States, Ethnic Studies cannot be ignored. To ignore it, as does the University of Wisconsin's Social Sciences Committee Report referred to above, is to be an ostrich with its head stuck in the sand, believing itself invisible.

W. E. B. Du Bois rightly stated in 1903 that "The problem of the twentieth century is the problem of the color-line,—the relation of the darker to the lighter races of men in Asia and Africa, in America and the islands of the sea."[2] Though we are nearing the end of the twentieth century, the problem of the color line, unfortunately, remains a problem still. If the problem is not resolved in this century, if the offensive color barrier is not removed altogether, greater and more massively destructive explosions will surely result. "What happens to a dream deferred?" asked

Langston Hughes several decades ago. We all know the answer. We witnessed the explosion thirty years ago, and we're witnessing it again. For the Bush administration to place the blame for the Los Angeles riots on the failed programs of the Democratic party several decades ago, programs that Bush and Reagan continually slashed, is to complain of the mote in their neighbor's eye and be blind to the beam in their own eye.

In the Los Angeles fires, we saw the fruits of racism, of despair. We saw the failure of the justice system as it relates to peoples of color. And all of us are implicated—inner-city African Americans, Korean immigrant grocery store owners, bystanders of all colors. We are all residents of one village, the national village called the United States of America and the global village called the planet Earth. Like it or not, our lives and our fates are intertwined. Please indulge me, an old English major, as I quote a well-known passage that seems particularly fitting here. It was written by a seventeenth-century poet and Anglican minister, John Donne, while lying on his sickbed and hearing the church bells tolling for someone's funeral:

> No man is an island, entire of itself; every man is a piece of the continent, a part of the main; if a clod be washed away by the sea, Europe is the less, as well as if a promontory were, as well as if a manor of thy friends or of thine own were; any man's death diminishes me, because I am involved in mankind; and therefore never send to know for whom the bell tolls; it tolls for thee. *(Devotions Upon Emergent Occasions*, XVII, 1623.)

The bell is tolling for all of us, if we cannot solve the problem of the color line and do it soon.

Comparative Ethnic Studies is one step in the right direction. Let us all learn more about each other. Let us repress no one's history. We, African Americans, American Indians, Asian Americans, Chicanos, Puerto Ricans, all need to unearth our own individual and unknown or silenced histories, but, at the same time, we also need to know how we can be constructively interrelated. What do we have in common besides a shared history of oppression at the hands of whites? What ideas of community, of environmental concern, of literary, artistic, philosophical and, yes, political vision can we bring from our various cultural backgrounds to contribute to the larger American society? How might we have contributed to the problems, and how might we help to solve some of these inequities facing all of us?

I think we Asian Americans have a great deal of work cleaning up our own house and getting ourselves motivated to concerted and communal action outside our narrow personal spheres. Sad to say, many of us are racist and chauvinist in our beliefs. The Chinese call their land the Middle Kingdom; all other nations are peripheral, barbarian. Though residents in the U.S., Chinese speakers of my mother's generation call white Americans *wai guo ren,* foreigners, reversing the center and the periphery against the facts, for wherever they are and who they are is the center, the norm.

At the same time, paradoxically, we recognize that this is the white man's land, that we are here on suffrage and that if we wish to remain here, if we wish to survive, we must lie low, remain silent and as invisible as possible. The following quote from Lin Yutang's *Chinatown Family* illustrates my point:

> Tom Fong, Sr., raised his head high . . . He had been pushed about in this country and he had made his way like water, that symbol of Taoist wisdom, seeking the low places and penetrating everywhere. Laotse's philosophy, as he heard it in Chinese proverbs, was the first philosophy of camouflage, of seeking the lowly and appearing foolish, of the strength of the gentle and the blessedness of the meek, the apparent dumbness of the truly wise, the stupidity of the garrulous, the tactical advantage of lying low, and the futility of strife and contentions. That philosophy was, in truth, Tom Fong's philosophy of living. Laotse was right; those who occupy the lowly places can never be overthrown.
>
> How do the rivers and seas become the Lords of the Ravines? By being good at keeping low. That was how they became the Lords of the Ravines.
>
> And so Tom Fong and his people sought the lowly places and penetrated everywhere and survived like the sea.
>
> The best of men is like water; Water benefits all things And does not compete with them. It dwells in the lowly places that all disdain—Wherein it comes near to the Tao.[3]

Lying low was the practice that enabled the thousands of Chinese railroad workers to escape what Maxine Hong Kingston called "The Driving Out" after the completion of their work on the railroads in 1870s. Taking up the lowly work disdained by other men—cooking, housekeeping, and washing dirty clothes—was the means of survival for thousands of Chinese men in the United States for many generations when they were barred from other work. Silence was the protection of illegal Chinese immigrants during the sixty years of the Chinese Exclusion Acts.

Silence is also a cultural tradition among the Japanese. They have a saying, "The nail that sticks out gets the hammer." The polar opposites of silence and speaking out provide the tension and differentiate the characters in Joy Kogawa's 1981 novel *Obasan,* which begins: "There is a silence that cannot speak. There is a silence that will not speak." Though the novel is itself a speaking out, it is nonetheless named for the aunt who is silent—Kogawa writes, "Obasan's language remains deeply underground."[4] Through the narrative incidents and through her rich imagery, Kogawa not only underscores silence as a Japanese cultural trait but makes this willed silence a counterpart of the unwilled silence of the natural world: of stone, water, moonlight, fiddlehead ferns, butterflies, and coulee grasses.

For Japanese Americans, thirty years had to pass and with these years a new generation's rising to maturity before the ramifications of Executive Order 9066 could be spoken about. Here is a poem from Mitsuye Yamada's *Camp Notes*, published in 1979:

Thirty Years Under
I had packed up
my wounds in a cast
iron box
sealed it
labeled it
do no open. . .
ever. . .

and traveled blind
for thirty years

until one day I heard
a black man with huge bulbous eyes
say
there is nothing more
humiliating
more than beatings
more than curses
than being spat on

like a dog.[5]

Silence is read in Asian cultures as a sign of dignity, of stoic endurance. But when viewed from a western perspective, silence is taken as a sign of meekness and weakness. Despite the Christian precept of turning the other cheek, if one takes abuse or oppression without protest, then one is seen as a "pushover," a spineless creature without the strength to stand up for itself. No one wants to be lord of the ravines in this society; everyone strives for dominance of the eagle heights. But if you belong to a race that is unwanted in this country, that was forbidden by law to testify in courts against any white person, that was ineligible for citizenship, that was barred for sixty years from immigrating altogether, then speaking up against injustice and discrimination was not something you could easily do.

I want to make clear that alongside the tradition of silence imported from the Asian countries of origin was also a tradition of resistance, of peasant revolt, of a warrior class. But because Asians in the United States have long been in the minority, violent resistance was not expedient, and silent compliance was more the general rule. Nonetheless, despite this cultural tradition of silence, historic pressures and events caused Asian Americans in the late 1960s to speak out.

When we look back over the length of 300 years of American history, we note that roughly every one hundred years there has been a revolution: in the 1770s the colonies fought to obtain independence from England, in the 1860s the Northern States fought to keep the Union together and to end the practice of slavery; in the 1960s African Americans and women began a bloodless social revolution for equal rights. Furthermore, for Asian Americans, the Vietnam War was the third war Americans fought in Asia in as many decades. For months that stretched into years, we ate dinner each night with images of Asian bodies bloodied and stilled, with Asian forests blasted and bombed. These images could not help but have an effect on even the most quiet and restrained of people. For me, personally, the image of the women and children lying in a deep pit, executed by Lieutenant Calley, was burned into my psyche. Despite Calley's very public trial for excessive violence, I found it hard to believe that his was an isolated case and I found it impossible to view this war dispassionately.

When the African American students struck at San Francisco State in 1969, Asian American students joined them, helping to form the Third World Liberation Front. The sit-ins and shattered windows of this longest student strike in history broke the Asian American conventional mold of silence and polite restraint, resulted in the creation of Ethnic Studies as an academic department and discipline, and brought about the realization that concerted action on a massive grassroots level could effect social change. Malcolm X had taught everyone an important lesson: "It's the squeaky wheel that gets the grease."

Clearly, the establishment of an Asian American Studies Program at the University of Wisconsin was the result of squeaky wheels, of student demands. There is a flip side of the coin, however, as one graduate student pointed out recently, "What's to prevent the squeaky wheel's being removed entirely and replaced with another one?" My answer was nothing except the impracticality of removing Asians from America. My answer, however, presupposes that all Asian Americans support Asian American Studies. This, unfortunately, is not the case and leads us to another area in which we Asian Americans have to get ourselves together.

Perhaps it is our geographic location in the rural midwest, or our being known as the Dairy State with a barn in the middle of campus and master's degrees given for new flavors of ice cream, but despite the fact that the University of Wisconsin has a total enrollment (in 1992) of 1,344 Asian American students and a total of 2,542 foreign students from Asian countries, only 28 students signed up for Asian American history when it was taught for the first time. (That it was scheduled for 8:45 a.m. may have been a factor in the relatively low enrollment.)

Using my own siblings as a small sample, I must admit that I am the only one in my family out of three with any interest in Asian American Studies. My brother's attitude is "The history is so painful; why dig it up? Who wants to dwell on it?" My sister remarked, "I don't even know any Chinese but you, and I've never experienced any racism." One University of Wisconsin professor who has lived in the U.S. for twenty years, is married to a Caucasian and has Amerasian children, said at my interview, "I'm Japanese. What is Asian American Studies and why do we need it here?"

Most Asian American students are pragmatic; they want to choose a major that will lead to a lucrative career. The majority are thus pre-med, business, or engineering majors. To these students, cultural literacy seems an extravagance. The problem in Wisconsin seems to be not how to persuade white students that Asian American Studies is relevant to them but how to persuade Asian American students of this fact. My classes in Asian American Women writers always enroll a majority of Euro-American students. I've been told that the preponderance of students in African American Studies courses, despite an undergraduate enrollment of 697 African American students, is also white. I'm delighted that white students are interested, but I'm concerned that students of color are not.

Another major challenge I see here is the fostering of intergroup interaction. Birds of a feather flock together here in Madison, probably because their numbers are large. The Chinese students from Hong Kong (there are 464 of them) stick together; those from Taiwan (495) have their own separate group; those from the People's Republic of China (385) still another group. The undergraduate Korean American students (over 200) have nothing to do with the graduate Korean students (395). I recently learned that the Hmong students felt betrayed when one of their numbers left their own association to join the Asian American Students' Union. Attempts to cross these boundaries, to see oneself as Asian American rather than as Indian or Japanese or Chinese is more the exception than the rule.

A final challenge for the Asian American Studies Program is community outreach. Community involvement has traditionally been an integral part of Ethnic Studies programs, but how do we as an academic program interphase with an extremely diverse community that has very different needs? Wisconsin has the third largest population of Hmong in the United States (16,373 people), following California and Minnesota. Madison has a large group of recent refugees from Tibet, as well as long established populations of Chinese, Japanese, and Koreans. According to 1990 statistics provided by the

State's Center of Health Statistics, Dane County (in which Madison is located) alone has 2,839 Chinese, 660 Japanese, 1,170 Asian Indians, 397 Filipino, 1,449 Koreans, 350 Vietnamese, 202 Cambodians, 561 Hmong, 270 Laotian, 106 Thai, and 583 "Other Asian" for a total of 8,587 Asian residents.

With only one person officially in the Asian American Studies Program at present, I cannot hope to cover all bases. Having no crystal ball, I cannot tell what the future will bring or what the prospects for Asian American Studies will be. I do know that in literature, we have been experiencing a florescence in all genres. Enough literature is currently being produced and being unearthed and reprinted that I could teach half a dozen different courses and not repeat a single work. More and more anthologies are being published in the different genres and disciplines and more are being planned, a sure sign that there is a market for this work. I have been bringing in speakers, writers, film programs focused on the variety of Asian American experiences in an attempt to bring together community and campus, and to draw together peoples of different Asian backgrounds. This aspect of the program, our special events, has been extremely successful.

It seems to me, finally, that the prospects for Asian American Studies depend not only on the political and intellectual climate of the institution and of the nation, but also on us all joining forces to pull together. Our numbers are too few for the in-fighting we too often engage in. The boundaries we erect among ourselves along an alarming variety of lines—national origins, gender, politics, generations—only weaken us further. As Lincoln said, quoting Jesus, "A house divided against itself cannot stand." The time we spend pulling each other down instead of supporting one another is precious time lost from working for the common cause. As for myself, I can only do my best one day at a time, believing firmly in the rightness and importance of the cause and glad to be a worker in the field.

Endnotes

1. I am grateful to my colleague, Michael Thornton, for bringing this article to my attention. See Jo Ann Cunningham, "Black Studies Programs: Reasons for their Success and Non-Success from Inception to the Present," *National Journal of Sociology* 5,1 (1991): 19-40.
2. W. E. B. Du Bois, *The Souls of Black Folk,* 1903. New York: Signet, 1969, 54.
3. Lin Yutang, *Chinatown Family,* 1945, John Day. Taipei: Mei Ya Publications, 1975, 148.
4. Joy Kogawa, 1981, *Obasan,* Boston: D.R. Godine, 32.
5. Mitsuye Yamada, 1979, *Camp Notes and Other Poems,* San Lorenzo, California: Shameless Hussy Press.
6. For detailed information about this strike, see the special issue of *Amerasia,* volume 15, number 1, 1989.

Chapter Eighteen

From Different Shores Again

Peter N. Kiang

At the concluding plenary session of the Association for Asian American Studies national conference in San Francisco in 1987, I announced to the rather jaded, majority California crowd that a "New Wave" of activity in Asian American Studies was sweeping the East Coast with regional and national implications.[1]

To illustrate my point at the time, I referred to a dinner conversation from the previous evening in which two of the Filipino faculty from the host campus were talking-story about riding the Pacific waves on their twelve-foot surfboards. Their tales of adventure seemed almost mythic compared to my East Coast reality. I realized that we *really do come from different shores!* And I wondered, how can we follow in the footsteps of Ten Toes Takaki or the many others who handle those big boards on the West Coast? To ride our new wave, I proposed that we would need to use smaller, lighter boards which, though lacking stability and power, provided quickness and flexibility. We did not know when the East Coast wave would crest and subside, but some of us were determined to ride it and find out.

Several years have now passed, and we are still riding. Since that first report of the New Wave in 1987, Cornell launched its landmark program, the first in the Ivy League, followed by the University of Wisconsin in the Big Ten. Queens College in New York City established an Asian/American research center while University of Massachusetts/Boston established a stable core of courses and a free-standing Institute for Asian American Studies. In 1993, new programs opened at the University of Connecticut and Hunter College. More courses are now offered on more campuses than ever before. Students have developed sophisticated networks while diverse, new communities have emerged.

At the same time, the recession has hit hard. Even institutions with billion-dollar endowments face retrenchment. Although new waves of needs and demands continue to pound the shore, the tide of institutional support is receding. With this in mind, the following commentary analyzes the continuing challenge to develop Asian American Studies on the East Coast, and outlines four parallels to historical struggles and survival strategies of Asian immigrant communities.

First, for East Coast Asian American Studies faculty, we recall the legacy of coolie contract laborers, following the crops from season to season, moving from place to place. These are typical patterns of work, and many of us have filled this role. In a typical semester of the 1980s, for example, Shirley Hune rode the trains from New York to Philadelphia every week; Betty Lee Sung migrated across state lines from New York City to Princeton, New Jersey once a week; Grace Yun covered the entire state of Connecticut from New Haven to Storrs to Hartford; while I taught three days at University of Massachusetts/Boston, one night at Boston University, and one day at Yale.

When students organize and demand courses at schools where existing faculty are unable to teach Asian American Studies, then temporary, adjunct positions are created—just like the Bracero programs that allow cheap migrant labor to enter the U.S. under contract, paid by the bushel, to harvest the crops. While teaching is by no means equivalent to farm work, the parallel is revealing. And, like the role of migrant laborers in building the economy, those contracted, adjunct faculty have played major roles in developing Asian American Studies on the East Coast.

A second connection relates to one's fate being determined by one's papers. Whether referring to the Chinese paper sons of the 1920s, or the Cambodians who could leave Thai refugee camps to resettle in the U.S. only if they had the right documents, or the Pakistani foreign students who disappear into the informal, under-the-table economy in order to stay here after their visas expire, Asian immigrants over the years have been vulnerable because their identity in society was linked explicitly to their status on paper. So it is with many of us who work to expand Asian American Studies on the East Coast but do not have the proper paper credentials. Graduate students, experienced community leaders, and especially undergraduate students and their campus organizations have done most of the hard work of developing Asian American Studies at schools like Columbia, Princeton, Brooklyn College, Wesleyan, and many others. But, their status, in not having the right papers, such as doctoral degrees, puts them in short-term, restricted, and ultimately, untenable positions.

Historically, pooling resources within the community has served as a strategy to counter these kinds of social, political, and economic restrictions. Organizations based on family name or village origin and community-based, rotating credit associations such as the Korean *kyo*, Chinese *hui*, Japanese *tanomoshi*, and Vietnamese *hoi*, have provided individual and group enterprises with networks and support with which to expand and develop—in spite of restrictive conditions imposed by mainstream institutions and the larger society.

This same *hoi* approach is a third parallel, taking shape in the form of regional consortia of colleges and universities to develop Asian American Studies on the East Coast. In the five-college area of western Massachusetts, for example, where Amherst College, Hampshire College, Mt. Holyoke College, Smith College, and University of Massachusetts/ Amherst are located, a five-college Asian American Studies Committee was established in 1991 which pools money to sponsor lectures, film showings, and Asian American Studies courses at one of the colleges each semester. Students from any of the participating five colleges are eligible to enroll in these courses or activities.

The hoi approach has also inspired discussions about developing Asian American Studies in Philadelphia through a regional consortium.[2] Recognizing how difficult it would be for any individual school to muster the resources and commitment to mount a strong program by itself, some have suggested a coordinated, regional effort through which Bryn Mawr, for example, might hire a literature scholar, Haverford a historian, Swarthmore a social scientist, University of Pennsylvania an anthropologist, and Temple University a faculty member in education. Such a coordinated plan of hiring, based on the *hoi* approach, might lead to a coherent, regional program with far greater impact than any individual campus could readily organize on its own.[3]

A fourth parallel recognizes that the community's ethnic economy has always played a major role in enabling immigrants to survive in this country. Excluded from primary labor markets and mainstream services, generations of Asian immigrants have turned to their communities for social and economic support. Our work at University of Massachusetts/ Boston illustrates how individual institutions can similarly rely on community resources.

For six consecutive years, beginning in 1988, University of Massachusetts/Boston faced hiring freezes and budget cuts; during the same time, the Asian American student population tripled and we began expanding Asian American Studies. As an urban, public university without a large base of wealthy alumni, and with no resources coming from the state legislature or the university, we turned strategically to the local Asian American communities for support.

By making a compelling case that we serve as "the community's university" through raising public awareness about the Asian American experience, training new generations of leadership for the various immigrant and refugee communities, and conducting relevant research on significant community issues, we established a university-based Fund for Asian American Studies in spring 1992. Within two months' time, the fund raised over $25,000 from nearly 400 community members to support new courses, library acquisitions, and planning for a Massachusetts-focused Asian American research and policy institute. More importantly, we strengthened an organic relationship with the community that will help to sustain us for the long-term, provided that we remain true to our mission.

We have no intention of asking the community to pay for our Asian American Studies program. This is clearly the responsibility of the university which the community's tax dollars already finance.[4] But during this period of retrenchment, we have consciously turned, first and foremost, to the community to provide a base of support that has enabled us to survive and grow. In the process, we have not only strengthened our Asian American Studies initiatives during a time of severe budget cuts, but we have also hearkened back to a long-standing tradition in Asian American history.

These are some of the parallels between the social and historical experiences of Asian immigrant communities and the ways in which Asian American Studies is now developing on the East Coast. This is by no means ideal. In every example, there is growth but not permanence—adjunct faculty riding trains, instructors and students not having proper papers or credentials, schools pooling scarce and scattered resources, new courses depending on community dollars. Few stable programs with real resources have developed during this period of the New Wave.

These examples illustrate what it means to surf with a small board, taking risks and maneuvering quickly amidst white water, but always with the threat of losing balance and control. Nevertheless, we have moved in many positive, exciting directions since I first reported on the New Wave in 1987. From this vantage point, it seems more important than ever for the Asian American Studies field to gaze East of California and consider different shores.

The East Coast needs to be recognized, in part, because thousands of students are raising legitimate, unmet demands at dozens of campuses. Furthermore, graduates of East Coast universities are playing leadership roles in the field. For example, three former presidents of the Association for Asian American Studies—Don Nakanishi, Shirley Hune, and Franklin Odo—each graduated from East Coast schools themselves. A fourth former president—Gary Okihiro—now directs the Cornell program.

But the East Coast has significance for more profound reasons. As both Jack Tchen and Sucheta Mazumdar suggest, relationships between

Asia and the Americas were established in the 1700s through the China and India Trades which were centered in New York and New England. Those historical connections generated an initial presence of Asians on the East Coast several decades before Chinese laborers dug for gold in California. More importantly, this confluence of the early India and China Trades established American elite and popular images of Asia and Asians that were inherited through the generations and which still influence our society today.

Sucheta Mazumdar has also pointed out that a large percentage of Indians currently on the East Coast and in the South have come from Uganda, as depicted in Mira Nair's film, *Mississippi Masala*. Similarly, many Chinese from Jamaica, Panama, and other nations of Central and South America are also forming new communities on the East Coast. They really do come from different shores! And they point to a reality of Asian Pacific America that is even more diverse and complex than that which we typically recognize.

If we do not continue nationally to develop and expand Asian American Studies east of California, then we, as a field, will fail to address the full complexity of our peoples' experiences, and we, as a movement, will fail to make full use of everyone who wants and needs to be included.

The surf is still up. Let's get back on board.

Endnotes

This article is adapted from a panel presentation on "East of California Programs" at the Association for Asian American Studies national conference in San Jose, California on May 29, 1992. The title, "From Different Shores Again," acknowledges the significance of Ronald Takaki's *Strangers from a Different Shore* (Boston: Little Brown, 1989) as a reference point in the writing and teaching of Asian American history.

1. See: Kiang, Peter Nien-chu. 1988. "The New Wave: Developing Asian American Studies on the East Coast" in Gary Y. Okihiro, Shirley Hune, Arthur A. Hansen, and John M. Liu (eds). *Reflections on Shattered Windows*. Pullman, Washington: Washington State University Press, 43-50.
2. This was a topic of discussion in the 1991 East of California conference at Cornell University.
3. In the meantime, the University of Pennsylvania agreed to hire an open rank Asian Americanist with responsibilities to launch a new interdisciplinary Asian American Studies program. This is a major step forward for the campus and the greater Philadephia area. The potential advantages of inter-institutional collaboration and pooling of resources, however, remain useful to consider.
4. In fact, the breadth and depth of the community's investment, both financially and politically, were crucial points of leverage in moving University of Massachusetts/Boston and the Massachusetts state legislature to approve an annual $200,000 line item for the new Institute for Asian American Studies beginning in 1993-1994, in spite of the university's continuing budget crisis.

Notes on Contributors

PETER BACHO teaches Asian American Studies at San Jose State University. He is the author of *Cebu* and numerous other short stories.

MALCOLM COLLIER teaches Asian American Studies at San Francisco State University.

SOO-YOUNG CHIN is an assistant professor and teaches Asian American Studies and anthropology at San Jose State University.

AMARPAL K. DHALIWAL is a doctoral candidate in the Department of Ethnic Studies at the University of California, Berkeley. Her research interests include the study of South Asian immigration to the United States, with an emphasis on Sikh migration, post-colonial and international feminist theory.

NEIL GOTANDA is an associate professor of law at Western State University College of Law in Fullerton, California.

LANE RYO HIRABAYASHI is coordinator of Asian American Studies at the Center for Studies of Ethnicity and Race in America, University of Colorado at Boulder.

BETTY NOBUE KANO designed the cover art for this volume and is an artist in Berkeley, California.

PETER N. KIANG is an assistant professor in the Graduate College of Education and American Studies Program at the University of Massachusetts at Boston. He was formerly the elected East Coast representative to the Association for Asian American Studies.

KICHUNG KIM is a professor of English at San Jose State University.

RACHEL LEE is a doctoral candidate in the Department of English at the University of California, Los Angeles. She is completing her dissertation entitled "The Americas of Asian American Literature."

AMY LING is the director of the Asian American Studies Program and a professor in the Department of English at the University of Wisconsin.

JAMES S. MOY is a professor in the Theatre Arts Department at the University of Wisconsin. He is the author of numerous scholarly articles and reviews on the subjects of theatre history and performance art. His most recent work is the book *Marginal Sights: Staging the Chinese in America*.

MIKE MULLEN is a graduate of the University of Washington and a free-lance writer in Seattle.

DAVID MURA is the author of *Turning Japanese: Memoirs of a Sansei,* which was the 1991 Josephine Miles Book Award from the Oakland PEN. He has also published a book of poetry, *After We Lost Our Way,* and *A Male Grief: Notes on Pornography and Addiction* and *The Colors of Desire.* He is currently working on an autobiographical book on race and Asian American identity.

GARY Y. OKIHIRO is professor of history and teaches in the Asian American Studies Program at Cornell University. He is author of *Cane Fires: The Anti-Japanese Movement in Hawaii, 1865-1945.*

WENDY L. NG is an assistant professor in the Sociology Department and Asian American Studies Program at San Jose State University.

R.A. SASAKI lives in Berkeley, California and is the author of *The Loom and Other Short Stories.*

ELLEN SOMEKAWA is a doctoral candidate in geography at the University of Pennsylvania.

SHARON SUZUKI-MARTINEZ is a graduate student in English at the University of Arizona. She is completing her dissertation on Asian American literature.

JAMES A. TYNER is a doctoral candidate in the Department of Geography at the University of Southern California. His research interests include Asian migration and population issues.

GEORGE UBA is an associate professor of English at California State University, Northridge. He has published criticism on Poe, Howells, Richard Wright, and a variety of Asian American poets. His most recent publication is "Friend and Foe: Decollaborating Wendy Wilder Larsen and Tran Thi Nga's Shallow Graves: Two Women and Viet Nam" in *Journal of American Culture.* Currently he directs the Japanese American San Fernando Valley Oral History Project.

TRAISE YAMAMOTO is an assistant professor in the Department of English at the University of California, Riverside. She is currently finishing a book on Japanese American female subjectivity.